THE
MARTYRDOM OF
ABOLITIONIST
CHARLES TORREY

Antislavery, Abolition, and the Atlantic World
R. J. M. Blackett and James Brewer Stewart, Editors

THE
MARTYRDOM OF
ABOLITIONIST
CHARLES TORREY

E. FULLER TORREY

LOUISIANA STATE UNIVERSITY PRESS

BATON ROUGE

Published by Louisiana State University Press
Copyright © 2013 by Louisiana State University Press
All rights reserved
Manufactured in the United States of America
First printing

Designer: Laura Roubique Gleason
Typeface: Kepler MM
Printer and binder: Maple Press

Library of Congress Cataloging-in-Publication Data
Torrey, E. Fuller (Edwin Fuller), 1937–
    The martyrdom of abolitionist Charles Torrey / E. Fuller Torrey.
        pages   cm. — (Antislavery, abolition, and the Atlantic world)
    Includes bibliographical references and index.
    ISBN 978-0-8071-5231-7 (cloth : alk. paper) — ISBN 978-0-8071-5232-4 (pdf)
— ISBN 978-0-8071-5233-1 (epub) — ISBN 978-0-8071-5234-8 (mobi) 1. Torrey,
Charles T. (Charles Turner), 1813–1846. 2. Torrey, Charles T. (Charles Turner),
1813–1846—Trials, litigations, etc. 3. Torrey, Charles T. (Charles Turner), 1813–
1846—Imprisonment. 4. Torrey, Charles T. (Charles Turner), 1813–1846—Death
and burial. 5. Abolitionists—United States—Biography. 6. Abolitionists—Maryland—Biography. 7. Underground Railroad—Maryland. 8. Antislavery movements—Maryland—History—19th century. 9. Fugitive slaves—Maryland—History—19th century. 10. Clergy—New England—Biography. I. Title.
    E449.T69T67 2013
    326.092—dc23
    [B]

                                                                    2013008666

For Halsey and Sandra

Although our brother lie asleep,
Man's heart still struggles, still aspires;
His grave shall quiver yet, while deep
Through the brave Bay State's pulses leap
Her ancient energies and fires.

—James Russell Lowell, "On the Death of
   Charles Turner Torrey," 1846

CONTENTS

PREFACE

"Martyr Charles Turner Torrey, the Abolitionist" was one of twelve names on the yellowing piece of paper to which my mother vainly tried to direct my attention. The paper was titled "Prominent Torreys," but despite sharing a few genes, distant relatives held little interest for a teenage boy. Besides, our family was definitely not the kind to produce martyrs.

Many years later, I came across Charles Torrey's name connected to the Underground Railroad in Maryland. That got my interest, so I queried the few references available. They revealed that Torrey had challenged abolitionist leader William Lloyd Garrison, had been called the "father" of the Underground Railroad, and had freed more slaves than had Harriet Tubman. One article also stated that "Charles T. Torrey is now generally forgotten by historians of antebellum America," which appeared to contradict his accomplishments. I therefore undertook additional investigation.[1]

This book is the product of that investigation, which unearthed a brief but rich life. As Henry Stanton described it at Torrey's funeral: "The events of Mr. Torrey's life, while engaged in those peculiar enterprizes which marked the two last year [*sic*] of his efforts in the anti-slavery cause, would, if written, possess all the charms of romance. All who can appreciate the thrilling interest which the history of these events would excite in every bosom where dwells a soul, will regard it as among not the least of the calamities of his death, that his graphic pen could not leave them to the world as the best vindication of his fame."[2]

Almost all Torreys in America are descendants of four brothers who landed in 1640 at the Massachusetts Bay Colony. Charles was a fifth-generation descendant of James, who settled in Scituate, and I am a ninth-generation descendant of William, who settled a few miles further north in Weymouth.

This book focuses on Charles Torrey's efforts to combat racism and slavery. The depth of the race problem in the 1830s and 1840s was extraordinary. For example, in 1836, James Hammond, a South Carolina congressmen and one of the leading defenders of slavery, suggested to Congress that all abolitionists deserved to be killed as "ignorant, infatuated barbarians." Regarding the freeing of slaves, he added:

> Although I am perfectly satisfied that no human process can elevate the black man to an equality with the white—admitting that it could be done—are we prepared for the consequence which then must follow? . . . Are we prepared to see them mingling in our legislatures? Is any portion of this country prepared to see them enter these halls and take their seats by our sides, in perfect equality with the white representatives of an Anglo-Saxon race—to see them fill that chair—to see them placed at the heads of your Departments; or to see, perhaps, some Othello, or Toussaint, or Boyer, gifted with genius and inspired by ambition, grasp the presidential wreath, and wield the destinies of this great republic? From such a picture I turn with irrepressible disgust.[3]

We sometimes forget how far we have come.

ACKNOWLEDGMENTS

Paternity of this book is attributable principally to two men. Stanley Harrold, professor of history at South Carolina State University, published the initial research on Charles Torrey, and without it this book would not have been conceived. Rand Dotson, an editor at Louisiana State University Press, saw promise in an earlier draft and persisted until I got it right; without him, it would not have been born.

Librarians are a biographer's best friends. I am especially grateful to Sean Casey, Kim Reynolds, and Barbara Davis at the Boston Public Library; Jessica Steytler and staff at the Congregational Library in Boston; Auburn Nelson at the Schomburg Center of the New York Public Library; Tammis Groft at the Albany Institute of History and Art; Katherine Carr at the University of Missouri Library; Nicolette Dobrowolski at the Syracuse University; and the library staff of the Uniformed Services University of the Health Sciences. Many people at historical societies also went out of their way to be helpful, including Diane Rofini at the Chester County Historical Society; Henry Peden at the Harford County Historical Society; Carol Miles at the Scituate Historical Society; Margaret Maxwell at the Medway Historical Society; Jocelyn Gould at the Massachusetts Historical Society; and Elizabeth Plummer at the Ohio Historical Society.

I thank the following for permission to quote from letters in their collections: the Chester County Historical Society in Pennsylvania; the Ohio Historical Society; the trustees of the Boston Public Library/Rare Books Collection; the Special Collections Research Center, Syracuse University Library; and the Congregational Library in Boston.

I am deeply indebted to the two historian reviewers of the manuscript, Professors James Brewer Stewart of Macalester College and R. J. M. Blackett of Indiana University. They deserve much of the credit for whatever merit exists in the final product. Robert Taylor, Jerry

Lynn, Halsey Beemer, and Judith Phelps also provided useful suggestions, and Chris Gillis contributed the map of Charles Torrey's Underground Railroad route. Lee Sioles and Stan Ivester guided the manuscript through the shoals of the editorial process in a skillful manner, and Judy Miller again provided excellent administrative and editorial support. And I am indebted to my wife, Barbara, for steering me to Charles Torrey and for cheerfully keeping dinner waiting and all the things that make writing a book possible.

THE
MARTYRDOM OF
ABOLITIONIST
CHARLES TORREY

Underground Railroad Route used by Charles Torrey, 1842–1844

Map by Chris Gillis

1

AN ABOLITIONIST SCHISM

Wednesday, January 23, 1839: It was, wrote Maria Chapman, "the largest anti-slavery gathering ever witnessed in Massachusetts, and a noble sight it was to look upon.... Bigotry and sectarism [*sic*] were pitted against religious liberty and Christian love.... It was a turning point in the cause. A strong and mighty wind had come to winnow the wheat from the chaff." The annual meeting of the Massachusetts Anti-Slavery Society would indeed be a pivotal point in the abolitionist movement, not only for Massachusetts but for the entire country. It would shape the future of the movement during a period that has been called "America's national adolescence."[1]

Well before the 10 o'clock opening, an "immense throng . . . packed Boston's Marlboro Chapel to the rafters." The chapel, which had been opened the previous year, was a large hall that, like Philadelphia's Pennsylvania Hall, "had been built by reformers and dedicated to 'the cause of humanity and free discussion.'" The comparison of the two halls was apposite for several of the attendees at the Massachusetts meeting; they had been at the antislavery convention in Philadelphia two years earlier, when a mob of proslavery activists had burned Pennsylvania Hall to the ground.[2]

The battle this day, however, was not to be between abolitionists and supporters of slavery. Rather, it was between two abolitionist factions—one led by William Lloyd Garrison, and the other, a group trying to oust Garrison from his leadership position, led by Charles Torrey, Amos Phelps, Alanson St. Clair, and Henry Stanton. The result of the battle would be "a division of the abolitionist host into separate and mutually hostile organizations [that] would take on the fearful name of *schism*." In the words of Maria Chapman, it was to be a "war to the knife's point," and one that would, for some of the participants, continue beyond the grave.[3]

William Lloyd Garrison, thirty-three years of age, was deceptively benign in appearance, leading adversaries to sometimes underestimate him. Five feet, seven inches, tall and slender, Garrison had a "long, earnest face, with its prominent nose, thin-lipped, straight mouth," wore wire-rimmed glasses, was completely bald, and was often dressed in a formal waistcoat. He was the middle of three children born to an alcoholic father who abandoned his family and an intensely pious mother who perpetually urged her children to lead strict Christian lives. Because of his family's poverty, Garrison received little formal education and at age thirteen had apprenticed himself to a printer. His background may explain in part Garrison's lifelong desire for respectability. At age twenty, although still poor, he was said to be "always neatly, and perhaps I might say even elegantly dressed," and had commissioned a portrait of himself. Some would later describe Garrison as "eager for notoriety and adulation" and "determined more than ever to secure both salvation and worldly fame."[4]

In 1828, when he was twenty-three, Garrison had heard a lecture in Boston by Benjamin Lundy, one of the early abolitionists. Intrigued by Lundy's description of the slavery problem, Garrison joined him in Baltimore to help edit Lundy's abolitionist newspaper. In Baltimore, Garrison observed slaves being sold at auction and whipped, scenes he said left "my blood boiling in my veins, and my limbs trembling with emotion." In 1829 Garrison named in the newspaper a ship owner who was transporting slaves to be sold in southern ports. Such men, wrote Garrison, are "*highway robbers and murderers,* and their final doom will be, unless they speedily repent, to *occupy the lowest depths of perdition.*" Garrison was successfully sued for libel by the ship owner and fined $100 (approximately $2,020 in 2010 dollars) or six months in jail. Unable to pay the fine, Garrison was jailed for seven weeks, during which time he wrote and distributed a pamphlet describing his case. The pamphlet was read by Arthur Tappan, a wealthy New York abolitionist who was Lundy's friend, and Tappan sent Lundy money to pay Garrison's fine.[5]

Garrison's experience in the Baltimore jail converted him to being a devout abolitionist. Believing that Lundy was too timid in his approach in his abolitionist newspaper, Garrison returned to

Boston to start his own, which he called the *Liberator*. On January 1, 1831, four hundred copies of the first edition were printed and circulated. It carried the following manifesto:

> I am aware, that many object to the severity of my language, but is there not cause for my severity? I *will be* harsh as truth, and as uncompromising as justice. On this subject I do not wish to think, write or speak with moderation. No! No! Tell a man whose house is on fire to give a moderate alarm; tell him to moderately rescue his wife from the hands of the ravishers, tell the mother to gradually extricate her babe from the fire to which it has fallen;—but urge me not to use moderation in a cause like the present. I am in earnest—I will not equivocate—I will not excuse—I will not retreat an inch and I WILL BE HEARD.

One year later Garrison and eleven others founded the New England (later to become the Massachusetts) Anti-Slavery Society, and the following year Garrison was one of the founders of the American Anti-Slavery Society when it was organized in Philadelphia.[6]

The New England Anti-Slavery Society was not the first such organization. The Pennsylvania Abolition Society, led by Quakers, had been active for many years. What made Garrison's efforts unique at that time and led to his preeminent role among American abolitionists were two things. First, he called for an *immediate* end to slaveholding in the United States. "All property in slaves should *henceforth* cease," said Garrison, and "anything which serves as a substitute for the immediate and absolute abolition of slavery is delusive, cruel and dangerous." As historian James Brewer Stewart noted, "immediatism was not a doctrine original to Garrison, but few before him had espoused it, and fewer still with his vehemence." In particular, Garrison had been influenced by a pamphlet published in 1829 by David Walker, a free African American man in Boston, who called upon slaves to free themselves. Immediatism became Garrison's gonfalon, and he flew it with pride; it stood in contrast to the gradualist efforts of the Pennsylvania society or the efforts of other abolitionists, referred to as colonists, to send free blacks, and ultimately all slaves, back to Africa. Immediatism implied freeing all slaves at once and giving them the same civil rights as other citizens.[7]

The second unique aspect of Garrison's abolitionist efforts was that they included blacks as full participants. Indeed, the New England Anti-Slavery Society was "the world's first integrated abolitionist society." The *Liberator* employed William Nell and other young blacks, and financial support from Boston's free blacks kept the *Liberator* alive in its early years. In fact, "of the nearly 400 first-year subscribers, Garrison tabulated that three-quarters were black." The *Liberator* printed essays by black writers as well as notices of black meetings, social events, and obituaries. Immediatism thus included blacks in the abolitionist efforts as previous abolitionists efforts had never done; "Garrison stood out, from the start," in this regard.[8]

In the intervening years from 1831 to 1839, William Lloyd Garrison had built the Massachusetts Anti-Slavery Society into the strongest such society in the country. On that January morning in 1839, Garrison was joined by most of his prominent supporters. Especially conspicuous was Wendell Phillips, a tall, wealthy graduate of Harvard College and Law School, president of the Boston Anti-Slavery Society, and said to be "among the most accomplished orators of New England." According to one Phillips biographer, "by early 1839 he stood in the forefront of Boston's abolitionist leadership." Samuel Sewall and Ellis Gary Loring, two wealthy lawyers who were financially supporting Garrison's efforts, and Samuel May, a Unitarian minister, were also there. Also noteworthy in the audience were many female supporters of Garrison. These included Maria Chapman, "a regal beauty with a razor-sharp mind," who was married to a wealthy Boston merchant. Her 1839 account of the meeting, *Right and Wrong in Massachusetts,* would be the most detailed account of what took place, although written, of course, from a Garrisonian viewpoint.[9]

Garrison's inner circle of supporters formed a tightly knit and intensely loyal clique. In *Gregarious Saints,* Lawrence Friedman described them as an extended family, with Garrison being the father. "A common loyalty, allegiance, and intense emotional warmth toward Garrison was a fundamental source of Clique cohesiveness." Wendell Phillips, for example, regarded Garrison as a "peerless saint

. . . the inspired visionary who had dispersed the clouds of ignorance and apathy that had hidden slavery for so long." Garrison's *Liberator,* according to Phillips, was "the first banner which was unfurled in our cause. . . . I regard the success of the *Liberator* as identical with that of the abolition cause itself." Another historian summarized Garrison's antislavery society as follows: "No other organization would ever capture that spirit of implacable hostility to slavery that characterized the parent Society, and no one could ever match Garrison's symbolic role as the spokesman of the American conscience, at least until John Brown appeared."[10]

Garrison and his supporters had no doubts about who was responsible for the challenge to them and to the Massachusetts Anti-Slavery Society. In a December 23, 1838, letter to his sister, Garrison described the evolving attempts to force him out, adding: "Torrey, of Salem (formerly of Providence), is one of the most active of the plotters." Five days before the meeting, Garrison publicly named Charles Torrey as the leader of the "conspiracy," which he described as an "insidious and wicked attempt to subvert the integrity of the abolition enterprise." He told other correspondents that the plot against him was being led by "Torrey and Co.," and "the Torrey group"; and in another letter he named the other members of the cabal: "Phelps and Torrey are foremost in the matter, backed up by Stanton, St. Clair, and others." Similarly, Maria Chapman, in her account of the challenge to Garrison, named Torrey as having been "particularly active" as well as St. Clair, Phelps, and Stanton.[11]

Charles Torrey was at this time a twenty-five-year-old Yale graduate, failed school teacher, and Congregational minister who had headed a church in Salem for the previous year. He had joined the abolitionist movement four years previously but had dropped out for a year because of having tuberculosis. Alanson St. Clair was a Unitarian minister who also worked in Salem and who had collaborated with Torrey as their challenge to Garrison had developed. He was at the time of the meeting still a paid field agent for the Massachusetts Anti-Slavery Society. Amos Phelps, who was Torrey's closest friend, was a thirty-two-year-old Congregational minister at Boston's Pine Street Church. He had attended the 1833 founding of the American Anti-Slavery Society along with Garrison, had been appointed as one of the Massachusetts society's first field agents, and had published *Lectures on Slavery and Its Remedy* in 1834. In that book he called slavery "a great and threatening evil . . . and crying national sin" and had urged abolitionists to become politically active, including amending the Constitution to prohibit slavery. Phelps's public challenge to Garrison in 1839, after six years of having worked with him, was especially awkward, since Garrison and his family were at the time subletting a house from Phelps.[12]

Henry Stanton, the fourth of the plotters identified by Garrison, was a thirty-four-year-old former theology student and journalist. In contrast to Torrey, St. Clair, and Phelps, who were connected to the Massachusetts Anti-Slavery Society, Stanton was a member of the executive board of the American Anti-Slavery Society in New York and represented that organization, which was, in theory, the parent organization for Garrison's society. Two years before the 1839 meeting, Stanton had been sent to Massachusetts to investigate allegations against Garrison and had concluded "that it would be no bad thing to purge the eccentric and difficult Massachusetts leadership" from the parent organization. At the 1839 Massachusetts meeting, Stanton was thus representing the leadership of the New York office. This included Joshua Leavitt, a Congregational minister and former lawyer; James Birney, a former Alabama slaveholder who had freed his slaves and become an abolitionist; Elizur Wright, a former mathematics professor, antislavery lecturer, and college classmate of Torrey's; and Arthur and Lewis Tappan, wealthy silk merchants who were financially supporting the New York office. By the time of the 1839 meeting, all these men had decided that Garrison had to go. As Birney phrased it: Garrison's "departure from us might be the best thing he could do for the cause of emancipation." Wright, the most outspoken member of the group, added: "Garrison is doing us more mischief than his neck is worth. . . . I have no more hope from him in the future than I have from the inmates of Bedlam in general."[13]

Politics, Religion, and Women's Rights

The issues that led up to Maria Chapman's "war to the knife's point" were manifold, but three were most salient: politics, religion, and women's rights. Politically, both sides favored immediate emancipation, but they differed profoundly on the best strategy. Garrison and his followers preached "moral suasion," by which they meant convincing people that slavery was wrong by using lectures, newspaper articles, pamphlets, and petitions. This strategy, argued Garrison, would lead to "a change in the moral vision of the people," which in turn would produce pressure for emancipation from northerners and the voluntary freeing of slaves by southerners. As explained by historian Bruce Laurie, "Garrison found it impossible to envision emancipation or racial equality without a thoroughgoing transformation of the hearts of men and women."[14]

Closely related to Garrison's belief in moral suasion was his advocacy of pacifism, or nonresistance, as he called it. During the 1830s he had been moving in a pacifist direction, but the events of October 21, 1835, had accelerated that movement. On that day Garrison, who had been lecturing to the Boston Female Anti-Slavery Society, was seized by a mob of slavery supporters. Led through the streets, "leased like an animal" with a rope around his chest, he heard threats of being hanged or tarred and feathered. Finally, he was rescued and turned over to the mayor, who promptly put him in jail for his own safety. "Never was a man so rejoiced to get into jail," Garrison had exclaimed. According to one biographer, "his brush with martyrdom had shaken Garrison. . . . staring into the violent face of the mob . . . he began to think about pacifism as a rule for living."[15]

Following his "brush with martyrdom," Garrison espoused pacifist doctrines increasingly strongly. In September 1838, he organized a pacifist meeting for approximately 160 people, including many of his abolitionist supporters, and formed the New England Non-Resistance Society. The meeting produced a "Declaration of Sentiments," written mostly by Garrison, which discouraged believers from participating in any political or government action, including holding office or voting. It read in part: "We cannot acknowledge allegiance to any human government. . . . Our country is the world, our countrymen are all mankind. . . . As every human government is upheld by physical strength, we therefore voluntarily exclude ourselves from every legislative and judicial body, and repudiate all human politics." Although Garrison had voted in the 1834 elections, he said that doing so was a sin, and he did not vote again until 1871. "The governments of this world," he said, "are all Anti-Christ." "Is there one man in the United States—in the whole world—who can honestly and truly affirm, before God, that by becoming a politician he has improved his manners or morals, his head or his heart, or has elevated the tone of his piety, or felt new emotions of spiritual life?"[16]

By the late 1830s most abolitionists, except for Garrison and his followers, had become convinced that moral suasion by itself was not going to be sufficient to free the slaves. Amos Phelps's 1834 *Lectures on Slavery and Its Remedies* had advocated a variety of political actions, and these actions were being widely discussed by other abolitionists. For example, there was increasing interest in the election of antislavery politicians to state and federal office. Following Garrison's formation of the Non-Resistance Society, James Birney "published a harsh attack upon the nonresistant abolitionists." Elizur Wright, in a letter to Maria Chapman, wrote: "With all due respect to Garrison, I consider his 'nonresistance' sheer lunacy—and sadly ill-timed, as it cuts the hamstrings of abolitionism just at the crisis of battle."[17]

The second issue that divided the abolitionists was religion. Garrison had been raised a Baptist but had little use for formal religion. As the 1830s progressed, he increasingly attacked organized religion, questioned clerical authority, and claimed that there was no biblical authority for the sanctity of the Sabbath and that not everything in the Bible was divinely inspired. "I am growing more and more hostile to outward forms and ceremonies and observances, as a religious duty," he wrote. When the churches refused to take a strong stand against slaveholding, Garrison publicly labeled them "heathenish," "disgraces to humanity," and "Bulwarks of slavery." In 1836, when the Methodist Church voted to prohibit the discussion of slavery, Garrison called them "a cage of unclean birds and a synagogue of Satan." To supporter Samuel May, a Unitarian minister, Garrison wrote: "Oh, the rottenness of Christendom! I am forced to believe that, as respects the greater proportion of professing Christians in this land, Christ died in vain."[18]

Such remarks further alienated Garrison from the majority of abolitionists, especially those who were theologically trained, such as

Torrey, Phelps, St. Clair, Stanton, and Leavitt, as well as those who were intensely pious, such as Arthur and Lewis Tappan. But Garrison's anti-church bias became even stronger following his meeting with John Humphrey Noyes in the spring of 1837. Noyes had been expelled from theology school in 1834 for claiming that the second coming of Jesus Christ had already taken place and that men could become perfect, like Christ, simply by fully accepting him. Noyes's beliefs were a variant of what was called Perfectionism, which was popular among some religious reformers in the early nineteenth century. Once a man became one with Christ and thus achieved perfection, according to Noyes, it placed him above the dictates of both the church and the government. Such ideas intrigued Garrison, and he began promoting perfectionist ideas to his abolitionist colleagues and in the pages of the *Liberator*.

Garrison's opponents viewed his perfectionist interests as a further diversion from the abolitionist cause. In late 1837 Elizur Wright wrote to Garrison: "I look upon your notions of government and religious perfectionism as downright fanaticism—as harmless as they are absurd. . . . It is not in the human mind (except in a peculiar and, as I think, diseased state) to believe them. . . . I beg of you, as a brother, to let other subjects alone till slavery is finished, *because* this is the work you have taken in hand, it is the most pressing and needs your whole energy. . . . What I fear is that they [the other subjects] will suck *you* into a vortex of spiritual Quixotism, and thus absorb energies which might have shaken down the citadel of oppression." Shortly thereafter, Wright wrote to Amos Phelps, indicating that he had given up on Garrison: "I have just received a letter from Garrison which confirms my fears that he has finished his course *for the slave*. . . . It is downright nonsense to suppose that the Anti-Slavery cause can be carried forward with forty incongruous things tacked on to it."[19]

Political and religious differences between Garrison and his opponents may have been sufficient by themselves to bring about a permanent rupture in the abolitionist movement, but the addition of women's rights made that outcome inevitable. It began benignly enough in early 1837, when Garrison invited Angelina and Sarah

Grimké, sisters who had grown up on a slaveholding plantation in South Carolina, to give public lectures in Massachusetts describing the evils of slavery. During three months the sisters gave twenty-eight lectures in various towns and were enthusiastically received by abolitionist audiences.

The problems began when the Grimkés began talking about the rights of women in addition to the rights of slaves. As Angelina Grimké observed, "The investigation of the rights of the slave has led me to a better understanding of my own." Anne Weston, Maria Chapman's sister, similarly noted that "we have only to go steadily forward ... in the overthrow of slavery [and] we may also overthrow the injurious prejudices relative to the real duties and responsibilities of women." The Grimkés asked Garrison to be "divinely directed" and include women's rights as well as slaves' rights in the *Liberator.* Garrison enthusiastically agreed, saying that the "two reformations" were inextricably joined under "pure practical Christianity." Garrison proceeded to publish Sarah Grimké's *Letters on the Equality of the Sexes,* and Maria Chapman included a long section on women's rights in the annual report of the Boston Female Anti-Slavery Society.[20]

This public espousal of women's rights took place eleven years before the first women's rights convention in 1848 and was regarded by many as radical. The Congregational ministers of Massachusetts issued a "Pastoral Letter" in July 1837 deploring the "unnatural" presumption of women's rights and "the dangers which at present seem to threaten the female character." Theodore Weld, a prominent abolitionist who would marry Angelina Grimké the following year, also urged the Grimkés not to make themselves "so obnoxious as to cripple your influence on the subject of slavery." He said that the women's issue was "producing alienation in our ranks and producing confusion. What is done for the *slave must be done now, now, now* whereas woman's rights are not a life or death business *now or never.*" Elizur Wright argued that tying women's rights to abolitionism was like "tying a tin can to the tail of our enterprise." Lewis Tappan complained that Garrison and his followers "have loaded the cause [of slavery] with their no-government-woman's-rights-non-resistant &c" agenda. Even Henry Stanton opposed Garrison's agenda, despite Stanton's feminist bona fides, which he established in 1840 by marrying Elizabeth Cady, the organizer of the 1848 women's rights convention.[21]

Garrison ignored the criticism, correctly calculating that tying the abolitionist cause to women's rights would attract more women to abolitionism in general and to his approach, moral suasion, in particular. His opponents feared that Garrison would use the additional women to outnumber them at antislavery meetings, which is exactly what he did.

Of all the women who allied themselves with Garrison, Abby Kelley was regarded as the most radical and outspoken. She was a young schoolteacher in Lynn when she first heard Garrison speak about slavery, and she eventually gave up her job to work as a full-time abolitionist. At a meeting of the Massachusetts Anti-Slavery Society she called clergymen, which included many of Garrison's opponents, "thieves, robbers, adulterers, pirates and murderers." On occasion she also walked into church services and lectured on slavery while the minister was preaching. Even her biographer described her as "sharp-tongued and intense." Abby Kelley was one of the first women to link women's rights to those of the slave: "In striving to strike *his* chains off, we found most surely that *we* were manacled too." And she strongly urged Garrison to open the *Liberator* to the women's issue: "The time is now *fully* come when thou will take a decided stand for *all truths*." Garrison called Kelley his "moral Joan of Arc," and she was regarded as one of his "five closest nonresistance associates."[22]

It is thus not surprising that it was Abby Kelley who in 1838 pushed to the forefront the most explosive rights issue of all—the rights of blacks and whites to marry. All abolitionists were aware that the public feared "amalgamation" as a consequence of abolitionism and that such fears were a major impediment to the success of the abolitionist movement. For example, during the 1834 anti-abolitionist riots in New York, mobs attacked two churches "because it was rumored that their ministers had performed interracial marriages." Mobs also "destroyed Arthur Tappan's house because allegedly he had entertained blacks there." As soon as the riots ceased, Tappan and other members of the American Anti-Slavery Society "posted handbills throughout the city" that stated, among other points, that "we entirely disclaim any desire to promote or encourage intermarriages between white and colored citizens." Similarly, in Philadelphia at an 1837 abolitionist convention, "it was reported that white men and black women, and black men and white women walked arm-in-arm." According to one account, such reports "had much to do with what followed" when, on the following day, a mob burned the convention hall to the ground. Historian James Brewer Stewart summarized the racial politics of this period as follows: "In nearly all of these thoroughly studied events, mob activity from 1831 to 1838 was triggered initially by a highly visible action that abolitionists regarded as part of their 'respectable' promotion of African American 'uplift' but that whites of all classes abominated as degrading racial and sexual 'amalgamationism.' . . . The white men who mobbed abolitionists and terrorized black neighborhoods until the late 1830s should be understood as having been absolutely correct when decrying their victims as racial 'amalgamationists.'"[23]

Garrison was well aware of the explosive nature of the "amalgamation" issue. In 1832 he had caused a sensation when he had written: "Inter-marriage is neither unnatural nor repugnant to nature, but obviously proper and salutary." He, along with Maria Chapman and Abby Kelley, had attended the 1837 Philadelphia convention and thus experienced the white working-class fears of racial integration. In light of this, it is puzzling why Garrison and his followers decided to petition the Massachusetts legislature in 1838, advocating repeal of the state law prohibiting interracial marriage. The petition was organized by Abby Kelley's Female Anti-Slavery Society in Lynn and sponsored by Wendell Phillips. It was signed by 786 Lynn women.[24]

The petition was summarily rejected by the legislature and ridiculed by the press. The *Boston Post* suggested that "some of these ladies despair of having a white offer and so are willing to try *de colored race*." A follow-up mocking petition was submitted by 150 men from Lynn recommending that the Lynn ladies be given "the exclusive right to marry any Negro, Indian or Hottentot." The submission of Abby Kelley's petition to the state legislature just prior to the impending annual meeting of the Massachusetts Anti-Slavery

Society confirmed to Garrison's opponents that he and his followers had clearly lost their abolitionist bearings.[25]

In addition to the political, religious, and women's rights issues that increasingly divided Garrison and his opponents, personal animus was also prominent. This was especially true between Torrey and Phelps on one side and Garrison on the other. Torrey referred to Garrison as "Lloyd Garrulous," cited Garrison's "belief that his mighty self was abolition incarnate," publicly called him "one of the most bigoted and unfair sectarians in our land," and is said to have referred to Garrison's followers as "infidels and prostitutes." Garrison reciprocated, calling Torrey "decidedly objectionable," "arrogant, aggressive and often irritating," "in spirit and in purpose . . . criminal," and comparing him to "the arch enemy of mankind," the devil. Similarly, the animosity between Phelps and Garrison was such that poet and abolitionist John Greenleaf Whittier, originally a Garrison supporter, said that he was tired of "the everlasting ding-dong" and suggested that Phelps and Garrison settle their differences by having "a regular set of fisticuffs" in the street. Theodore Weld, who attempted to remain neutral in the fray, noted the "deep, irreconcilable, *personal* animosities and repulsions" on both sides and said that such feelings make "cooperation impossible." After Torrey's death, his wife wrote that her husband had been "partially insane upon some subjects"; Garrison was surely one of the subjects to which she was referring.[26]

It is interesting to speculate why Torrey and Garrison disliked each other so intensely. For starters, their backgrounds were completely different. Garrison's pedigree included an alcoholic father who had deserted his family, a mother who had had to work at menial jobs to support her children, and a brother who was a public drunk. Torrey, by contrast, could recite his eminent Puritan forefathers, including a grandfather who had been a member of Congress, and he claimed that his family background placed him "in the highest and purest class of society." There was also the issue of education. Garrison had had little and had become a printer's apprentice at age thirteen. On one occasion, Garrison described himself as "a poor, self-educated mechanic." Torrey had gone to Exeter, Yale, and

Andover Seminary, qualifying him as a fully educated Boston Brahmin. For Torrey, education was everything, since "piety and knowledge, in the masses, are ever unified." Religion was yet another milestone for which, in Torrey's opinion, Garrison fell short, for he had been raised a Baptist. Torrey wrote that among Baptist ministers, "a large portion of their predecessors were extremely illiterate, and themselves in many cases, filled with prejudices against learning in the ministry." Torrey, by contrast, belonged to the Congregational Church, the religion of the Massachusetts Bay Colony and the predominant religion of abolitionist leaders.[27]

Torrey and Garrison also had profoundly different personalities. Torrey aspired to be the prototypical "Christian gentleman" esteemed in New England at that time. According to historian Michael D. Pierson, such a man "controlled his bodily appetites . . . stayed away from tobacco and alcohol . . . and most of all regulated his sexuality." Such "personal self-control, when joined with hard work, punctuality, and scrupulous honesty . . . would secure him a place in heaven." As Daniel Walker Howe noted in his history of this period, those are the "standards we now term 'Victorian,' which laid increased emphasis on impulse control and strict personal accountability."[28]

According to Garrison's opponents, such standards did not apply to him. "Always disorderly and unpunctual," Garrison was vilified as being "negligent, polygamous, imperious, and the pawn of a female 'prime minister,'" Maria Chapman. According to Lewis Tappan, Chapman was "a talented woman with the disposition of a fiend," who could control Garrison "as easily as she could untie a garter." Garrison "experienced sharp strains early in his marriage" and displayed "interest in intellectual reformist-oriented women, especially Ann Weston," an unmarried sister of Maria Chapman. Rumors regarding Garrison's personal life were further fueled by his admiration for John Humphrey Noyes. In addition to beliefs in perfectionism, Noyes promoted ideas about "spiritual wives" and "free love," ideas that he would put into action by establishing communes in Vermont and New York in the 1840s. By at least 1841 Garrison was rumored to be "associated" with persons "advocating the right and propriety of unlimited intercourse of the sexes." Such persons were said to be "promoting the most shameless libertinism, under the guise of anti-slavery."[29]

The intense enmity between Charles Torrey and William Lloyd Garrison continued from 1839 until Torrey's death in 1846 and would even follow Torrey to his grave. It dominated the relationship between the two men and affected the relationships of many of their friends as well. The relationship of the two men had a certain poignancy, given that they both hated slavery intensely, and both devoted their lives to its abolition.

The Meeting

When William Lloyd Garrison entered Marlboro Chapel on the morning of January 23, 1839, he saw a sea of female and black faces. He had prepared carefully for the meeting. Maria Chapman, Abby Kelley, and other female members of his inner circle had spread the word to every women's rights activist in the area—be there if you want the *Liberator* to continue publishing on women's issues! Notices of the meeting had also been sent to Boston's three black churches with a notation that anyone "who set Garrison at naught" would not thereafter be regarded as a "genuine abolitionist." The strength of Garrison's support among Boston's free blacks can be inferred from men such as David Walker, who named his son after Garrison, and John Smith, who said he regarded Garrison as second only to Moses.[30]

Garrison had worked assiduously to inform his supporters about the nature of the threat by Torrey and his colleagues. It was, he said, a "deplorable and alarming conspiracy" being carried out "in a mean and treacherous manner." He warned friends that "the clerical snake was coiling in the grass for a spring" and said "that you must be present at our annual meeting on [January] the 23d instant, if practicable, and induce as many sound, *ultra* abolitionists to attend as you can." The "clerical abolitionists," he cautioned, "are working in darkness, and secretly endeavoring to transfer our sacred cause to other hands. . . . The plot is extensively laid, and the wires are pulled skillfully." The plot, Garrison explained, was to change the governing board of the society, "then to get a vote for the establishment of a new weekly paper, to be under the control of the new Board, and to be the organ of the Society. How mean, how ungrateful, how contemptible is conduct like this!"[31]

Having complete editorial control of the *Liberator* was a great advantage for Garrison, and he used it skillfully. He warned readers about the plot and urged them to come to the meeting to support him: "Strong foes are without, insidious plotters are within the camp. A conflict is at hand, —if the signs of the times do not deceive us—which is to be more hotly contested, and which will require more firmness of nerve and greater singleness of purpose, . . . than any through which we have passed to victory." Garrison was willing to do whatever was necessary to retain control of the abolitionist movement, which he regarded as his own. Nobody was going to take it from him. "We have blasted the rocks . . . and macadamised the road," he wrote, "and now the big folks are riding upon it in their coaches as proudly as if they had made it all. . . . they mean if possible to monopolize it all, and to transfer the credit of its design and completion to themselves!"[32]

Garrison's opponents were equally active in fomenting plans to unseat him. Their strategy was to attack Garrison on his opposition to political action in general and to voting in particular, and to advocate for a new abolitionist newspaper, one that would focus exclusively on the issue of slavery. Accordingly, they went to local chapters of the Massachusetts Anti-Slavery Society and introduced resolutions. These stated that "every abolitionist is duty bound . . . to go to the polls and throw his vote for some man known to favor it [the freeing of slaves]," and also that "a weekly and ably-conducted anti-slavery paper . . . is now greatly needed in Massachusetts."[33]

The first local chapter that passed these resolutions was in Fitchburg, so the proposals became known as the Fitchburg resolutions. Since there were eighty-six local branches of the state society, covering them all involved considerable effort. As described by Maria Chapman: "Mr. Phelps, Mr. Stanton, Mr. Torrey and Mr. St. Clair were hurrying from meeting to meeting with the Fitchburg resolutions . . . and dwelling strongly on the importance of sending up large delegations [to the January 1839 meeting], instructed to vote in its favor." A review of correspondence between Torrey and

Phelps during this period shows them discussing strategy in military terms: "We must be prepared for war," wrote Torrey. "But yet, our battery must be mounted with *5,000* guns before one is loaded or a shot fired. We must be content to suffer a little, as Nelson was, from the enemies' broadsides at first. But if we keep cool, we can fight the harder by and by." Torrey sometimes called Phelps his "brother plotter." It was an especially difficult period for Phelps, who was severing his longstanding ties to Garrison. Phelps's wife was also dying, and Torrey thus assumed much of the advocacy burden. That is probably why Garrison perceived Torrey to be primary leader of the plot.[34]

At 10 o'clock on January 23, Francis Jackson, Garrison's benefactor and close friend, gaveled the annual meeting of the Massachusetts Anti-Slavery Society to order. The first item on the agenda was Garrison's reading of the society's annual report, which was "heavily freighted with criticism of his opponents." Before they could reply, however, Wendell Phillips moved for the immediate consideration of the Fitchburg resolutions.[35]

Alanson St. Clair led off, describing for more than an hour the deficiencies of the *Liberator* and the need for a new paper. He was followed by Charles Torrey, who detailed the misuse of the *Liberator* for women's rights, non-resistance, perfectionism, and other issues unrelated to slavery. He identified St. Clair, Phelps, Stanton, and himself as the origin of the idea for a new paper and "said that it was contemplated to obtain the services of some first-rate editor— Elizur Wright or John G. Whittier." Wendell Phillips "argued earnestly against the . . . resolution" and was followed by Samuel May. "We have never wanted means of communication with the public," May claimed; "when the Massachusetts Society wants an *organ*, she sounds the trumpet." Before a vote could be taken on the resolutions, "a doubt was raised by Mr. Phelps and Mr. St. Clair as to the right of women to a voice in the decision." The decision by Francis Jackson surprised no one: "The Chair rules that it is in order for women to vote."[36]

On the second day Henry Stanton led the attack against Garrison. "It is not that other subjects are introduced into the *Liberator,*" said Stanton, "but it is that *such* other subjects are introduced—subjects so injurious to the cause." "To the utter astonishment of the meeting," according to Maria Chapman, Stanton then accused Garrison of having "lowered the standard of abolition" and being a "recreant to the cause."[37]

Garrison was on his feet at once, "grim-faced, to say that he had been regarded as the friend of the black man and the slave and hoped he still had their confidence." "You have! You have!" shouted the free blacks. "Am I recreant to the cause?" he asked. "No! No!" shouted the audience, followed by "a cheer that spoke more eloquently and sincerely than the tongue of man ever did." Maria Chapman captured the ambience of the moment: "His words opened the flood-gates of many memories. Instantly rushed through the minds of abolitionists all that had passed since he first stood among them, the trusted and beloved; their guide—their companion—their own familiar friend." Garrison's supporters sprang to his defense. John Hilton, a black clothes dealer, said that he had stood by "Brother Garrison" when he "was living on bread and water to sustain the *Liberator*. . . . If Brother Garrison was not a simon pure, sincere abolitionist, then neither he nor his colored brethren would ever trust or confide in a man with a white face again."[38]

When the crowd quieted, Stanton pressed on. He accused Garrison, who was urging abolitionists to not vote or participate in politics, of having himself voted in the 1834 elections and of having urged his supporters to do likewise. "It is false!" Garrison shouted. Stanton, having prepared carefully, "pulled out a sheath of quotations from the *Liberator* and requested to read them." "Garrison knew he was trapped, and so did his followers, for they refused to allow Stanton to proceed." Stanton then confronted Garrison directly on the voting issue. "Mr. Garrison, do you or do you not believe it is a sin to go to the polls?" Garrison perceived the trap immediately; if he said no, he would be endorsing political action, and if he said yes, he would be accusing many of his followers of having sinned. After a long pause, he cleverly replied: "Sin for *me*." Stanton slowly repeated his question and again got the same reply. It then developed into a standoff, with Stanton accusing Garrison of retarding the abolitionist cause by his failure to support political action, and Garrison responding by asking Stanton questions. "Why had Stanton waited so long to break silence? Why had he joined 'the sectarian party' in the first place—to destroy anti-slavery or merely to discredit veterans like himself? Who could prove that the *Liberator* hurt the cause? Where was the man who could deny his devotion to the slave? When Stanton tried to interrupt, his complaints were drowned out by roars and cheers."[39]

The outcome was foreordained. The convention voted overwhelmingly, 180 to 24, to reject the creation of a new abolitionist paper and to accept Garrison's annual report, "which advocated women's rights, censured the clerical party in Massachusetts, recommended nonresistance, and criticized political action." The delegates even voted down a mild resolution by Alanson St. Clair suggesting that it was the "duty of every abolitionist who could conscientiously do so to go to the polls," with "women supplying a powerful number of nays." At this time, of course, women did not yet have the right to vote anyway.[40]

The outcome of the meeting did not surprise Garrison's opponents. They had long since agreed that, if they were unable to oust Garrison from the *Liberator,* they would form a new organization with its own paper. In fact, their plans were so far advanced that "arrangements for a new paper were complete within less than a week," and the first issue of the *Massachusetts Abolitionist* appeared on February 7, just two weeks following the meeting. The lead editorial was headlined "Political Action" and "proposed concerted political campaigns to destroy slavery in the territories and the District of Columbia and to ban the interstate slave trade." "The political action we ask of you," it continued, "is to undo by your *votes,* the mischief that your votes have done, and those of your fathers. *Votes* make the men that make the laws that make the slaves." The political abolitionist movement was underway and would diverge profoundly from Garrison's moral suasion. As Henry Stanton correctly noted at the time, "the split is wide, and can never be closed up."[41]

2

DISCOVERING GOD AND SLAVES

The road Charles Torrey traveled to reach his 1839 confrontation with William Lloyd Garrison was not easy. He had been born on November 21, 1813, in Scituate, a coastal town south of Boston. Later in life, Torrey recalled the "wide marshes, covered with short salt grass, through which curves for many a mile old North river." The river, he said, was "famed for its excellent fisheries, and still more for its shipbuilding. Here our carpenters launched the first American vessel that ever doubled the stormy Cape Horn, and coasted the western shores of our continent."[1]

When Torrey was not quite two, his father, a twenty-four-year-old Scituate merchant, died from tuberculosis. Six months later his baby sister died, and one year later, when Torrey was three-and-a-half, his mother also died from tuberculosis. Death was therefore an acquaintance from his earliest childhood. Then, when he was seven, his closest childhood companion died. At that time he had a dream that he later described as "the most permanent influence that has acted on my life":

> I dreamed I was dead and in hell! It seemed not unlike the scenery of our world. Its devil, not unlike a smiling man. He offered to the lost, beautiful and fragrant fruits, that turned to bitter ashes in the mouth; and still he smiled! . . . Full of anguish at being shut up with the wicked, I approached the low wall that seemed to divide the place from heaven! Child as I was, I could see over it; but had no power to climb it. It seemed as if help must come from the heavenly side. I looked around for it. Presently, the forms of my venerable grand-parents seemed to pass by, mingled with throngs of happy faces. I called for help. They only looked at me mournfully, and passed

on. I could not blame or envy them. "*It is right, it is just*," was the feeling irresistibly impressed on my mind.

Thus, death for Torrey was like an anomalous old man you occasionally pass on the street. You nod, but he does not appear to notice. The man becomes familiar, but not a friend.[2]

Following his mother's death, Torrey was taken to Norwell, four miles away, to live with his maternal grandparents and grandmother's sister, Aunt Fanny. She "loved Charles with the fondness of a mother," and "his doubly fond grandparents . . . always abundantly supplied every want." Despite being orphaned, many of Torrey's childhood memories were happy ones: "I revisit every old haunt, think about where I plucked the butter-cups and violets; and the old moss grown nut tree, the button wood where the oriole hung her nest of fine thread, far beyond the reach of the most daring; the dear old mansion where my early youth was passed so rapidly."[3]

Torrey's maternal grandfather, Charles Turner, was especially influential in his grandson's development. He had served in the Massachusetts House and Senate, then been elected to the U.S. House of Representatives for two terms, from 1809 to 1813. After Torrey came to live with him, Turner continued to be politically active at the local level in Scituate. Beginning at age five, Torrey regularly accompanied his grandfather to town meetings, where he "watched every proceeding, counted every vote, and was able to carry home a correct account of all that transpired there." It was at this time that his grandfather officially changed Charles Torrey's middle name to Turner. Thus, it was said of Torrey that he had grown up "sprightly in his manners, with uncommon knowledge, ability, and self-confidence, and swayed by passions which yielded to no control."[4]

Torrey took special pride in his Puritan heritage and having descended from one of America's earliest settlers. In 1640, James Torrey and his three brothers had sailed from Somerset, England, to start a new life in the Massachusetts Bay Colony. James bought land in Scituate from the Matakeeset Indians and settled there. Perhaps unknowingly, Charles Torrey exaggerated the feats of his ancestor, writing that James had been "the first white settler" in Scituate, "twenty miles from any habitation of a Christian man." In fact, there were about seventy-five white families in Scituate when James arrived.[5]

Twenty-five years later, James Torrey met with a dramatic, if untimely, demise. According to a contemporary account, he was ordered to prepare the town's gunpowder supply for a possible attack by Dutch colonists coming from New York. He went to the Tickner house, where the powder was being stored, and started to spread it out on boards to dry. However, "by some accident, G. knows what, ye powder was fired, both that in ye house and that abroad, and ye house blown up and broken in pieces." Goodwife Tickner, her child, and Torrey were all severely burned and died within hours. James Torrey had made a major mistake that cost him his life, a pattern that would be repeated by Charles Torrey five generations later.[6]

When Torrey was eleven, his grandparents moved to Charlestown, and two years later, to Chelsea. At that time, he was sent to Exeter Academy in New Hampshire for the final two years of his secondary education. He apparently did well and in the fall of 1830 was admitted directly into the sophomore class at Yale University, despite being only sixteen years old. He was, according to Joseph Lovejoy's memoir, written after Torrey's death, "at that age when the magazine of passion is almost to be uncovered, and sparks are flying around it in all directions. The pure minded boy joins the older circle of companions, and must for himself choose the good or perish by the evil."[7]

For Torrey, good and evil were not abstractions. As noted in a diary he kept at Yale, he believed that man is born with "indwelling sin and corruption of the heart," a consequence of Adam's fall, and this "is sure to get the mastery if the Christian does not continually watch unto prayer." The devil, hell, and everlasting damnation were tangible. "That old serpent," wrote Torrey, could be identified by "his cloven foot" and "fiendish nature." "Why is it," Torrey asked, "that Christians, almost invariably, become cold and careless about the concerns of eternity?" Torrey's God was not a forgiving God. Not only were sinners to be eternally damned, but the sins of the fathers would also be visited upon their children in what Torrey called "that fearful law of retribution." This principle, said Torrey, "is designed to restrain men from crime by the before-known judgments their sins may bring upon the objects of their warmest love." The sufferings of the children, though they may be "pure and innocent victims of a parent's crimes, still more impressively show the evil nature of sin."[8]

During his college years, Torrey was continuously challenged by the devil. "Procrastination," he wrote, "has been my ruin. The habit of reading newspapers in the morning, when I should have been praying, has been a serious injury to me." More menacing was the problem of lust: "I find my resolution broken nearly as soon as formed, my purpose of holy obedience turned aside by my lusts, and my soul in misery...." Lust threatened to subjugate his soul and send him straight to hell: "Have sinned *much* within a few days past, in unholy thoughts, desires, and actions. It seems to have a giant power over me; and I have indeed felt a little of the misery of a body of sin and death, and the need of a Savior who is *mighty* to deliver out of every device of the evil one, and from the deceits and vileness of my own heart, which is indeed a sink of iniquity." Thus, at Yale, Torrey was initially confronted with the challenge of becoming a "Christian gentleman," one who was able to resist the lustful wiles of the devil. He would be ever reminded of his childhood dream in which he found himself in hell, being justly punished for unknown sins. "'*It is right, it is just*,' was the feeling irresistibly impressed on my mind."[9]

Salvation for Charles Torrey came in the spring of 1831 in the form of a religious revival. Such revivals were taking place throughout the northeastern United States as part of the Second Great Awakening. Charles Finney was the most prominent of many contemporary revivalist preachers. In 1821 Finney had "met the Lord Jesus face to face," received a "mighty baptism of the Holy Ghost," and vowed to sow the word of God. By 1831 Finney had become America's foremost evangelist, ultimately credited with saving half a million souls. It may well have been Finney himself who saved Torrey's soul in the spring of 1831, since Finney is known to have been preaching in New York early that year and also held revivals in Providence and Boston later in the year. Finney and other revivalists demanded that believers give their lives totally to God. They "should accept self-discipline while also engaging in long-term moral self-improvement, sometimes called 'sanctification.' . . . In short, the believer was expected to remake himself or herself into a new person—to be 'born again.'"[10]

Torrey was profoundly affected by his revival experience and committed his life to serving God. He had found "a Savior who is *mighty* to deliver out of every device of the evil one, and from the deceits and vileness of my own heart." On Sunday evening, March 13, 1831, Torrey set forth in his diary a formal agreement with God:

> Whereas my attention has been for some time called to the all-important subject of my soul's salvation, I . . . do now resolve that I will be, in every deed, his disciple; that I will take him in Christ as my only portion and hope, for time and for eternity, putting away all lusts and everything inconsistent with his honor and glory and the devotion of my whole heart and life to his cause: that I do now and forever consecrate myself to his service; that he shall be my God, and I will be his child. And may God, in his infinite mercy and love, enable me, in reliance on the Savior, to keep this resolution: to which I now, in his presence, affix my hand.

Torrey documented the agreement as being signed at precisely 9:31 p.m. and added: "I feel that I am acting no trifling part; that my future state has now been decided." Indeed it had.[11]

In later years, writing in prison, Torrey claimed that his dedication to God had been initiated by his dying mother. Previously, however, Torrey had written: "I remember very little about my parents or sister; perhaps nothing; for impressions may have been made on my mind so in unison with what may have been my feelings at the time, that I remember them." Was this his memory of the actual scene, or what Aunt Fanny had told him, or of a dream? Such cerebral fragments are lodged together and as time passes increasingly lose their labels of origin.[12]

Following his conversion, Charles Torrey was a changed man. All pleasures, he pledged, were to be subordinated to the service of God. Six months later, he asked: "When shall I feel that God *is* and *must* be the *only* source of my joys—the *only* object of my devotion in *time* as well as in eternity." And later: "In his service I find all the enjoyment I obtain. . . . In his cause I will spend my life, my all." Drinking, dancing, sexual relations, and all other pleasures were sinful insofar as they were not done to glorify God.[13]

These beliefs did not make Torrey a fun-loving friend. During a visit to two young ladies, Torrey persuaded them to give up coffee and tea and donate the money saved to a missionary society. In his diary, Torrey proudly noted that this would amount to "*thirty* dollars, if not more, in consequence. So much saved from sensual indulgences to the cause of Christ!" Torrey also joined Yale's "missionary circle" and suggested that the college should "*adopt* China with its 350 millions, and take up the work of converting it to God, as a business to be effected by the instrumentality of its students."[14]

Torrey's friends noticed the change in him. Writing some years later, Torrey described an episode after he had returned home following his first year at Yale, shortly after his conversion. He was at a social event with a female cousin, of whom he was very fond, and other friends. Describing himself in the third person, Torrey wrote: "He had been telling his youthful associates of the love of Christ, and exhorting them to flee to the same refuge for the guilty [and] trying to persuade her [his cousin] to become a Christian that very night." His cousin was offended, saying: "You are very queer tonight, cousin!"[15]

A few years later, following the death of his cousin's husband, Torrey implied that his cousin had been indirectly responsible for her husband's death because she had loved him more than God: "Three years ago you made choice of your companion. Which was dearest to your heart, he or your God? . . . I weep over your sorrows. But I cannot alleviate them by suggesting any ailment for a sinful heart. . . . I beseech you, turn not away from the view of your own sinful heart. Let your mind dwell on it, till by God's Spirit, you discover, as I did, in my own bosom, its dark, deadly depravity." This was apparently Torrey's idea of a letter of condolence. "The timid and sluggish shrink from a bold conflict with human passion," he wrote. Torrey had found God and would never be accused of being either timid or sluggish.[16]

It was during his years at Yale that Charles Torrey became aware of the slavery issue. Slavery had existed in America since the seventeenth century and was a fixture in the nation's landscape. Beginning with George Washington, five of the first seven presidents were slaveholders, as were "the majority of cabinet members and

. . . justices of the Supreme Court." Demonstrations against slavery dated to Quaker protests in the seventeenth century but became common in the late eighteenth century, at which time Vermont, then Pennsylvania, Massachusetts, New Hampshire, Rhode Island, Connecticut, New York, and New Jersey passed laws making slavery illegal.[17]

The legal status of slavery was ambiguous, a product of compromises necessitated by the drafting of the federal Constitution in 1787. The Declaration of Independence had proclaimed that "all men are created equal, that they are endowed by the Creator with certain unalienable rights, that among these are Life, Liberty and the Pursuit of Happiness." But the Constitution, written eleven years later, had included three clauses that appeared to permit slavery. One, the fugitive slave clause, said that all slaves must be returned to their owners. A second clause permitted the slave trade to continue for another twenty years, at which time it would be abolished. A third clause declared that slaves counted as three-fifths of a non-slave for purposes of determining representation in Congress. Thus, one man in Alabama who owned ten slaves counted the same for purposes of representation as seven men in Massachusetts who owned no slaves. This provided southern states with a disproportionate representation in Congress and allowed southern congressmen to control many key committees. According to a letter from James Madison to Thomas Jefferson written during the Constitutional Convention, these clauses were compromises necessitated by the fact that South Carolina and Georgia "were inflexible on the point of slaves."[18]

By 1830 the United States had approximately 2 million slaves among its total population of 12.5 million. The slaves were critical for the growing of cotton, which according to historian Daniel Walker Howe, was becoming "a driving force in expanding and transforming the economy not only of the South but of the United States as a whole—indeed of the world." Between 1800 and 1820, American cotton production increased tenfold, at which time the United States surpassed India as the world's leading producer. In 1820 cotton constituted 39 percent of American exports, and by 1840 this had increased to 59 percent. Most of the exports went to textile mills in England, but increasingly they also went to mills in New England, making the Northeast increasingly dependent on the growing of cotton. Shippers and bankers in cities such as Baltimore, New York, and Boston also depended heavily on the cotton trade, thus explaining in part the resistance to the abolition of slavery among many northerners. As Howe noted, the American South in the nineteenth century "was to be the most favored place for the production of a raw material of global significance . . . as the oil-rich Middle East would become in the twentieth." Because of the economic importance of cotton, slavery was said to be the most powerful institution in early-nineteenth-century America. . . . Those who owned human property exercised enormous economic, social, and political influence over the whole country."[19]

At the same time, many Americans acknowledged that slavery was an evil and a solution needed to be found. During the early years of the nineteenth century, one of the most commonly proposed solutions was to return freed slaves to Africa. Known as colonization, this policy was promoted by the American Colonization Society, formed in 1816, and by many ministers who viewed favorably the sending of blacks as potential Christian missionaries to convert Africa's heathen. Initially, American freed slaves, or blacks who had been born free, were sent to Sierra Leone, a free black colony that had been established by Great Britain. In 1821 the United States established its own African colony and called it Liberia. By the late 1820s, however, colonization had fallen out of favor; both free blacks and white abolitionists increasingly viewed it as a violation of the rights of black citizens and a way for slaveholders to get rid of troublesome free blacks and slaves. It was at this time that William Lloyd Garrison and other abolitionists, influenced by the increasingly public criticisms of colonization by free blacks, began advocating for the *immediate* freeing of all slaves.

The slavery controversy became prominent in New Haven during the same years that Charles Torrey was at Yale. There had been growing racial tensions in many northern cities during the 1820s, with race riots having occurred in Boston, New Haven, New York, Philadelphia, Pittsburgh, Cincinnati, and other cities. Working-class whites were increasingly threatened by the growing number of free blacks who often competed for the same jobs. Northerners and southerners alike were also becoming uneasy by reports of possible slave uprisings. The most prominent of these was an 1822 planned uprising in Charleston, led by Denmark Vesey, a free black. The plot was uncovered at the last minute, and Vesey and thirty-four others were hanged. Also disturbing to whites was the 1829 publication in Boston of a pamphlet entitled "An Appeal to the Colored Citizens of the World, But in Particular, and Very Expressly, to Those of the United States of America." The pamphlet's author, David Walker, a free black, warned his countrymen to educate and free the slaves or suffer the consequences: "I speak Americans for your good. We must and shall be free I say, in spite of you. You may do your best to keep us in wretchedness and misery, to enrich you and your children; but God will deliver us from under you. And wo, wo, will be to you if we have to obtain our freedom by fighting." Walker disseminated his pamphlet widely, provoking fear and anger among whites. According to historian Peter Hinks, "nothing like this had ever been seen before in the South." Even William Lloyd Garrison called the pamphlet "a most injudicious publication" but also warned of an impending race war if slaves were not freed: "Blood will flow like water—the blood of guilty men, and of innocent women and children."[20]

In case anyone had not gotten the message, on August 22, 1831, it was writ large. Nat Turner, a slave in southeastern Virginia who believed himself destined to lead all slaves to freedom, initiated an insurrection. After reading an eclipse of the sun as a sign from heaven, Turner and his slave confederates, armed with knives and axes, "burst into his master's house, and murdered every one of the white inmates." They then proceeded to the next plantation and repeated the slaughter, then to the next, and the next, increasing their slave army as they went. In order to strike maximum terror into those who would discover the destruction, they "most shockingly mangled the bodies of their victims. . . . The head of the youthful maiden was in one part of the room and her mangled body was in another." Within twenty-four hours, they massacred fifty-seven white men, women, and children, until they were stopped by the militia and military forces. Almost all of the participants, including Turner, were hanged, many without benefit of trial.[21]

The effect of Nat Turner's insurrection was profound. According to one account: "To describe the state of alarm to which this outbreak gave rise is impossible. Whole states were agitated. . . . For months the entire South remained in a fever of excitement." The governor of Virginia "was convinced that the Nat Turner rebellion was attributable to abolitionist writings, and especially to William Lloyd Garrison's *Liberator,* and "laws were passed forbidding blacks from preaching or from circulating incendiary pamphlets." Every southern state except Kentucky passed legislation limiting the freedom of speech and of the press, and Maryland and Tennessee "made it a felony for any free black to receive an abolitionist newspaper."[22]

The news of Nat Turner's slave uprising arrived in New Haven at the same time that Charles Torrey was returning from summer holidays and amidst a heated local racial debate. Two months earlier, Simeon Jocelyn, a Congregational minister in New Haven, had proposed the building of a "Negro training school" close to the Yale campus where blacks could study "agriculture, horticulture and the mechanic arts [along] with the study of literature and the sciences." Jocelyn got the support of Garrison as well as Arthur Tappan. Tappan was so enthusiastic about the plan that he moved to New Haven, pledged an initial gift of $1,000 ($20,200 in 2010), promised to match other gifts of up to $20,000 ($404,000), and purchased twenty acres of land for the school.[23]

In late August, a week after Nat Turner's insurrection, a New Haven town meeting was held to debate the merits of the school. The proposal was deemed to be "incompatible with the prosperity if not the existence of the present institution of learning [Yale]," and the crowd voted 700 to 4 to reject it. In order to leave no doubt about the outcome, a "garbage-throwing mob" then proceeded to Arthur Tappan's house, where his "wife and children awoke to hear shouts . . . mingled with the 'most obscene and blasphemous' curses and the noise of shattering window glass." The crowd then "moved into New Haven's colored community . . . for two nights of mayhem," including vandalizing black-owned establishments and destroying some black residences. New Haven's leaders deplored the riot but blamed "abolitionist 'firebrands' as the agents of provocation." Arthur Tappan thereupon sold his home and moved back to New York, terminating any plans for a school. Charles Torrey and the other Yale students had received an important lesson in both the politics and the violent dimensions of the slavery question.[24]

In June 1833, at the age of nineteen, Charles Torrey graduated from Yale. He was substantially in debt, having had to borrow funds to complete his education. His father had left him a "small patrimony," but Torrey was careless with money, purchasing "a library, and other useful things, which it would have been better to have remained without, till he really needed them, or was able to pay for them." Indebtedness would follow Torrey all his life, a pecuniary pestilence from which he would never be free.[25]

He needed a job in order to repay his debts, so he decided to teach, a common vocation for educated young men of that era. It was also consistent with his heritage; the Puritans placed great emphasis on education, opening the first public school and college (Harvard) shortly after arriving in America. The purpose of education was to enable people to read the Bible, which Puritans regarded as the word of God and the scriptural basis for all authority.

Torrey was accepted for a teaching position at a school in West Brookfield, a village on the stage route midway between Worcester and Springfield. He traveled there in October 1833 and in his diary outlined his ideas regarding the purpose of education: "The true and only proper end of education is to train the soul for an eternal existence; to train the intellect and the passions, *the whole man,* for eternity. It is to teach the young immortal to think clearly, correctly, to feel aright, and to act aright, in time and in eternity." Such a philosophy did not encompass the pleasures of learning, or learning for learning's sake. It was aimed solely at the saving of souls, and one would predict that the children of West Brookfield would have had less interest in the fate of their eternal souls than Charles Torrey had.[26]

From the first day of class on November 2, for which only five pupils appeared, the teaching went poorly. Although the class increased to twenty, Torrey wrote that he had "been discouraged by my small number and want of success in several respects. . . . I have not secured the affection of all the pupils, though in most cases I think I have. . . . About every difficulty originates either in my ignorance of human nature, or in want of self-control." Torrey added that "my difficulties out of school have affected my countenance and tone in school too often, rendering me, I fear, a little irritable."[27]

Torrey's difficulties out of school included social isolation, financial hardship, and sin. West Brookfield was but a village, its social center being Ye Olde Tavern, opened in 1760 but off limits to the teetotaling Torrey. In his diary Torrey wrote that "womankind avoided me." He may have lodged with the widow of Daniel Merriam, who took schoolteachers and others as boarders for one dollar and a half per week. Her husband had been a local printer and had published Noah Webster's *Spelling* book; a decade after Torrey was in West Brookfield, two of Merriam's sons set up a printing business in nearby Springfield and published the Merriam-Webster *Dictionary*.[28]

Financially, Torrey's income was in part dependent on the number of his students. In his diary, he described his "pecuniary embarrassment; for at this moment I have not one cent on hand; the number of pupils small; some considerable debts; . . . In truth, I have been, for some time, quite discouraged having no rational prospects of better times." And then there was the ubiquitous specter of sin, from which he could not break free. He wrote: "I struggle feebly with my chain, and then it seems riveted more firmly than ever. Oh! for relief from the chain of sin." Finally, in early March, four months after beginning his teaching career, Torrey resigned and left West Brookfield. It would be the first of three failed careers; only in his fourth, as an abolitionist, would he achieve success.[29]

Torrey returned to his grandparents' home in Chelsea feeling older than his twenty years. He was aware that he had to "go to work to pay my debts," but he was uncertain what to do. He briefly considered going to China to convert the heathen, but, he wrote, "the way to China seemed hedged up with difficulties. What shall I do?" He wished to serve God, but the path was obscure. After much deliberation and prayer, Torrey decided that the most logical way to serve God was to become his representative on earth, a minister. In October 1834, Torrey therefore registered as a student at the Andover Theological Seminary.[30]

At Andover in late 1834, a major topic of conversation was slavery.

Since leaving Yale, Torrey had followed the news as the American abolitionist movement gained traction. In August 1833, the British House of Commons had abolished slavery in the Commonwealth, including Canada and the West Indies. It was the culmination of a forty-six-year battle led by William Wilberforce and Thomas Clarkson. For American slaveholders, this "was ominous indeed.... Southerners concluded that they must take every possible action to prevent a repetition of the events that had transpired in Britain." It also meant that, if American slaves could reach Canada or the West Indies, they would be free. For American abolitionists, the termination of slavery in the British Commonwealth gave them great hope and encouragement, even calling it "the greatest event in history since the founding of Christianity."[31]

Two months after the British abolished slavery, in October 1833, "a menacing crowd of over a thousand threatened the inaugural meeting" of the New York Anti-Slavery Society, forcing Arthur and Lewis Tappan to relocate the meeting at the last minute. Then, in December 1833, sixty-two abolitionists from ten states met in Philadelphia and formed the American Anti-Slavery Society (AASS). Arthur Tappan was elected president, with Elizur Wright and William Lloyd Garrison elected as secretaries. The delegates signed a declaration of sentiments: "Pledging ourselves that, under the guidance and help of Almighty God, we will do all that in us lies, consistently with this declaration of our principles to overthrow the most execrable system of slavery that has been ever witnessed upon earth ... come what may to our persons, our interests, or our reputation— whether we live to witness the triumph of Liberty, Justice, and Humanity, or perish untimely as martyrs in this great, benevolent, and holy Cause."[32]

The 1833 organization of the American Anti-Slavery Society was, in retrospect, a pivotal point in the evolution of the abolitionist movement. Up until that time gradualism, as espoused by the Pennsylvania Abolitionist Society, and returning the slaves to Africa, as advocated by the American Colonization Society, had been the dominant strains of the American movement. Neither of these approaches was immediately threatening to slaveholders and their allies. The founding of the AASS changed this by committing itself to the *immediate* freeing of slaves, and this was to be done by abolitionists willing to "perish untimely as martyrs in this great, benevolent, and holy Cause." A national organization had thus been formed to coordinate and provide leadership for the increasing number of state and local antislavery societies committed to immediatism. The magnitude of the threat posed by this new organization was reflected by a Philadelphia newspaper one week after the AASS meeting. It called the immediate abolition of slavery "a wild and visionary scheme" that would force "every slaveholder to release his sable thrall and offer his throat meekly to the knife of the semi-savage." The shadow of Nat Turner continued to loom large.[33]

When Charles Torrey arrived at the Andover Theological Seminary in October 1834, seminary students were discussing recent events that had taken place at the Lane Theological Seminary in Cincinnati. There, for eighteen evenings, a public debate about the ethics of slavery had taken place, and the audience had concluded that slaveholding was a sin. The seminary students had been led by thirty-year-old Theodore Weld. Among the spectators at the debate was Harriet Beecher, the daughter of Lane's president, Lyman Beecher; eighteen years later, she used stories she had heard during the debate in her widely influential novel, *Uncle Tom's Cabin*.[34]

In the weeks following the debate, some Lane students began teaching classes to free blacks in Cincinnati and also opened a library for them. The reaction of the Lane Board of Trustees was vehement; they abolished the student society, expelled Theodore Weld, and prohibited all antislavery activities. In response, thirty-eight of the forty Lane Seminary students resigned and went to northern Ohio, where they became the first students at Oberlin College. The events at Lane "stirred the entire college world" and "reverberated throughout the nation." A meeting of college presidents "unanimously agreed that the times imperiously demanded that all antislavery agitation should be suppressed," and copies of a resolution to this effect were sent to every college in the nation. Weld, who was described as being "as eloquent as an angel and powerful as thunder," was singled out for special opprobrium by university authorities, thereby launching him on a career as one of the national leaders of the abolition movement.[35]

Torrey became involved in the ongoing discussion at Andover and joined the nascent Andover Anti-Slavery Society. Theodore Weld seemed to Torrey to be just the kind of model Christian activist who should be emulated. By early 1835 Torrey had become the leader of the society and the official corresponding secretary for reports to the Massachusetts Anti-Slavery Society, directed by William Lloyd Garrison. In his duties as corresponding secretary, Torrey did not report to Garrison but rather to Amos Phelps, one of three paid agents Garrison had hired in 1834 to promote the growth of local antislavery societies around the state.

Although Phelps was seven years older than Torrey, he and Torrey shared similar backgrounds and many interests. Phelps had grown up in a small town in Connecticut and had also graduated from Yale. He had then become a Congregational minister and had initially taught at Andover Theological Seminary before assuming a position at Boston's Pine Street Church. He had become interested in the slavery issue in 1830 and, with Garrison, had attended the founding meeting of the American Anti-Slavery Society. Garrison had then appointed him one of the first three field agents of the Massachusetts Anti-Slavery Society, with the task of developing more local societies, as Torrey was helping to do at Andover.[36]

Phelps's 1834 book *Lectures on Slavery and Its Remedy* was being widely read by abolitionists at the time he and Torrey were becoming friends. Phelps stated unequivocally that "slavery in our land is a great and threatening evil [and] a great and crying national sin." Therefore, "every man whether he live at the North, South, East, or West, is personally responsible, and has personal duties to discharge in respect to it." Phelps argued forcefully that the colonization movement would not work and that the only solution was "Immediate Emancipation." Such statements were included by Phelps under a "Declaration of Sentiment" signed by 124 clergymen, whom Phelps listed; they included Joshua Leavitt, Elizur Wright, and Theodore Weld. Phelps believed that clergymen had a special responsibility to oppose slavery since it was a sin.[37]

Prophetically, Phelps also foresaw a terrible struggle if slaveholders did not voluntarily free their slaves: "The spirit of freedom is abroad, and to a greater or lesser extent, it will breathe itself into the entire mass of slaves. It has already done so. It will continue to do so. . . . Slaveholders have but one alternative, either to emancipate their slaves voluntarily, and thus escape the dangers they dread, or to have the slaves emancipate themselves by force. . . . If they will not have the former, they must have the latter. And when it comes, it will be violent indeed." As reflected in a letter to his wife at this time, Phelps believed that the shedding of blood would probably be needed to accomplish the emancipation of slaves.[38]

Charles Torrey was immediately attracted to Amos Phelps's ideas and adopted him as a mentor. Phelps believed that slaveholding was "the *strong hold of Satan*" and "*the* means by which he maintains his cruel sway on earth." The abolition of slavery in Britain, the founding of the American Anti-Slavery Society, and the antislavery riots in New York in July 1834, in which Arthur Tappan's house and some black businesses were attacked, were all events pointing to the looming battle. This would not be merely a political fight but rather a battle between Good and Evil. This was a battle for which Torrey had longed, a battle in which true Christians could distinguish themselves by demonstrating their devotion to God. If Torrey had lived six hundred years earlier, he would have been one of the first Crusaders to go to the Holy Land; freeing the slaves was Torrey's opportunity to capture Jerusalem.[39]

In addition to believing that slaveholding was a sin, Phelps and Torrey also agreed that it was the worst kind of sin—sexual sin. In his 1834 book, Phelps was one of the first abolitionists to explicitly discuss the problem of coerced intercourse between masters and slaves: "The condition of the colored female in the slave States is, in this respect, most dreadful. . . . She is her master's property, and is subject to his control in the matter of sexual intercourse as much as in any other." Phelps cited examples, such as a "female professor of religion, who keeps one of her handsomest slaves as a mistress for her son," and a "minister of the gospel, the owner of a plantation, who once refused to protect a poor slave girl from the licentiousness of his own overseer, though the girl herself requested such protection." As proof of his allegations, Phelps pointed to "the rapid increase of mulattoes." Indeed, said Phelps, defenders of slavery say that freeing the slaves would lead to miscegenation and amalgamation, but in fact, "the process of amalgamation is going on with vastly greater rapidity now, than it probably would, if the blacks were free."[40]

Many abolitionists used such sexual licentiousness as one of their strongest arguments against slaveholding. They argued that "the Southern states are one great Sodom," "the sixteen slave States constitute one vast brothel," and "a Turkish harem is a cradle of virgin purity" compared to the South. President James Madison's sister claimed that "a planter's wife is but the mistress of a seraglio." Census data supported such accusations; "among free blacks in southern cities in 1860, close to forty percent were of mixed blood," many of whom had been freed by the slaveholders who had fathered them. Abolitionists cited such examples when speaking to audiences. Phelps, for example, often "gripped the attention especially of the females in the audience when during his appeal for support he 'brandished . . . the slave driver's whip such as had lacerated the back of women.'"[41]

Given his challenges in controlling his own sexual impulses, the licentiousness of slaveholding was of great repugnance to Charles Torrey. In contrast to Christian gentlemen who control their bodily appetites, "the South was a society in which man's sexual nature had no checks put upon it." The lack of such self-control was, for Torrey, abhorrent, and he condemned the "vile conduct" of an acquaintance who got a girl pregnant. Torrey shared "the perspective of black families attempting to preserve themselves and protect the virtue of daughters and sisters threatened by sale into prostitution." Writing to his wife, he described how listening to a "nearly white" slave woman describe her situation filled him "with new energy to make war upon that hateful institution." His zeal was fueled by scenes such as the following, which he later described: "I have seen a woman, apparently as refined, as lady-like, ay, and as white as any women in Scituate—an humble Christian, too, but, alas! a slave—in this district, held by the laws of congress, clasping her hands in anguish too deep for words, because she was made the sport of a tyrant's lust!" The sexual aspects of slaveholding were thus an important part of Torrey's intense feelings about the subject and a motivating force that helped determine his future conduct.[42]

* * *

By mid-1835, Charles Torrey was working closely with Amos Phelps, exchanging ideas regarding the most effective strategies for abolishing slavery. The abolitionist movement was expanding its reach; what had been a handful of antislavery societies in 1833 had become two hundred local chapters by 1835. Whereas previously, abolitionists had been dismissed as a small fringe group not to be taken seriously, increasingly this was no longer the case, as was strikingly demonstrated during the summer of 1835 in what became known as the "great postal campaign." Antislavery societies, such as that at Andover, flooded the mails with antislavery tracts, periodicals, and sermons destined for southern states. In 1834 antislavery societies had sent 122,000 such mailings; in 1835 the number increased almost tenfold, to 1.1 million. Southerners, whose memory of Nat Turner was still fresh, were alarmed. As David Grimstead noted in *American Mobbing,* "the mail campaign provided the smoking gun between the strength of abolition and the reality of insurrectionary threat: the abolitionists were preaching servile war to the slaves." The prominence of the postal campaign and battle over slavery can be illustrated by a story published in the *New York Sun* at this time. Using telescopes, the paper reported that four-foot-high "winged humans" had been seen standing on the moon "engaged in conversation." When the story was subsequently exposed as a hoax, the paper justified its publication by explaining that it was merely an attempt at "diverting the public mind . . . from the bitter apple of discord, the abolition of slavery."[43]

Southern slaveholders reacted with intense anger to the postal campaign. A letter in a New Orleans newspaper commented on the perpetrators: "The murderous designs of these fiend-like fanatics would not only place the firebrand in our dwelling, but prepare their knives for the cutting of our throats." In Georgia the legislature passed a law providing for the death penalty "for the publication of material tending to incite slave insurrections." It also offered bounties for the capture of prominent abolitionists, such as $10,000 ($209,000) for Amos Phelps, and $50,000 ($1,043,000) for Arthur Tappan, who was believed to be financing the postal campaign. In South Carolina the governor suggested that "every community should punish this species of interference by death without benefit of clergy." In North Carolina a U.S. congressman "sent a piece of rope to Arthur Tappan, and the South hugely enjoyed the joke." And in Virginia a "grand jury indicted and demanded the extradition of all the key personnel of the [national] Anti-Slavery Society." Ex-president Andrew Jackson called the abolitionists "monsters" and accused them of stirring up "the horrors of a servile war." In reaction, on July 30, "a mob of three thousand burned bundles of antislavery literature looted from the Charleston, South Carolina, post office."[44]

Opposition to the abolitionists was not confined to the South. In northern states there was also a widespread fear of what would happen if the nation's two million slaves were freed. As historian Stanley Harrold noted: "Most white Americans—both northern and southern—regarded slavery as the best means of controlling a growing black population that they regarded as alien, inassimilable, and dangerous." As noted previously, many northerners profited economically, either directly or indirectly, from the slave trade, since slaves were important not only for the cotton, rice, and tobacco industries but also for others such as lumbering, shipping, and banking. A prominent example of this was the New England textile industry, which was heavily dependent on cheap cotton from the South to manufacture competitively priced clothing for export to Europe. Thus, it was said that the "lords of the loom" in New England were dependent upon the "lords of the lash" in the South.[45]

Fear and economic considerations were important antecedents of northern opposition to the abolition of slavery. At the simplest level, this opposition was demonstrated at antislavery speeches by hecklers, some of whom became more substantive in their expression. On one occasion, Theodore Weld had an egg thrown in his face. According to an observer, "he wiped it away calmly . . . and proceeded as deliberately as if he had paused to take a draught of water." On another occasion while he was speaking, a stone was thrown through a window and hit him on the head. He "paused for a few moments till the dizziness had ceased, and then went on and completed [his] lecture." For Torrey, Weld represented one of the major attractions of the antislavery movement: the opportunity to prove oneself worthy of salvation. Weld expressed this dilemma in a letter to a friend: "Let every abolitionist debate the matter once and for all, and settle it with himself . . . whether he can lie upon the rack—and grasp the fagot—and tread with steady step the scaffold—whether he can stand at the post of duty, and having done all and suffered all . . . fall and die a martyr 'not accepting deliverance.' . . . God gird us all to do valiantly for the helpless and innocent. Blessed are they who die in the harness."[46]

On numerous occasions, northern opposition devolved into riots. This was especially true in 1835, when according to a study by David Grimstead, forty-six proslavery riots occurred. For example, Utica, a town of ten thousand in upstate New York, had a large textile industry and thus was dependent on cotton. When a state Anti-Slavery Society meeting was scheduled to take place at the local Presbyterian Church, many of Utica's leading citizens planned a proper reception for the delegates. Just as the meeting was starting, a large group of men, led by U.S. Congressman Samuel Beardsley, "burst through the church doors, rushed down the aisle, and headed for the pulpit. About half-a-dozen men ripped the clothing off one abolitionist's back. Others threw hymnals or tore up antislavery documents and papers." The mob continued to shout down the meeting until the delegates gave up and adjourned. It was at this time that the mobbing of William Lloyd Garrison in Boston also took place.[47]

The events of 1835 and his friendship with Amos Phelps confirmed for Charles Torrey that he had found his métier. He would be a Congregational minister, a representative of God on earth, and lead a model Christian life by waging war against the greatest of all sins, slaveholding. For Torrey, an activist ministry was the only possible ministry; if ministers did not lead the fight against sin, they could not expect other people to do so. Slavery was evil incarnate, and Torrey would fight it, literally, to the death.

There was, however, one major problem: Torrey was facing his own possible death before he had even had a chance to go into battle. During 1835 he had become progressively weaker and sicker with a fever and cough. Torrey knew the implications of his symptoms—tuberculosis—for it had killed his father and mother. The Puritan writer John Bunyan had called it "the captain of all these men of death." The severity of Torrey's illness at that time can be assessed by later comments he made regarding "my old disorder, which so nearly killed me in 1835" and the fact that "physicians regarded him as almost incurable."[48]

Torrey was seriously ill and had no money. Although it must have been an extreme disappointment to him, he had no choice but to leave Andover Theological Seminary and try to recuperate. His decision was memorialized by an official letter, dated October 19, 1835, from an Andover trustee: "Mr. Charles T. Torrey, the bearer, has been a member of this seminary one year; and when his health has permitted, he has regularly pursued his theological studies. While resident here he has maintained a Christian character. On account of the feeble and precarious state of his health, and his pecuniary circumstances, he is now, at his own request, dismissed from the seminary."[49] His career as a minister and abolitionist appeared to be over before it had even begun.

Torrey returned to his grandparents' house in Chelsea and prepared to "devote nearly a year to the sole business of regaining health." Although various folk remedies and bromides were used to treat tuberculosis in the nineteenth century, rest was the only effective treatment. The specter of his disease would shadow Torrey for the rest of his life, never far from consciousness. For example, he later wrote to Amos Phelps that "some of my people begin to fear my health won't hold out if I do too much." Torrey's fervent wish to prove himself worthy of everlasting life did daily battle with that most implacable adversary, time.[50]

Tuberculosis, however, is a capricious disease, unpredictable in its remissions and relapses. By early 1836 Torrey's health had modestly improved, so he went to Scituate, where he resumed his theological studies with a Congregational minister, the Reverend L. A. Spofford; such private studies were a common arrangement at that time.[51]

In 1835 Scituate had an antislavery society with seventy members. Through the society and his correspondence with Amos Phelps and other friends at Andover, Torrey followed events as the antislavery drama unfolded. In Washington Congress refused to admit Michigan to the Union as a non-slave state until Arkansas could also be admitted as a slave state, thus preserving the balance in Congress.

Of greater concern to abolitionists were proposals to annex a province of Mexico where American settlers had revolted, declared Texas to be a slave republic, and then been defeated at the Alamo by the Mexican army. Those who favored the annexation of Texas "loudly declared that anywhere from five to nine new states could be carved out of this southwestern domain, and slavery could be lawful and profitable in every single one of them."[52]

Even more alarming to abolitionists was the passage by Congress of what became known as the "gag rule." Throughout 1835, abolitionists, as part of their "great postal campaign," had flooded Congress with petitions signed by thousands of citizens demanding that slavery be abolished. Citizens had been petitioning Congress since the founding of the United States, and publicly noting petitions submitted by their constituents was a perfunctory duty of every member of Congress. However, by late 1835 many southern members of Congress had tired of the increasingly lengthy daily drone of abolitionist petitions, and a proposal was made to no longer read them. This was initially put forward by a prominent defender of slavery, South Carolina Congressman James Hammond, who argued that slavery was "the order of Providence" and that the emancipation of slaves "would be followed instantly by a civil war between the whites and blacks . . . accompanied with horrors such as history has not recorded." A formal notion to institute a gag rule for that session of Congress was introduced in January 1836 and passed four months later. Henceforth: "All petitions, memorials, resolutions, propositions, or papers, relating in any way, or to any extent whatsoever, to the subject of slavery or the abolition of slavery, shall, without being either printed or referred, be laid on the table and that no further action whatever shall be had thereon." One of the most effective guns in the abolitionists' arsenal was, at least temporarily, being silenced.[53]

As Torrey's health continued to improve, he was anxious to return to the abolitionist trenches. In June 1836 he left Scituate to go to West Medway, a village in Norfolk County on the stage road between Boston and Hartford. The reason for going to Medway was to continue his theological training with the Reverend Jacob Ide, a Congregational minister well known to Amos Phelps and noted for his activist abolitionist views. A farmer's son, Ide had graduated from

Brown University as class valedictorian, then obtained theological training at Andover. In 1833 he had been a founding member of the American Anti-Slavery Society, and in 1836, when Torrey arrived, he was vice-president of the Massachusetts Anti-Slavery Society. Like Torrey, Ide had briefly tried teaching and had had major health issues early in his career. For Torrey, he was thus an ideal mentor.[54]

Charles Torrey's move to West Medway proved fortuitous for yet another reason. Ide's eighteen-year-old daughter, Mary, described as "possessing a sprightly, active and amiable disposition," was said to have inherited "much of the acumen of her [maternal] grandfather Emmons," a highly respected theologian and active abolitionist. He had called her "Little Miss Dispute It" when she was a child. She was also an accomplished writer and would later publish pamphlets and articles for religious newspapers. Twenty-two-year-old Torrey and Mary Ide were immediately attracted to each other and, within six months, he was writing to "My beloved Mary" about his gravest concerns: "Pray for me, dear Mary, that I may be kept from sin, and led in the path of duty to God. And how is your heart, dearest? God has given me some peace since I left you, though I have had some bitter struggles with *evil thoughts*.[55]

By October 1836, Charles Torrey had completed his theological training and largely recovered his health. He was licensed as a Congregational minister and needed to find employment, both to pay off his debts and to have a secure income so he could marry. What he *really* wanted to do was to rejoin the antislavery fight but saw no way he could get paid for doing so. He carefully followed the various skirmishes, however. For example, in Nashville, Amos Dresser was publicly whipped for distributing abolitionist literature. In Washington, D.C., Reuben Crandall, a white physician, was charged with "criminal and seditious libel and with inciting insurrection" for possessing antislavery pamphlets. Crandall's pamphlets claimed that blacks had as valid a right to deport whites to Europe as whites had to deport blacks to Africa "under the pretext that we shall there be prosperous and happy." The prosecuting attorney was Francis Scott Key, a Maryland native who, two decades earlier, had written the words for the *Star-Spangled Banner*. Crandall was found not guilty "due to a technical deficiency in the indictment."[56]

What Torrey longed for most in the fall of 1836 was to join the men being recruited by Theodore Weld to become agents of the American Anti-Slavery Society. They were to be "men of the most unquenchable enthusiasm and most obstinate constancy" who would be called "The Seventy," after the seventy men in the Bible sent out to convert the world to Christianity. In November 1836, the recruits gathered in New York City for three weeks of rigorous training under Weld. One-third of them were Weld's colleagues from the Lane Seminary, and the majority of the rest were recruited from other seminaries. Weld focused their training on slavery as sin and "exhorted the agents to create 'an abiding inwrought, thoroughly intelligent feeling' that would make people's hearts ache for the slave and 'leap into our ranks because they cannot keep themselves out.'" This group was tailor-made for Charles Torrey, but practical concerns dictated that he must first find a job and, he hoped, secure Mary's hand in marriage.[57]

Charles Torrey's career as a Congregational minister was as unsuccessful as his career as a teacher had been. After being ordained he sought a position, giving sermons and being interviewed by church committees in various New England towns. Finally, in late March 1837, he was hired by the Richmond Street Congregational Church in Providence, and on March 29, he and Mary wed. However, six months after starting his ministry in Providence, he was asked to leave because of a strong impression "that he is not the proper person," according to a letter from a church member to Amos Phelps. Three months later Torrey was hired by the Harvard Street Congregational Church in Salem, just in time to move Mary into their new home, where on December 27, 1837, she delivered their first child, Charles Henry Torrey. The Salem job lasted eighteen months, at which time church leaders there asked him to leave as well.[58]

The reasons for Torrey's failure as a minister are not difficult to ascertain. According to letters written by people who heard him, he was a "miserable preacher" and provided "a most indifferent sermon." The style and content of Torrey's preaching can be gleaned from his own assessments of other ministers. He praised a minister whose "style of preaching was bold, fearless, manly, full of reasoning, sometimes lofty in thought, and sublime in denunciation of woe to the guilty." He criticized another who was "amiable in his social character, gentle in his manner, a lover of children" but who failed to utter "the truths of religion." For Torrey, religion for church members was not merely "something intended for the Sabbath, the sick bed, or old age" but rather "the guide of their daily life in all its actions, civil, as well as individual and social." He especially decried the desecration of the Sabbath, which he said had become "a day of jollity, of social visits, of idle talk, of rides, of wandering in the fields to pick berries; a day of pleasure, instead of a season of worship." He also advocated denying church membership to individuals who were not living what he considered to be a true Christian life. "Who would respect a church," he asked, "when its richest member was openly alleged, without denial, to be an immoral man?" In short, Torrey's preaching style was akin to that of revivalist preachers. Heard once or twice, they may invoke pious thoughts, but heard week after week, they soon wear out their welcome.[59]

The largest reason for Torrey's failure as a minister, however, was his obsession with slavery. He aspired to be a minister focused on the sin of slavery, but in reality he was becoming an antislavery zealot posing as a minister. This became clear in Providence, which had had anti-black riots in the 1820s, where anti-black feelings were "very bitter," and where abolitionists were comparatively sparse. Torrey was aware of this, writing in a letter at the time he took the job that "my abolitionism . . . might cause a few [church members] to leave," but he was unable to modulate his message.[60]

In contrast to Providence, Salem had an active antislavery society and was much more sympathetic to Torrey's interests, but even there his obsession with slavery grew tedious. In a series of letters he wrote to another minister at the time, Torrey argued "that *sometimes* a particular object may have claims upon the attention of the humane and pious paramount, for the time being, to all others" and that slavery was such an object. Indeed, he added, "if Paul and Peter were now living, it doubts not that to exterminate slavery from this *Christian and free land,* Paul would joyfully become 'secretary' and Peter 'general agent' of the Massachusetts Abolition Society." In Torrey's view, churches should be the fuglemen of God's antislavery army: "Let Zion awake, and put on her garments of beauty, and make war upon slavery; and she shall be more 'terrible than an army with banners.'"[61]

In retrospect, it is surprising that Charles Torrey lasted as long as he did as a minister in Salem before being asked to leave. Arriving in Salem in December 1837, Torrey reconnected with Amos Phelps and reimmersed himself deeply in abolitionist activities, leaving little time for the usual tasks of ministers. At the time, William Lloyd Garrison was espousing perfectionism, pacifism, and women's rights and was alienating many abolitionists. In October 1837, Phelps had written to a friend: "I cannot pardon such isms as those which Garrison is now linking with his abolition. . . . I have pretty much given up on him. He falls if he falls." It was at this time that Phelps, Torrey, and Alanson St. Clair, another Salem minister, began serious discussions regarding how Garrison might be replaced.[62]

Two events in December 1837 gave impetus to their plans to try to oust Garrison. The first of these was the death of thirty-five-year-old Elijah Lovejoy, who would be anointed as the first martyr of the abolitionist movement. Born in Maine, Lovejoy had attended Colby College and Princeton Theological Seminary, then gone to St. Louis to begin a Presbyterian newspaper. St. Louis at the time was dominated by southern businessmen who were unsympathetic to Lovejoy's New England views. In 1836 Lovejoy observed Francis McIntosh, a free black man who had killed a white deputy sheriff, being dragged from jail by a mob, chained to a tree, and then "roasted alive over a slow fire of green wood." Lovejoy's editorial denunciations of such lawlessness resulted in his office being sacked and his press thrown into the Mississippi River. At the invitation of local Presbyterian ministers, Lovejoy relocated his offices to Alton, Illinois, twenty-five miles upriver, where he increased the volume of his antislavery attacks. His press was destroyed once, then again when he proposed the organization of a state antislavery society, and twice more as he continued to excoriate slaveholding. Each time his supporters purchased a new press, but by October 1837 Lovejoy's supporters and opponents had both armed themselves and the drama was moving toward a denouement.[63]

On November 3, 1837, Lovejoy was summoned to a courthouse

meeting by the town's leaders. They announced that he must close his press and leave Alton immediately. To do so, they added, would be the proper Christian thing to do, just "as Paul had fled from Damascus." Lovejoy responded slowly and passionately:

> I do not admit that it is the business of this assembly to decide whether I shall or shall not publish a newspaper in this city. The gentlemen have, as the lawyers say, made a wrong issue. I have the *right* to do it. I know that I have the right freely to speak and publish my sentiments, subject only to the laws of the land for the abuse of that right. This right was given to me by my Maker; and it is solemnly guaranteed to me by the Constitution of the United States and of this state. . . . I am hunted as a partridge upon the mountains. I am pursued as a felon through your streets; and to the guardian power of the law I look in vain for protection against violence, which even the vilest criminal may claim. . . . You may hang me up as the mob hung up the individuals of Vicksburg. You may burn me at the stake as they did McIntosh at St. Louis; or you may tar and feather me, or throw me into the Mississippi as you have often threatened to do; but you cannot disgrace me. I, and I alone, can disgrace myself; and the deepest of all disgrace would be, at a time like this, to deny my Master by forsaking his cause. He died for me; and I were most unworthy to bear his name, should I refuse, if need be, to die for him. . . . Sir, I dare not flee away from Alton. Should I attempt it, I should feel that the angel of the Lord with his flaming sword was pursuing me wherever I went. It is because I fear God that I am not afraid of all who oppose me in this city. No sir, the contest has commenced here; and here it must be finished. Before God, and you all, I here pledge myself to continue it, if need be, till death. If I fall, my grave shall be made in Alton.

The conclusion came quickly. Four days later, Lovejoy's new press arrived, and his supporters took it to a warehouse, prepared to defend it. The mob attacked, shots were fired, and one young man among the attackers fell dead. The roof of the warehouse was then set afire, and Lovejoy, with two supporters, emerged to put it out. More shots rang out, and Lovejoy fell, mortally wounded, with "four balls in his breast."[64]

According to one historian, "the Alton tragedy rocked the North to its foundations." John Quincy Adams said the death sent "a shock as of an earthquake throughout this continent." Meetings protesting Lovejoy's death were held in cities and towns throughout the North. At one such meeting, in Hudson, Ohio, a man named John Brown stood up and proclaimed: "Here, before God, in the presence of these witnesses, from this time, I consecrate my life to the destruction of slavery." In Springfield, Illinois, state legislator Abraham Lincoln decried mob law and called the events in St. Louis and Alton "perhaps the most dangerous in example and revolting to humanity."[65]

On December 8, a meeting was held in Boston in Faneuil Hall, with five thousand people, including Charles Torrey, in attendance. James T. Austin, the attorney general of Massachusetts, criticized Lovejoy for having been "presumptuous and imprudent," saying that the mob had a perfect right to kill him and that he had "died as a fool dieth." Most other speakers praised Lovejoy. Especially eloquent was Wendell Phillips, a socially prominent Bostonian and Garrison supporter who stated that "the gun which was aimed at the breast of Lovejoy brought me to my feet. I can never forget the agony of that moment."[66]

Conspicuously absent that day in Faneuil Hall was the voice of Garrison himself. In the *Liberator,* Garrison had regretted that Lovejoy's "friends in Alton should have allowed any provocation, or personal danger, or hope of victory, or distrust of the protection of Heaven, to drive them to take up arms in self-defense." Garrison added that "they have certainly set a dangerous precedent in the maintenance of our cause." Lovejoy was a martyr, Garrison conceded, but he was not "a Christian martyr." Torrey, Phelps, and other abolitionists were outraged at Garrison's condemnation of Lovejoy's actions as non-Christian. This is what Garrison's pacifism would lead to, they said. Torrey spoke for many when he said that he was "opposed to talk without definite action."[67]

The second event in December 1837 that reinforced the decision of Torrey, Phelps, and their colleagues to challenge Garrison's leadership was the further extension of the gag rule by Congress, whereby it would continue to be prohibited to publicly read petitions pertaining to slavery. When the rule had been passed in 1836, most people had assumed that the ban would be temporary. During 1837 abolitionists had therefore continued to collect petitions. One 1837 petition alone, containing 51,862 signatures, was described as an "immense roll of paper . . . about the size of an ordinary barrel." The reimposition of the gag rule meant that it could be extended indefinitely, thus depriving abolitionists of their most effective means of public debate.[68]

Phelps acted immediately. He printed a circular denouncing the reimposition of the gag rule and added: "Shall the people of Massachusetts bow the neck, in tame and dumb submission to this fresh outrage on their rights? Rather, let them rise en masse against it." Rising en masse implied political action, such as electing abolitionist supporters to Congress and even amending the Constitution to ban slavery. Such political action was not going to happen under the no-government leadership of William Lloyd Garrison. As one abolitionist commented at this time: "Too many seem to think that all our objects are to be effected by resolutions." It was time for action, and it was clear that Garrison had to go.[69]

Thus, by the beginning of 1838, the plans to try to oust Garrison from the leadership of the Massachusetts Anti-Slavery Society had been set in motion. The year would be spent by Torrey, Phelps, St. Clair, and their Massachusetts colleagues trying to get local support for their plans and in conferring with Henry Stanton and others at the New York office. The tectonic battle for the future direction of the abolitionist movement was under way.

3

POLITICAL ABOLITIONISM

The 1839 meeting of the Massachusetts Anti-Slavery Society would be a watershed for American abolitionism. In the early years of the century, the abolitionist movement's dominant theme had been gradualism—the belief that the emancipation of slaves could be brought about slowly in a series of graduated steps. These included the freeing or manumission of slaves by slaveholders, as George Washington had done at his death; allowing slaves to purchase their freedom; and changing state laws to gradually abolish slavery, as the northern states had done by the 1790s. The problem with gradualism was, in the words of one abolitionist, that it would bring about emancipation "sometime between now and never." In the 1820s colonization, the sending of free blacks and slaves to Liberia, emerged as another form of gradualism. Given this history, William Lloyd Garrison's call for the *immediate* emancipation of slaves by moral suasion was regarded as radical and rhetorically aggressive, especially by slaveholders themselves.[1]

The schism of 1839, however, gave birth to political abolitionism as an alternative tactic for achieving emancipation. Garrison viewed political abolitionism as a threat to moral suasion and to his leadership, and insofar as political abolitionism was successful, it weakened Garrison's authority. Bruce Laurie, in *Beyond Garrison*, claimed that "in the 1840s Garrison's camp was dwarfed by political antislavery and was probably smaller still a decade later.... Garrisonianism and political abolitionism ... were headed in different directions by the middle of the 1840s, with the former in decline and the latter on the rise." Howard Temperley, in *British Antislavery, 1833–1870*, noted that "even in Garrison's native Massachusetts his followers constituted a minority of the antislavery body." Reinhard Johnson, author of *The Liberty Party*, similarly claimed that "by 1845 ... the Garrisonians were a numerically weak, though vocal, segment of Massachusetts abolitionism. Key Garrisonians privately lamented the diminution of their following and acknowledged that almost all abolitionists adhered to the Liberty party." Johnson is one of the few historians to have focused on the importance of Torrey, Phelps, St. Clair, and the other breakaway abolitionists in helping to establish political abolitionism and its public persona, the Liberty Party.[2]

The official name of the organization created by the dissidents was the Massachusetts Abolition Society, but Garrison and his followers usually referred to it as the New Organization. Similarly, Torrey, Phelps, and others generally referred to Garrison's group as the Old Organization. From its beginnings, the New Organization was set up to use political means to fight slavery. Membership was restricted to gentlemen who were, in Phelps's words, "sober, serious and prayerful," and voting for abolitionist candidates was incumbent on everyone. The political abolitionists' power was to come from the ballot box, and this, they said, would make them "*feared* as they never would have been had they remained in the quiescent land of abstractions."[3]

Immediately following the schism in January 1839, a fierce fight ensued between the New and Old organizations for the fealty of local abolitionist societies. According to observers, "Amos Phelps and his fellow ministers organized day and night to convince local antislavery societies to break with the Massachusetts Anti-Slavery Society and affiliate with" the New Organization. "Private letters *innumerable* have been written in every direction, especially by Phelps." Garrison and his followers worked equally hard to undermine "the clerics," as they referred to Phelps, Torrey, St. Clair, and so forth. When Garrison successfully persuaded the Essex County Society to oust Torrey as its corresponding secretary, Garrison called it a "grand meeting." In the end, some local societies remained affiliated with Garrison, others affiliated with the New Organization, and still others split into two societies. Women in the Boston Female Anti-Slavery Society voted 142–10 to affiliate with the New Organization, despite the fact that the New Organization did not admit women as full members, because "it was found impracticable to remain united with . . . their no-government friends." The schism also affected surrounding state societies. Rhode Island continued to follow Garrison, whereas Maine, where Garrison "was almost universally disliked for his anti-clericalism and aggressive manner," followed the New Organization.[4]

Much of the fighting took place on the pages of the two organizations' newspapers. Elizur Wright, Torrey's Yale classmate, came to Boston from the American Anti-Slavery Society's New York office to edit the *Massachusetts Abolitionist*. Wright was a capable editor, and the paper's emphasis on political action appealed to many abolitionists. By late spring, the circulation of the *Massachusetts Abolitionist* had reached more than 3,000, compared with the *Liberator*'s approximately 2,300. Alarmed, Maria Chapman warned that the newspaper "must be put down or it will put down the Mass. [Anti-Slavery] Soc." Garrison attacked the *Massachusetts Abolitionist* incessantly but to little avail. Lydia Maria Child, another staunch Garrisonian, even suggested that Garrison's attacks were backfiring: "I am convinced that every move Garrison can make against the Abolitionist re-acts against the Liberator."[5]

As the New Organization progressively gained strength in 1839, its fight with Garrison's group became increasingly bitter. In March, at the quarterly meeting of the Massachusetts Anti-Slavery Society, Henry Stanton, James Birney, and Lewis Tappan came from the New York office to ask Garrison why his organization had not paid its national dues. The New Yorkers took the occasion to again chastise Garrison for his no-government stand. Such a philosophy, they argued, was producing "an Association having a proposed end without any prescribed means for attaining it which . . . would render the act of associating *useless*." They also accused Garrison of, in the past, having voted and having urged others to vote, to which Garrison simply replied: "Whereas we were then blind, now we see; and greatly do we rejoice in the light."[6]

The next confrontation between the two organizations took place two months later in New York at the May 1839 annual meeting of the American Anti-Slavery Society. Garrison brought with him almost one hundred supporters, including many women, to reinforce his position. For the first day and a half, the two sides argued about whether women should be allowed to vote. Torrey and Lewis Tappan argued strongly against it; Torrey also introduced an amendment to the constitution of the society to alter voting procedures so as to neutralize Garrison's women. Garrison ultimately won on this issue but lost on the political issue. The conference attendees declared that voting was important, "so as to promote the abolition of slavery, [and] is of high obligation—a duty which, as abolitionists, we owe to our enslaved fellow countrymen, groaning under legal oppression." During the meeting, Garrison decried the effects of the schism, saying that he "could weep tears of blood over this division, if it would avail to stay its evils." Torrey responded dryly that "to see the gentleman weep tears of blood, would indeed be a curious physiological fact."[7]

Thus by May 1839 political abolitionism had become established. The Massachusetts Abolition Society was growing steadily and by the mid-1840s would have "twelve county and two hundred local auxiliaries." In May, Torrey also committed the society to the "improvement of the free people of color, in this their native country," and "hired a black man, Jehiel C. Beman, to coordinate projects for 'colored youth.'" The major question facing Torrey and his colleagues at this time was how to use political abolitionism most effectively to free the slaves. A new and interesting idea was being privately discussed by Torrey's colleagues at the New York meeting, and they agreed to set up a national conference in Albany in July to discuss it and other "great principles" of political abolitionism.[8]

The new idea that so intrigued Charles Torrey at the New York meeting was the creation of a new political party devoted to abolitionism. The idea had been initially suggested in January 1839 by Alvan Stewart, president of the New York State Anti-Slavery Society, at a meeting of the executive committee of that organization. Stewart was a lawyer from upstate New York and was described as "an imposing figure—tall, dark and muscular— . . . [who] blended immense learning with mordant humor." Stewart argued that an abolitionist party was needed because other strategies were not working. He ridiculed Garrison's moral suasion, saying that "to hope to flatter, persuade or convince a majority of slaveholders in this nation that it is their duty to let their slaves go free is a task beyond the highest conquest of moral suasion." He also characterized as "infinite absurdity" the idea that either the Whigs or the Democrats would ever adopt a platform that included abolitionist principles. What was needed, Stewart contended, was a third political party, devoted to abolitionist principles, to challenge the Whigs and the Democrats. Since slavery rested on political power, it must be counteracted by political power. "Shorn of political power," he said, "slavery would fall by its own weight and die of its own imbecility." If more aggressive political action was not adopted by the abolitionists, Stewart warned that "murderous slave insurrections were perfectly justifiable—indeed natural and inevitable unless human bondage was soon destroyed."[9]

One month after having proposed the formation of an abolitionist party, Stewart's suggestion received unexpected support. Abolitionists had long since given up on the Democratic Party, since it staunchly supported slaveholding. Many abolitionists, however, still had hopes for the Whigs, especially after 1838, when several Whig congressmen sympathetic to abolitionism—such as Seth Gates of New York, William Slade of Vermont, and Joshua Giddings of Ohio—had been elected. It was widely assumed that Henry Clay would be the Whig nominee for president in 1840, as he had been in 1824, 1832, and 1836. Clay was a senator from Kentucky who owned slaves but who, early in his political career, had publicly opposed the perpetuation of slavery and was therefore thought to be privately sympathetic to abolitionist goals.

Such abolitionist hopes were shattered on February 7, 1839, when Clay, in a speech in the U.S. Senate, delivered a scathing denunciation of the political abolitionists. In an attempt to get southern support for his expected presidential bid, Clay said that political abolitionists "should no longer be regarded as an imaginary danger. . . . It is because those ultra-Abolitionists have ceased to employ the instruments of reason and persuasion, have made their cause political, and have appealed to the ballot box, that I am induced, upon this occasion, to address you. . . . The liberty of the descendants of Africa in the United States is incompatible with the safety and liberty of the European descendants." Clay concluded his speech by warning the political abolitionists "to pause in their mad and fatal course." Elizur Wright called Clay's speech "diabolical," and the speech was widely reprinted in abolitionist newspapers.[10]

On July 31, 1839, almost five hundred abolitionists gathered in Albany for a National Abolition Convention to discuss the formation of an abolitionist political party and other strategies for abolishing slavery. Charles Torrey, Alanson St. Clair, Orange Scott, and Daniel Wise represented the New Organization, while William Lloyd Garrison brought sixty-three supporters to represent the Old Organization. Alvan Stewart was made president of the convention and delivered a strong appeal for an abolitionist party to challenge the Democrats and Whigs, by nominating candidates for office at the local, state, and national levels. Because Henry Clay's speech was still fresh in their minds, Stewart's proposal received more serious consideration from the delegates than it otherwise would have. Although the majority of abolitionist leaders were opposed to the idea, a "considerable number of influential abolitionists seemed disposed, on the whole, to favor the *ultimate* organization of a third party," according to one observer.[11]

For William Lloyd Garrison, it was not a good meeting. According to John Thomas's biography of Garrison, "he was outvoted both on non-resistance and woman's rights and presented with the title 'prince of disorganizers.'" Garrison attempted to head off the movement toward a third party, arguing that it would attract "a swarm of unprincipled aspirants" and make abolition "a marketable commodity to be sold to the highest bidder." Although Garrison himself had advocated the formation of "a Christian party in politics" five years earlier, by 1839 he strongly opposed it. As historian Richard Sewell noted in his *Ballots for Freedom,* "establishment of an antislavery political party would surely dilute Garrison's own influence. At every turn, in every way possible, therefore, Garrison and his disciples strove to head off 'the party movement.'"[12]

Charles Torrey enthusiastically endorsed Alvan Stewart's proposal for an abolitionist party. Stewart was a man, said Torrey, who was not only willing to *talk* about freeing the slaves but willing to *act* as well. This new political direction had great appeal.

At this time, however, Torrey had other problems. Charles Turner, his grandfather, who had been like a father to him, had died in May at age seventy-nine. Then, in July, just prior to the Albany meeting, Torrey had been dismissed from his pastorate in Salem. Since Torrey had been functioning as virtually a full-time abolitionist and neglecting his church duties, the dismissal was not unexpected. As Joseph Lovejoy in his *Memoir of Rev. Charles Torrey* politely phrased it, "his numerous labors in the antislavery cause diverted his mind from his duties to his own charge, and he found it necessary to yield the one or the other." Since some supporters of Garrison were also members of Torrey's congregation, it seems likely that Torrey's ongoing fight with Garrison may have also contributed to his dismissal.[13]

Once again, Charles Torrey was without a job and, as usual, in debt. To make matters worse, Mary was pregnant with their second child, a daughter who would be born January 29, 1840, and named after her. At this point in his life, Torrey desperately needed to find a way to contribute both to the abolitionist cause and to his family's support. As an interim measure, Torrey asked Amos Phelps to designate him as a lecturer for the Massachusetts Abolition Society, to be paid $1,000 ($20,200) per year plus travel expenses. Phelps agreed, and by August, Torrey was lecturing in Williamstown and Pittsfield. On one occasion, when he was harassed by proslavery young men who threw pennies at him, he wrote Phelps saying that he "would willingly be pelted till doomsday by money for the cause of the poor." Torrey continued to give antislavery lectures in western Massachusetts throughout the latter months of 1839. He worked assiduously at what had become his primary mission in life, deterred by neither opposition nor obstacles. In December, traveling in bad weather, he was thrown from his wagon and spent ten days in bed recovering from his injuries.[14]

As he continued his abolitionist labors in late 1839, Torrey carefully followed the ongoing attempts to form an abolitionist political party. Following the Albany meeting, Alvan Stewart had gone to Pennsylvania and attempted, unsuccessfully, to get the Pennsylvania Society to nominate "a pair of good antislavery Whigs" for president and vice-president and publicizing that ticket in the *Pennsylvania Freeman.* Myron Holley, a graduate of Williams College and, like Stewart, a lawyer from upstate New York, then held a meeting in

Rochester in September to nominate antislavery candidates for the New York State Assembly. Several surrounding counties, including Monroe, Ontario, and Oswego, nominated antislavery candidates for local office; Oswego County abolitionists even "formally organized themselves as a [political] party—complete with a central committee." In October, Holley traveled to Cleveland to try to convince Ohio abolitionists of the necessity for a third party. Undeterred by such failures, in November, Stewart and Holley convened a meeting of abolitionists at Warsaw, near Rochester, and nominated James Birney for president and Francis LeMoyne, president of the Pennsylvania Anti-Slavery Society, as vice-president; both nominees immediately declined.[15]

In Massachusetts the New Organization was also considering the formation of an abolitionist party more seriously. Alvan Stewart had convinced Elizur Wright of its necessity, and by October, Wright was enthusiastically advocating for it in the *Massachusetts Abolitionist*. Wright assured his readers that, if an abolitionist party was formed, "both parties and religion will gain by it. Politics will be ennobled and religion will be *humanized*." In a letter to Henry Stanton, Wright detailed seven reasons why abolitionists should support a third party, including that it would provide "something practical for every man to *do*" and would strike terror "to the hearts of the South, from [Henry] Clay downwards."[16]

Torrey and his colleagues strongly supported Wright's suggested course of action, but many other Massachusetts abolitionists did not. They claimed that Wright was trying to turn the Massachusetts Abolition Society into a political party. According to Richard Sewell's *Ballots for Freedom*, Wright's advocacy of a third party in the *Massachusetts Abolitionist* lost him many subscribers.[17]

In addition to disagreements among its members regarding the best political course of action, the New Organization was also preoccupied by its ongoing, and seemingly interminable, fight with Garrison and his followers. This came to a head in October 1839, when Garrison obtained a copy of a private letter Elizur Wright had sent to Henry Stanton. In it, Wright complained that "*our New Organization here is a gone case. It has been, inter nos, shockingly mismanaged. Everything has been made to turn upon the woman question.*"

Garrison was so delighted to be able to use this letter to denigrate the New Organization that he reprinted it in the *Liberator* "seven or eight times as the schismatics *coup de grâce*." John Whittier, who had once been a close friend, said that Garrison had developed "a perfect incapacity of tolerating those who differ from him"; Garrison's obsession with the New Organization would appear to support this assessment.[18]

In December 1839 the Whigs held their nominating convention and emerged from it with a surprise candidate. Henry Clay was passed over, and instead the Whigs chose William Henry Harrison, a military hero who had led troops against the Indians in the 1811 Battle of Tippecanoe, as their nominee for president. John Tyler, a Virginia slaveholder, was selected as the Whig candidate for vice-president. Abolitionists would spend much of the following year trying to assess the abolitionist credentials of Harrison, who actively courted their votes. At one point, Harrison even gave "private assurances that if elected he would do nothing to block abolition [of slavery] in the District of Columbia," one of the primary goals of the abolitionists.[19]

By the end of 1839, significant progress had been made toward forming an abolitionist political party. A majority of abolitionists, in addition to Garrison's group, were still opposed, but those in opposition were growing fewer. In late 1839, two important leaders—Joshua Leavitt and Gerrit Smith—had been persuaded of the necessity of a third party. Leavitt was the editor of the *Emancipator,* the official newspaper of the American Anti-Slavery Society and an influential voice among the New York abolitionists. Gerrit Smith, an extremely wealthy landowner from upstate New York, was potentially a crucial link in making it happen, since he gave generously to causes he supported. In the past, abolitionists had depended on the wealthy Tappan brothers for funding, but they had been devastated by the 1837 financial panic. Beginning in 1840, therefore, the most important source of abolitionist funds would come from Gerrit Smith, including funds for Charles Torrey and, later, for John Brown.

Charles Torrey had many good qualities, but patience was not among them. Tiring of the seemingly endless arguments on the pros and cons of forming an abolitionist party, Torrey "set the ball rolling in late January with a call for a national convention to meet in New York City in May." James Birney complained that he had not been consulted and wrote to Amos Phelps: "Mr. T. is hardly sufficiently known to take such a matter as the call of a Convention in hand." A few days later, however, at an abolitionist meeting near Rochester, Myron Holley and Gerrit Smith agreed with Torrey's suggestion but thought May would be too late in the year to mount an effective campaign for the December elections. They therefore set the meeting for April 1, to take place in Albany.[20]

During early 1840, Torrey and Phelps forcefully promoted the formation of an abolitionist political party among their New Organization colleagues. Torrey recruited supporters from Massachusetts and Maine to attend the Albany meeting, while Phelps countered the reservations of skeptics. To those who opposed the new party because of the risk that its nominees might become corrupt, Phelps responded that hanging on to the nominees of the Democratic and Whig parties to avoid possible Liberty nominee corruption "is like hanging on to the plague to keep clear of t[he] itch. The latter to be sure is rather uncomfortable, but it admits of an easy cure." During these months, Torrey and Phelps were increasingly forced into leadership roles on the third-party issue because Elizur Wright, who had been forcefully promoting it as editor of the newspaper, had fallen into disfavor. Wright had become increasingly hostile to organized religion and had become, some said, an atheist. In May, following the Albany meeting, Wright was fired.[21]

A late winter storm made travel to the Albany meeting difficult. According to an account of the meeting, "the state of the roads was perhaps never worse, owing to the melting of the later snows. . . . One man walked 90 miles, through the mud, and over the hills from Vermont, to attend." Only 121 delegates were able to attend, but "abler discussions we have seldom, if ever, heard . . . [and] the meeting was eminently characterized by good feeling."[22]

Alvan Stewart was made president of the meeting, an appropriate choice, since his call for a third party had been the first. In his address, Stewart noted that for abolitionists to try to continue working with the Democrats and Whigs would be "of as little avail as it would be for a man to stand on an iceberg and whistle to the northwest wind to warm the atmosphere." Myron Holley and Charles Torrey were vice-presidents of the convention, and Joshua Leavitt was secretary; all argued strongly for the creation of a third party. Although Gerrit Smith did not come because of illness, he sent a message urging delegates to form a party and make nominations for national office. To not do so, he argued, "will be a failure most disastrous to our dear antislavery cause. The dogmatism and arrogance of Mr. Garrison will then know no bounds."[23]

On the second day of the convention, a vote was taken on whether to form a third party and make nominations for national office. The vote was 44 for, 33 against, with the remainder of the delegates abstaining. The convention then nominated James Birney for president, and Thomas Earle, a Pennsylvania abolitionist, for vice-president. Although the name of the new party was not officially adopted until a year later, Gerrit Smith had referred to it as the "liberty party," and the name stuck. The party platform had but a single plank, which was "the absolute and unqualified divorce of the General Government from slavery," with special emphasis on abolishing slavery in the District of Columbia and the interstate slave trade. Garrison, predictably, ridiculed the entire proceedings as an "April Fools" convention that had had "the folly, the presumption, the almost unbridled infatuation" to nominate candidates for the nation's highest offices.[24]

Reinhard Johnson, who wrote a definitive history of the new party, claimed that "the most distinctive features of the Liberty Party were its high-toned moralism and religious orientation." "At least one-third of all Liberty Party editors were ministers. . . . Liberty newspapers frequently had biblical quotes on their mastheads, and their columns were filled with religious imagery." The party's slogan was "vote as you pray and pray as you vote." Some even regarded the Liberty Party as a "surrogate religious denomination." Temperance was also highly valued, and "virtually all Liberty leaders seem to have been temperance persons" during the party's early years. Charles Torrey stated that the association between the Liberty Party and temperance was "not from policy, but from principle."[25]

Following the Albany convention, Torrey and his colleagues

returned to Massachusetts and formalized a state chapter of the Liberty Party. At a meeting in May, they nominated William Jackson, a prominent abolitionist, for governor, and Roger Leavitt for lieutenant governor on the Liberty Party ticket. Jackson, in a letter to Torrey and others, said he thought such a nomination was premature, so he declined. Leavitt accepted the nomination but then died two months later.[26]

Although some historians have claimed that the New Organization died out several months after splitting off from Garrison's group, that is a misunderstanding of events. What happened was that the New Organization essentially became the Massachusetts state chapter of the Liberty Party. The *Massachusetts Abolitionist* became the *Boston Free American,* the Liberty Party's official organ. Amos Phelps "suggested removing Charles T. Torrey as agent of the Massachusetts Abolition Society and employing him as an agent of the state [Liberty Party] central committee to organize the towns and congressional districts," but some abolitionists opposed the use of their resources for such political purposes. William Lloyd Garrison viewed the New Organization and Liberty Party as one and the same. In October 1840 he told a friend: "The third party is only another name for new organization. They twain are one."[27]

Garrison and his supporters "missed no opportunity to snipe at the new party." They "combined with others opposed to independent nominations to pass resolutions against the third party" at state antislavery meetings and personally attacked the motivations of the Liberty Party leaders. Garrison called them "a small but talented body of restless, ambitious, men, who are determined to get up a third party, come what may—in the hope, doubtless, of being lifted by it into office." The *Ninth Annual Report of the Massachusetts Anti-Slavery Society,* written by Garrison at the end of 1840, reflects his thinking at this time. The majority of the report details what Garrison called "the most absurd, the most false and flagrant charges . . . wicked and monstrous accusations. . . . This unnatural and criminal opposition has arisen from the spirit of sectarianism." On page after page, Garrison obsessively detailed the criticisms that had been leveled at him during the year by Phelps, Torrey, St. Clair, and other members of the New Organization. Each of the criticisms was followed by a detailed refutation. It was as if each arrow that had been shot in his direction was still embedded in his flesh, and he was determined to methodically dissect each detail to prove that he was right.[28]

During 1840 Garrison achieved an additional organizational victory over his New Organization rivals. In early May, one month after the Liberty Party convention, the American Anti-Slavery Society was scheduled to hold its annual meeting in New York. Since Garrison had obtained the right for women to vote at the 1839 meeting, it was anticipated that he would again pack the meeting with his supporters and thus dominate the agenda. Charles Torrey had foreseen this in November 1839 when he told Amos Phelps that they should simply let Garrison take over the existing American Anti-Slavery Society and instead form a new national organization without him. Arthur and Lewis Tappan, the major financial backers of the society, agreed with this plan. Therefore, prior to the May meeting, the Tappans transferred the ownership of the *Emancipator,* the society's newspaper, to the New York Anti-Slavery Society and transferred all the assets of the society, including its books and pamphlets, to individual members. The society was thus declared to be insolvent. The Tappans also drafted a constitution for a new society.[29]

None of this was apparently known to William Lloyd Garrison on Monday, May 11, 1840, as he assembled his supporters at the railroad depot in Boston. His wealthy Boston backers had chartered two trains to take them to Providence, where they boarded a chartered steamship to carry them overnight to New York. The steamship carried 450 Garrison supporters, including many described by his opponents as "Lynn shoemakers on holiday." At least 100 more Garrison supporters, including 25 women, came from Pennsylvania and New York.[30]

When the meeting opened at the Fourth Free Church on the afternoon of May 12, Arthur Tappan, president of the American Anti-Slavery Society, failed to appear, instead simply sending a note saying that he had resigned. One of Garrison's supporters then took the chair, appointed Garrison chairman of the business committee, and submitted a list of committee members that included Abby Kelley. A shouting match ensued, described by the New York newspapers as "a fight among alley cats," and the meeting was adjourned for the day. The following morning, a vote was called on Abby Kelley's nomination, and it was approved, 571 to 451. Thereupon Lewis Tappan, Amos Phelps, and their many supporters got up and walked out, reassembling downstairs, where they formed the American and Foreign Anti-Slavery Society, elected Arthur Tappan as president, and approved the society's constitution, which Tappan had previously drafted. Garrison and his supporters were left upstairs with a society in name only, since it had no assets. In a letter to his wife, Garrison described it as "a glorious triumph. . . . We made clean work of everything." He had won the organizational battle but was losing the war.[31]

Immediately following the meeting of the American Anti-Slavery Society, William Lloyd Garrison left for England to attend the World Anti-Slavery Convention. He was joined by Wendell Phillips and several female followers, even though Garrison had been told that only gentlemen would be admitted as delegates. James Birney, the Liberty Party nominee for president, and Henry Stanton represented the New York abolitionists, and Rev. Nathaniel Colver represented the New Organization. Neither Charles Torrey nor Amos Phelps ever went to Britain to raise funds, as so many American abolitionists did, but it is likely that John Scoble, secretary of the British and Foreign Anti-Slavery Society, had met them when he visited Boston in 1839. Upon Torrey's death, Scoble and Thomas Clarkson, president of the British society, signed a society resolution praising Torrey's actions.[32]

The British meeting was another setback for Garrison and his colleagues. The meeting was opened by Clarkson, then eighty years old, who had been one of the leaders in the forty-six-year fight preceding passage of the 1833 Slavery Abolition Act. Wendell Phillips then argued strongly that women should be seated as delegates, but the motion was voted down. Garrison, in protest, refused to be seated, "preferring to sit with the women in the gallery, thus causing, according to Birney, 'a good deal of merriment' among the British delegates." According to Howard Temperley's book on the British antislavery movement, the British leaders "never entirely trusted" Garrison, especially "his way of linking antislavery with extraneous causes. . . . Above all they objected to his rejection of political action."[33]

Meanwhile in the United States, Charles Torrey and other Liberty Party advocates were attempting to organize support for the December elections. They faced formidable political obstacles. In May the Democratic Party not only had renominated President Martin Van Buren for a second term but also had included a plank in the party platform explicitly prohibiting Congress from interfering on the slavery issue. Van Buren was widely viewed as a staunch defender of slavery and was hated by the abolitionists. Whig William Henry Harrison, by contrast, was actively soliciting the abolitionist votes, and most abolitionists had previously counted themselves as Whigs. As Henry Stanton summarized it, "49/50th of our friends are in that [Whig] party," most of whom "would wade to their armpits in molten lava to drive Van Buren from power." Thus, a vote for Birney and the Liberty Party would be one less for Harrison and the Whigs, thereby improving Van Buren's chances of reelection. Many prominent abolitionists, therefore, publicly declared their support for the Whigs.[34]

In addition to these political obstacles, Liberty Party supporters had limited fiscal resources and little time to get organized. Despite this, Charles Torrey and Amos Phelps were among the most active Liberty Party workers in Massachusetts and were joined, surprisingly, by Samuel Sewall, a respected lawyer who had been one of Garrison's earliest supporters. According to Reinhard Johnson's book on the Liberty Party, the workers "held numerous rallies, printed electoral tickets, distributed Extra editions of newspapers and tracts, and lectured constantly." Torrey also campaigned for the Liberty Party at this time in upstate New York, in towns such as Auburn, Syracuse, and Clinton. In the midst of his campaigning, on September 29, Nathaniel Emmons, the maternal grandfather of Charles Torrey's wife, died at age ninety-five. Emmons, who had been an eminent Congregational minister, had been an early supporter of the abolitionist movement, as Mary Torrey's father had also been.[35]

The voter turnout for the election on December 2, 1840, was 80.2 percent of the qualified electorate, one of the highest turnouts in American history. William Henry Harrison and the Whigs swept to victory, amassing 234 electoral votes to only 60 for Van Buren. Birney and the Liberty Party received only 7,056 votes out of the almost 2.5 million cast. Their strongest showing was in Massachusetts, where they received almost 1 percent of the votes, despite the active opposition of Garrison and his followers.[36]

Abolitionist hopes for Whig support rose briefly on March 4, 1841, when William Henry Harrison was inaugurated as president. Such hopes fell abruptly one month later when Harrison died from pneumonia and Vice-President John Tyler assumed the highest office. Tyler was not only a Virginia slaveholder but also, like Thomas Jefferson, "he left behind black people claiming descent from him."[37]

In the eyes of many abolitionists, this setback made the Liberty Party more necessary than ever. Torrey resumed his work for the party in both Massachusetts and Maine. In an August 1841 letter to his wife, written from Maine, he described having "lectured *every evening*, about two hours, each night; besides one afternoon lecture of 2 3/4 hours. I have given, therefore, eighteen lectures already. . . . I will go hence to Waldoboro, Thomaston, Camden, Belfast . . . and then up to Waterville, and other towns, on the river from Hollowell." Torrey also described being homesick: "Tell Charlie, Pa loves him, and prays for him, every day, that he may be a good boy, and love God, and mind mother, and love sister. Kiss little Mary for me, and don't let her forget papa; and may the love of God rest upon all the members of my dear household." It is likely that Torrey's Liberty Party efforts were being supported at this time by Gerrit Smith. The previous year, Amos Phelps had asked Smith to support Torrey's work. Such support is also suggested by this having been the only time in his life when Torrey appears to have had any discretionary income, and he purchased $1,000 ($21,500) worth of land in Maine.[38]

As Charles Torrey and his colleagues labored to strengthen political abolitionism throughout 1841, William Lloyd Garrison attacked them at every opportunity. "Torrey is engaged in vilifying the old anti-slavery organization and its friends, and manufacturing political moonshine for a third party," he wrote to one friend. In another letter he referred to "Colver, Phelps, Torrey, St. Clair etc" as "disorganizers and defamers . . . priestly conspirators . . . to make capital for [the] New Organization, and to bring a false accusation against the leading friends of the old organization." According to William Goodell's 1858 history of this period, Garrison continued to characterize the New Organization as "a hateful form of pro-slavery" designed to cripple "the only efficient abolitionists," his own organization. According to Goodell, "the repetition of these charges [by Garrison] has been incessant." At this time, Garrison's group was working primarily to racially integrate Boston's schools, trains, and steamships. In addition to criticism from Garrison, Torrey was apparently acquiring a reputation beyond Massachusetts. A June 24, 1841, letter to him from a minister in Savannah, Georgia, said: "God Almighty bless your soul to Hell. . . . What are you thinking about you Son of a Bitch, don't you know you have a soul to save?"[39]

Throughout the fall of 1841, Torrey continued to build an infrastructure for the Liberty Party. In September and October, he published a series of articles on the "Policy of the Liberty Party" in the *Boston Free American*. The series included an economic analysis of slavery, especially "the contest between free and slave labor and its resulting favors for the South." According to historian Reinhard Johnson, Torrey was also "a candidate of the [Liberty] party in Boston in 1841," although Johnson does not indicate for what position.[40]

As Charles Torrey labored for the Liberty Party in 1841, he began to think about alternative means for freeing the slaves. Political abolitionism was certainly proving to be more promising than Garrison's moral suasion, but getting enough abolitionist politicians elected to make a real difference could take a very long time. As always, Torrey's time horizon did not extend to the distant future. In his August 21, 1841, letter to his wife, written from Maine, Torrey described being "regularly tired out . . . rested again *almost* every day, not quite. But I feel better and stronger than I did last week." The possible recurrence of his tuberculosis could never have been far from his consciousness.[41]

Torrey's thinking about other means of freeing slaves was profoundly affected by an event in June of 1841. While in Boston attending an abolitionist meeting, Torrey heard about an escaped slave named John Torrance and immediately took action. Torrance was a slave from New Bern, North Carolina, who had escaped by hiding on a schooner bound for Boston. Torrance had previously purchased freedom for his wife and child, who had gone to Philadelphia, and he wished to join them. Four days into the voyage, Torrance was discovered. The captain wanted to stop in Norfolk to put Torrance ashore, but the crew refused, so they continued to Boston. There Torrance was chained and forcibly kept on board the ship until arrangements could be made for his return to North Carolina. Hearing of the situation, Torrey argued that Torrance had become a free man once he arrived in Boston and therefore filed charges of kidnapping against the captain and first mate, alleging that they "did forcibly seize and confine John Torrance . . . against his will, with intent to cause the said John Torrance to be sent out of this State against his will."[42]

The captain and mate were arrested, and the case presented to a grand jury on June 5. Appearing as counsel for Torrance was Richard H. Dana, a Boston lawyer and abolitionist. Dana was also a well-known writer and the previous year had published *Two Years Before the Mast*. Dana presented five witnesses who verified the facts of the case, which were not in dispute. The captain testified that he had had to return the slave to North Carolina or he would no longer be able to trade with the southern states. The grand jury refused to indict the captain and mate and set them free.

Torrey was apoplectic and published a scathing, full-page rebuke to the members of the grand jury, naming them in the *Boston Free American*. All legal authorities, he wrote, including the district attorney, who was defending the captain and mate, agreed that the grand jury had "greatly erred" in not finding an indictment. The grand jury's decision was, said Torrey,

> Monstrous! What is this but a *proclamation* that the laws of Massachusetts should *yield* to those of North Carolina, whenever the two conflict? *Worse still,* it says that whenever *southern slavery* and *northern freedom* conflict, the latter shall bow down in slavish subjection! . . . You [members of the Grand Jury] will hear notes of indignant rebuke and remonstrance that will reach you even in your counting houses, where you may, perhaps, be reckoning up the gains of trade in cotton, rice, sugar, tar, pitch, turpentine, corn and lumber, for which the liberties of the people of the North are to be sold! . . . Has

Massachusetts, has Boston, have the merchants engaged in trade with the South, sunk so low?[43]

The Torrance case received extensive coverage in the Boston newspapers and nationally in the abolitionist press. At a Boston meeting of over four hundred people, Torrey used the occasion to organize a Boston Vigilance Committee, patterned after those in New York and Philadelphia, to prevent future kidnappings. Ellis Gray Loring, a wealthy Boston lawyer who was one of Garrison's most important supporters, joined the committee and was rebuked by Maria Child for doing so. "A pang shot through my heart," Child wrote, "when I saw your name by the side of Torrey's." Joshua Leavitt sent a letter congratulating him, and Torrey was broadly praised for his actions by almost everyone except Garrison, who wrote: "It is unfortunate for the prosperity of this [Boston Vigilance] Committee, that one so decidedly objectionable as is Charles T. Torrey to so large a portion of the abolitionists of this Commonwealth, should be its Secretary and Agent."[44]

Torrey was deeply moved by John Torrance's fate. Here was a man who had bought freedom for his wife and child and was merely trying to free himself to join them. He had even reached Boston, yet because of the lack of northern assistance, he had been sent back to North Carolina, where he almost certainly would have been taken to New Orleans and sold. As Torrey wrote, "John Torrance should *never again see his wife and child!*"[45]

The attempt by Torrance to free himself reminded Torrey of the Amistad affair, which had been prominent in the news during 1840 and early 1841. Here was another example of slaves trying to free themselves, this time successfully. Fifty-three slaves from West Africa were being taken on the schooner *Amistad* from Cuba to be sold in the South. While at sea, the slaves broke their chains, killed the captain, and took over the ship. Sailing northward, they were taken into custody by the U.S. Navy off Connecticut and imprisoned in New Haven. Extensive litigation ensued regarding their legal status, with abolitionists arguing that they should be freed. Torrey and Amos Phelps helped raise defense funds, which they sent to Lewis Tappan, who was coordinating help for the slaves. The case was ultimately appealed to the U.S. Supreme Court, which heard it in February 1841. Arguing for the freedom of the slaves was former President John Quincy Adams, elected to the House of Representatives after he lost his bid for reelection in 1828 to Andrew Jackson. Adams's brilliant defense of the slaves before the Supreme Court resulted in their release.[46]

One month after the denouement of the Torrance case, another attempt of slaves to gain freedom was prominently reported. On July 1, 1841, three young white men—Alanson Work, James Burr, and George Thompson—rowed a boat across the Mississippi River from Quincy, Illinois, to the Missouri side in a prearranged plan to free some slaves. Two of the men were missionary students and the other a teacher at the Mission institute in Quincy, and all were deeply religious. Their plan was detected, and the three were seized and jailed in Palmyra, Missouri. On September 10–13, the men were brought to trial, found guilty, and sentenced to twelve years in state prison. While awaiting trial, Work had written: "I now feel my interest, my life, my liberty, my all [are] identified with those of the slave. I design to search some pillar on which slavery rests, and through the prayers of God's people, hope to be endued with power from on high to lay hold of it, and if I perish, perish Samson-like."[47]

Torrey admired these men and was angered when other abolitionists criticized them. Here were men that Torrey wished to emulate, men who valued actions over words. At this time, Torrey was increasingly wondering whether his real usefulness was in giving lectures in Williamstown and Waldoboro to increase the Liberty Party vote. Directly helping slaves seemed like a much more attractive option.

The Liberty Party organization work of Charles Torrey and his colleagues paid off in the 1841 local Massachusetts elections. In the gubernatorial race, the party captured over 3 percent of the vote. The following year, the figure increased to over 5 percent, thus preventing either the Whigs or Democrats from obtaining a majority, and throwing the election to the state legislature. In 1842 the Liberty Party "also placed at least six representatives" in the state legislature, which was evenly divided between Whigs and Democrats. The "six Liberty representatives" therefore "held the balance of power" in the legislature. Even Garrison, writing in the *Liberator,* had to reluctantly concede that the Liberty Party's elected officials "were sufficient to determine the political character of the State government."[48]

By the time of the 1841 election, however, Charles Torrey was on his way to Washington, D.C. His career as a political abolitionist had come to a close, and he had a new career in mind.

4

THE FIRST ARREST

Charles Torrey arrived in Washington in early December 1841. His ostensible job was to be a Washington reporter for the *Boston Daily Mail,* the *New York Evangelist,* and several other small abolitionist papers. Joshua Leavitt, the former editor of the *Evangelist,* may have helped Torrey get the assignments. As an accredited reporter, Torrey applied for and was given a desk in the House of Representatives.[1]

At this time, Washington was a city of forty-four thousand people. It had been planned in a grand design by Pierre L'Enfant, a French-born architect, and the cornerstone for the Washington Monument had just been laid; the city, however, was notably unfinished. Torrey viewed it as "a cluster of four or five villages . . . owing to the nature of the site which is low and marshy." Charles Dickens, who visited Washington three months after Torrey arrived, called the city "the headquarters of tobacco-tinctured saliva" and described it as follows:

> I walk to the front window [of the hotel room] and look across the road upon a long, straggling row of houses, one story high, terminating, nearly opposite, but a little to the left, in a melancholy piece of waste ground with frowzy grass, which looks like a small piece of country that has taken to drinking, and has quite lost itself. . . . It is sometimes called the City of Magnificent Distances, but it might with greater propriety be termed the City of Magnificent Intentions; for it is only on taking a bird's-eye view of it from the top of the Capitol, that one can at all comprehend the vast designs of its projector, an aspiring Frenchman. Spacious avenues, that begin in nothing, and lead nowhere; streets, mile-long, that only want houses, roads and inhabitants; public buildings that need but a public to be complete; and ornaments of great thoroughfares, which

only lack great thoroughfares to ornament—are its leading features. One might fancy the season over, and most of the houses gone out of town for ever with their masters. . . . Few people would live in Washington, I take it, who are not obliged to live there.

Among Torrey's initial impressions were the ubiquitous "grog-shops . . . and the free drinking of very many occupying stations of the highest influence" as well as gambling houses that "occupy many prominent points between the Capitol and the White House."[2]

Torrey's strongest impression of Washington, however, was the conspicuous curse of slavery. Washington was the center of the nation's interstate slave trade. Two large slave pens, known by their owners' names, Robey and Williams, stood at Eighth and B Streets (B Street is now Independence Avenue) and Seventh Street and Maryland Avenue SW, just off the National Mall. An English visitor described one of them as set "right against the Capitol, from which it is distant about half a mile, with no house intervening." From these pens and from slave auctions, slaves were often taken to the Franklin and Armfield slave pen at 1315 Duke Street in Alexandria, part of the District at that time, from which over a thousand slaves a year were shipped for sale in New Orleans, the nation's third largest city at that time. When Torrey arrived, the Williams slave pen was in the news because of a "daring November escape" of several slaves. On the streets of Washington, pedestrians were regularly confronted with slave auctions. The fact that such sales took place in the shadow of the Capitol highlighted the hypocrisy of slavery, "the voices of patriotic representatives boasting of freedom and equality, and the rattling of the poor slaves' chains comingled." One northern newspaper described the scene: "Under the very dome of the Capital, beneath the stars and stripes of the nation, women, Christian women, are sold by the appointed officer of the President, and the money put into the bag of the United States Treasury. Judas, for his thirty pieces of silver, hardly did worse than this." Profoundly disgusted by what he saw, Torrey described Washington as "that mock metropolis of freedom, and sink of iniquity."[3]

Torrey's decision to go to Washington had been a deliberate one.

The city had long been the center of the interstate slave trade; when the District of Columbia had been created by carving pieces out of Maryland and Virginia, these two states had "contained over half of the slave population of the entire nation in the first census." Moreover, the District of Columbia was a federal territory and thus under the authority of Congress. As historian Daniel Walker Howe noted: "Since Congress had no power to abolish slavery in the states, the District of Columbia became a favorite target for abolitionists wishing to focus national attention on their cause."[4]

The abolition of slavery in the District of Columbia had been a goal of abolitionists from the earliest years of the movement. In the early 1820s, Benjamin Lundy "promoted a complete plan of gradual emancipation, one that began with abolition in the territories and the District of Columbia." In 1828, encouraged by Lundy, U.S. Representative Charles Miner of Pennsylvania introduced legislation to abolish slavery in the District. Miner noted that the taxes paid by northerners "helped pay for jails used as holding pens for slaves awaiting sale." The Massachusetts Anti-Slavery Society and the American Anti-Slavery Society both cited the abolition of slavery in the nation's capital as one of their main goals, and the Liberty Party did as well. Slavery in the District was such a sensitive issue that in 1850, when the state of Georgia "listed possible northern actions that would require it to secede from the Union, it put the abolition of slavery in the District first."[5]

Charles Torrey went to Washington with ideas of carrying out activities other than merely newspaper reporting. During his first week there he began attending the black churches in order to establish contacts with both the free blacks and the slaves who attended them. He described his initial visit to the African Methodist Church on the corner of Fourth and D Streets SE, four blocks from the Capitol, in a letter to his wife:

> In the afternoon, I went to a colored church, one of the "Wesleyan," so called, a denomination of Methodists, who have separated entirely from white slaveholding churches; they are all colored. There was no sermon, only a class-meeting;

but I have not enjoyed the "communion of saints," so much, for a long time, as when mingling with that little band of despised colored people, partly slaves; and, when one of the poor women, nearly white, spoke of the "persecution" she endured, with sobs, I felt my heart filled with new energy to make war upon that hateful institution that so crushes the disciples of the Lord to the earth. I have determined to commune only with the colored churches, while I stay here; I will strive to be pure from the blood of the poor.

Torrey later wrote that he had "witnessed much warmth of heart, much humility, much fervor of devotional zeal" in the black churches and that "the standard of piety and morals . . . will compare with that in the white churches—in some respects it is higher." He was less enthusiastic about "the extravagancies, such as shouting, jumping, and dancing, which I have witnessed seem to be *habitual* with many; and I have no doubt that the *physical* enjoyment of this union of religious and bodily activity is its great charm."[6]

At the same time that he was making the rounds of Washington's black churches, Torrey sought out the abolitionist leaders in Congress. The person who provided him with the introduction was Joshua Leavitt, who was in Washington as a correspondent for the *Emancipator* newspaper. Torrey and Leavitt had become friends during the April 1840 nominating convention of the Liberty Party. Although Leavitt was nineteen years older than Torrey, the two had much in common. Both were from small towns in Massachusetts; both had attended Yale; and both had been ordained as Congregationalist ministers. Both also shared a close friendship with Amos Phelps and a strong dislike of William Lloyd Garrison; on one occasion Garrison had even suggested that Leavitt had "a disturbed state of mind." Like Torrey, Leavitt was also described as having "great confidence in his abilities and the soundness of his opinions." He "believed so deeply in the causes he supported that he at times felt compelled to personalize the battles," the consequence of which was an occasional "combative nature . . . obstinacy, pugnacity, etc." However, Leavitt also "could be extremely generous and caring toward friends, perhaps especially those . . . whom he considered victims of injustice." Torrey would subsequently be the recipient of such caring and regarded Leavitt as one of his closest friends.[7]

Joshua Leavitt had discovered slavery as a cause in 1825, even before William Lloyd Garrison had done so. He published an article entitled "People of Colour" in the *Christian Spectator* in which he discussed "the dangers that slavery posed to the nation and the need for Americans to discuss the issue and develop some plan of action." He acknowledged that he did not have a solution to the problem but said that, "if God is just, something will be done." By 1834 he had joined with other white abolitionists and black clergymen in New York to sponsor adult schools, libraries, and reading rooms for blacks in the city, and on a trip to Washington that year he had visited the slave pen in Alexandria. While living in Washington in 1842, Leavitt, like Torrey, often attended black churches.[8]

In 1842 there were three leading abolitionist members of Congress—Joshua Giddings of Ohio, Seth Gates of New York, and William Slade of Vermont. Torrey was especially impressed with Giddings, who had been elected to Congress in 1838 from the abolitionist-friendly Western Reserve section of northern Ohio. Giddings, who was an imposing six-foot-two, 225 pounds, had grown up as the youngest of seven children of a poor farmer, and had taught himself to read and write. He had then become a successful lawyer and speculator in real estate until the financial panic of 1837, which had almost bankrupted him. Following a deep depression and religious awakening, he was elected to Congress at age forty-three.[9]

Giddings entered the abolitionist edifice relatively late in his career. Prior to 1837, he had shown no special interest in the issue, but his experience in Washington quickly changed that. On January 30, 1839, while wandering the streets of the city, he saw a "coffle of about sixty slaves . . . chained together on their way south," driven by a slave driver "with a huge bullwhip in his hand." Giddings called it a "barbarous spectacle," an outrage that was reinforced a few days later when he observed a slave being severely beaten by his owner and the owner's son: "The master and his son then took him and dragged him through the street as they would have done a dead hog to a stable and left him there." Two days later, Giddings attended a slave auction on Pennsylvania Avenue. He observed the fear in a twenty-six-year-old black man, who apparently had been a free black but had been kidnapped; "as the bidders one after another raised the price of their fellowman, his eyes followed them and the deep horror and agony of his soul was portrayed in the contortions of his countenance."[10]

Joshua Giddings had thus been transformed into an ardent abolitionist, writing to his wife that "slaves are sold right before the Capitol, and in sight of the door." He told a friend, "I must do my political duty and leave the consequences to God." On February 13, he rose during a House debate on the budget for the District of Columbia and made his maiden speech. He urged that the sale of slaves in Washington be abolished, since such spectacles are only condoned in "barbarous and uncivilized nations": "On the beautiful avenue in front of the capitol, members of Congress, during this session, have heard the harsh voice of the auctioneer, publicly selling human beings, while they were on their way to the capitol. They also have been compelled to turn aside from their path to permit a coffle of slaves, males and females, chained to each other by their necks, to pass on their way to this National slave mart." Congressman Julius Alford of Georgia, seated near Giddings, suddenly exploded, saying that he would "sooner spit on Giddings than listen further to his abolitionist insults" and urged the Speaker to stop him. Giddings continued, at which point Alford "leapt to his feet, began shouting threats, and headed straight for Giddings," until he was restrained by his colleagues. Giddings later described it as "a perfect scene of disorder and uproar."[11]

It was a memorable maiden speech for a new member of Congress, and Giddings's career was suitably launched. Over the next three years, Giddings on numerous occasions confronted the men he called "southern Bullies." He was convinced that the southerners had intimidated his northern colleagues but said he would not follow suit. "This kind of fear I have never experienced, nor will I submit to it now," he confided in his diary. He submitted multiple resolutions, such as asking Congress "to investigate and report on how many slaves in the District of Columbia had committed suicide within the previous five years, rather than submit to being sold and sent away from their families." The abolition of slavery in the District of Columbia was his paramount issue, but he also lobbied for the rights of free states to protect slaves once they reached their territory as well as for the "slaves' constitutional right to seize their own freedom, violently if necessary." For the remainder of his life at his home in Ohio, Giddings "kept a particular chamber in his house ... for the use of refugees" and "contributed money for the transportation of runaway slaves by rail from that point to Cleveland."[12]

It is thus not surprising that, when Charles Torrey met Joshua Giddings in December 1841, they developed an immediate friendship. Both had a Puritan heritage and Congregational affiliation. Like Torrey, Giddings also spent time with blacks and was sought out by them because he was known to be sympathetic to their plight. For example, once when Giddings was being interviewed by a Cleveland newspaper reporter, "a woe-begone looking colored man, the picture of despair," knocked on his door and implored his help: "O sar ... our people told me that you had more feeling than the other men here." Southern congressmen regularly castigated Giddings for this "disreputable habit" of associating with black people. After spending an evening with Giddings, Torrey described him to his wife as "a plain, frank, open-hearted man" and added, "I feel quite attached to him." Giddings allowed Torrey to use his post-office box to receive mail and addressed him in correspondence as "my dear friend."[13]

Giddings, along with William Slade, Seth Gates, and Joshua Leavitt, lived in Ms. Sprigg's boarding house on First Street, just behind the Capitol, where the main building of the Library of Congress now stands. Because of the politics of its boarders, the house was often referred to as the Abolition House. Its most famous boarder would be Abraham Lincoln, who arrived in 1847 after being elected to the House of Representatives. Torrey lived in Ms. Padgett's boarding house on Thirteenth Street, close to the White House. Many Washington boarding houses, including those of Mss. Sprigg and Padgett, employed slaves owned by other people to staff the establishments. This provided individuals living in these boarding houses with as much social contact with the slaves as they wished to have.

For several slaves working in these two boarding houses, this interaction would prove to be particularly felicitous.[14]

As a congressional reporter, Torrey dutifully filed his stories. Not surprisingly, he focused special attention on the ongoing fight over the gag rule originally passed in 1835, which effectively prohibited discussion of slavery by Congress. Each year the gag rule continued to be passed by Congress by an increasingly narrow margin, and by late 1841 supporters of abolition believed they were close to having the votes to overturn it. In his newspaper dispatches, Torrey described John Quincy Adams's efforts to skirt the gag rule and present petitions under other guises, as well as the "*trickery*" of proslavery forces "to destroy the right of petition, and stifle all debate on the subject of slavery."[15]

Torrey was not at all impressed by Congress, calling it "a far less dignified assembly than most of our State Legislatures." He noted that a Tennessee congressman had called a New Hampshire congressman "a descendant from a Scotch body-snatcher and murderer." He described one congressional debate as "a scene of noise and folly . . . which lasted half an hour, during which nobody knew or cared who spoke, or what was said: each member striving to talk as fast and as loudly as might be." In the end, said Torrey, "the nation should be grateful to them [the members of Congress] for the little *evil* wrought by them. It was *only* a waste of time and of public funds."[16]

Torrey was especially disgusted by southern members of Congress who defended slavery even as they were using their female slaves as mistresses. Many stories circulated among the abolitionists in Washington, but two were noteworthy. One account concerned Kentuckian Richard Mentor Johnson, a member of the U.S. House and Senate from 1807 to 1837 and vice-president under Martin Van Buren from 1837 to 1841, who fathered two children by one slave mistress; then, when she died, he took another as his mistress, and later her sister as well. Another prominent example was James Hammond, a former U.S. congressman and later U.S. senator and governor of South Carolina. Hammond was one of the staunchest defenders of slavery, claiming "it to be the greatest of all the great blessings which a kind Providence has bestowed upon our glorious nation." He added: "I do firmly believe that domestic slavery, regulated as ours is, produces the highest toned, the purest, best organization of society that has ever existed on the face of the earth." According to his diaries, Hammond took as his mistress an eighteen-year-old slave who had a one-year-old daughter; then, when the daughter was twelve, he took her as his mistress as well. Hammond also acknowledged having abused his four teenage nieces "with everything short of direct sexual intercourse." Such stories deeply offended Torrey's sense of what was right. He later observed that it was common for "slaveholders in the Baltimore-Washington area not only to have children by their female slaves but to have additional children by their enslaved daughters and to sell them all to traders."[17]

On January 12, 1842, Charles Torrey traveled to Annapolis to attend a convention of Maryland slaveholders. It was the first such slaveholders meeting held in the United States. Leavitt, Giddings, and other abolitionists in Washington encouraged Torrey to go and report on the convention.[18]

Maryland's slaveholders had organized the convention "to take measures to protect the interests of the slave system." The slaveholders were concerned because the state's long northern border with Pennsylvania, a free state, invited slaves to run away, and the slaves were doing so increasingly often. Once across the border, the slaves were helped by Quakers and others who provided food and temporary shelter. Runaways, the slaveholders charged, were being encouraged by abolitionist literature from the North as well as by free blacks. The latter was a particular problem for Maryland, which had more free blacks in 1840—over 62,000—than any other state; in fact, Maryland had as many free blacks as North Carolina, South Carolina, Georgia, Alabama, Mississippi, Arkansas, and Louisiana combined. The slaveholders were also concerned because Baltimore was growing rapidly in population, and since power in the state legislature was based on population, the slaveholding southern and eastern counties were losing power.[19]

As Torrey would later write, proposed solutions offered at the slaveholders' convention focused on preventing runaways and preventing an increase of free blacks in the state. For the former, the slaveholders proposed actions such as "officers to be appointed to watch the arrival and departure of all steamers, railroad cars, etc., to prevent runaway slaves from traveling in them." For the latter, solutions included such proposals as a legal prohibition against "all emancipation," a prohibition against free blacks' purchasing the freedom of their enslaved spouse or children, and the following: "All children of free colored people, over eight years of age in 1844, to be taken from their parents and bound out, the females until eighteen and the males until twenty-one, to white persons, and then to be induced, if possible, to leave the state and not to be allowed to return."[20]

From the time he arrived in Annapolis, Torrey wrote, "I noticed looks of suspicion and inquiry cast upon me, and an occasional whispered remark, or finger pointed towards my seat." On the second day, the convention's president asked all persons who had not been officially accredited as members of the convention to retire to the lobby, at which time Torrey was accused of being an abolitionist. He protested that he was a reporter and that he should have the right to cover the convention for his newspapers. After much debate, the officers of the convention ordered him to leave, but by then "a lawless and drunken mob was excited against me" and followed him down the street. Various threats were made by the mob, including tarring and feathering him and hanging him. Torrey later described the scene: "I was perfectly cool, collected, fearless of evil, as I ever was in my life. Not that there was no real danger, or that I was unconscious of it; for no one could be so, with several hundred raging and menacing around him." As the mob was debating his fate, a police officer arrived with a warrant for his arrest, and he was taken to jail.[21]

Torrey described the Annapolis jail as "old and ruinous" for which "a jack-knife would free any prisoner in two hours." He was provided with no bedding but obtained some by paying the jailer for it. The jail was occupied by thirteen black men, women, and children, making up two families; they had been emancipated by their master upon his death but then seized by the master's creditors and were being sold back into slavery to pay off his debts. Torrey was very moved by the plight of these families, destined to be separated as they were sold back into slavery. As he later recalled: "I could not help weeping as I looked at the two little infants . . . in their mothers' arms, mewling in sweet unconsciousness of the bitter doom their parents were anticipating, a sale to the trader." At this time in Maryland, the sale of slaves south "shattered approximately one slave marriage in three and separated one fifth of the children under fourteen from one or both of their parents."[22]

The news of Torrey's arrest spread quickly. Two respected local lawyers offered to represent Torrey without charge; in addition, the Massachusetts delegation to Congress sent a prominent Massachusetts lawyer, who was in Washington on a case before the Supreme Court, to Annapolis to further assist Torrey. After four days in jail, Torrey was given a hearing, at which the state attorney tried to show why he should be charged with writing "incendiary" material. Torrey was ably defended, and it became clear he had broken no laws. Two days later, the judge so ruled and Torrey was released.

Torrey's arrest received widespread newspaper coverage in the North and propelled him into public prominence. Some papers called him "imprudent" for going to the slaveholders' convention, but most praised him. "It seems," said one, "that although a cat may look upon a king, yet an abolitionist may not look upon a convention of slaveholders." Another noted that "Mr. Torrey has been precluded from obtaining the full reports which he intended on the doings of the Convention, but he has done more by his imprisonment than he could by any report, to open the eyes of the body of people in Maryland to the machinations of a handful of slaveholders."[23]

Charles Torrey's experiences with the slaveholders and the black families in jail shaped his remaining days. He wrote to his wife that "the old Bastille of slavery was shaken more effectually by the [his] arrest and its consequences, than it could have been in any other way, in five years." He also told her that in jail he had reconsecrated himself "to the work of freeing the slaves, until no slaves shall be found in our land. May God help me to be faithful to that *pledge made in Annapolis jail.* In that cell, God helping me. . . . I will celebrate the emancipation of the slaves of Maryland, before ten years more roll away." He had developed more specific ideas during his days in jail of how he intended to accomplish this.[24]

Following his release from the Annapolis jail, Charles Torrey returned to his reporter's desk in the House of Representatives. He described his reception in a letter to his wife: "Since I returned here, I have been treated with unusual respect and kindness. A few slaveholders swear about me a little, to *exercise their venomous tongues*; but that does no harm to anything but their souls. They are civil to me, personally, though some of them *look* rather hard at me. . . . On the whole it will give me character and influence wherever our language goes; so that I shall have no great reason to regret it." Similarly, Theodore Weld reported in a letter: "Torrey, as you know, has been here at his post now a full week. Nobody molests him. His imprisonment at Annapolis as an abolitionist everybody knows here, and it has once been referred to by a member of Congress in a speech on the floor, but he is not molested." In a report to the *New York Evangelist,* Torrey claimed, with a mix of hopefulness and some exaggeration, that his imprisonment was having far-reaching effects. "Not only do the leading papers of Maryland come out against the doings of the Slaveholding Convention, but public meetings begin to be held to condemn it. The State is full of agitation, and slavery is tottering. Another such blow as it has recently received would destroy it wholly."[25]

Torrey's return to Washington was just in time to witness a remarkable spectacle—the so-called "trial" of John Quincy Adams by his congressional colleagues. Seventy-four-year-old Adams was a human textbook of American history. At age seven, he had watched with his mother as the colonial militia confronted British forces on Bunker Hill in the early stages of the Revolutionary War. At age fifteen, he had watched his father negotiate the Treaty of Paris to officially end the war. After graduating from Harvard and studying law, Adams had been appointed ambassador to the Netherlands by President Washington; ambassador to Prussia by his father; and ambassador to Russia and then Britain by President Madison. At home he had served one year in the Massachusetts State Senate; five years in the U.S. Senate; eight years as secretary of state under President Monroe; and four years as president, from 1824 to 1828. After being defeated for a second term by Andrew Jackson, Adams had run for a seat in the House of Representatives and by 1842 had served for ten years. One member of Congress estimated that Adams had more political experience "than the rest of us combined."[26]

In addition to having experience, Adams also had an agenda. According to one biographer, "Adams was particularly bitter about his defeat" by Jackson and "blamed the defeat and its stigma mainly on southern slavemasters and their northern sycophants." Adams's foremost interest as a congressman, therefore, was to seek revenge on southern slaveholders, and he did this by becoming a leading congressional abolitionist. After the gag rule was instituted in 1836, banning the reading of petitions related to slavery, Adams used every available trick and legal stratagem to circumvent the rule. Each petition introduced by Adams "roused Southern Representatives to increased fury," and they frequently referred to Adams as the "Mad Man from Massachusetts." On one occasion, Adams said he wanted to present a petition from some slaves themselves, which had never before occurred; he then watched as an uproar ensued as southern congressmen tried to block its presentation. When he was finally allowed to read it, Adams said that the slaves had petitioned "to protect them from the abolitionists lest their welfare be harmed." One historian called it "the best and most effective practical joke in the history of Congress."[27]

Adams was a short man, "about five foot seven with a slight pot belly, a round face, and a bald head surrounded by a crown of white hair and white sideburns." He was described as "a cantankerous old man, sour and uncharitable, more than a bit paranoid," but to his abolitionist friends he could be magnanimous and kind. For example, following Joshua Giddings's maiden speech in Congress, in which he castigated his southern colleagues, "Adams, his full face wreathed by a glowing smile, walked over to Giddings's seat, laughed heartily, and congratulated him." Adams was also known for his energy. When he was president, he not only "skinny-dipped in the Potomac" but also "swam against the tide for over ninety minutes at a stretch."[28]

By early 1842, Adams's southern colleagues had long since tired of his antics and were looking for a way to get rid of him. On January 24, one week after Torrey had returned from Annapolis, Adams gave his enemies an opening, when he presented a petition from citizens in Massachusetts, asking Congress to dissolve the Union of North and South because "the South was a constant drain on their pocketbooks." Despite the fact that some southern congressmen had threatened to do exactly the same thing, they were shocked that a northern member of Congress would raise the issue. One reporter compared the southerners' fury to "a hen with her head cut off," and they immediately moved to officially censure Adams for misconduct and "high treason." The former president of the United States was essentially to be put on trial by his colleagues to determine whether he should be expelled from Congress. That was exactly what Adams wanted, for it would provide him with a public forum to debate the slavery issue *in extenso.*[29]

What the southern congressmen did not know was that Adams and his abolitionist colleagues had been planning for just such an event. Two months earlier, they had hired Theodore Weld to come to Washington to help them. Weld had led the abolitionist forces during the Lane Seminary debates in 1834 and was regarded as an expert on the history of slavery. The abolitionists provided Weld with a bed at Ms. Sprigg's boarding house and a desk at the Library of Congress, located at that time in the Capitol building, and he went to work preparing material for Adams's use. Weld was a deeply religious and self-disciplined man who was a vegetarian, used neither alcohol nor coffee, exercised for an hour every morning before breakfast, and took a daily bath in cold water "no matter what the weather or how great the inconvenience."[30]

The other person who assisted Weld in preparing material for Adams was Torrey's friend Joshua Leavitt. Since Leavitt lived in Mrs. Sprigg's boarding house with Joshua Giddings, Seth Gates, and William Slade, Giddings referred to the foursome as the "Select Committee on Slavery." Although Torrey was available to help with these efforts and was good friends with both Leavitt and Giddings, Weld did not include him because he didn't like him. Weld had married Sarah Grimké, one of William Lloyd Garrison's most enthusiastic followers. Torrey had also been a leader in the challenge to Garrison that had resulted in the breakup of the Massachusetts Anti-Slavery Society, an event Weld had deplored because of what he called "contentious and personality feuds . . . among the abolitionists." In addition, Torrey had played a role in the formation of the Liberty Party, which Weld had also strongly opposed. Thus, it was not surprising that, in a letter to his wife, Weld described Torrey as "an exceedingly vain, trifling man with no wisdom or stability. All impulse and imprudence and ostentation."[31]

Torrey observed the events of the Adams trial with great interest and reported on them in detail for the *New York Evangelist*. He admired Adams for his aggressive approach to abolitionism; in one public speech, Adams had declared: "May the slave in the South be free, even if it should be through blood." On the opening morning of his congressional trial, "long before the hour for the house to convene, the spacious galleries were filled to the utmost capacity, and all approaches to the hall were crowded with anxious men and women, endeavoring to get where they could hear the proceedings." The man chosen to read the charges against Adams was Thomas Marshall, nephew of the man John Quincy Adams's father had appointed as the chief justice of the Supreme Court. When Marshall suggested that Adams should visit the South to ascertain the truth about slavery, Adams interrupted him and said that he would be lynched if he visited. Marshall: "Doubtless you would be lynched." Adams: "Still, you advise me to go!"[32]

When his turn came, Adams put on a brilliant defense. He proposed to "take up nearly all the relations of *slavery* to this government" and did so for six days, receiving each evening from Weld and Leavitt additional material for the following day. He argued that the Founding Fathers of the country had all opposed slavery and he could prove it because they had all been his friends and one had been his father. He even had the clerk read the Declaration of Independence to demonstrate that its framers had foreseen the possibility of disunion: "that whenever any form of government becomes destructive of those ends, it is the right of the people to alter or to abolish it." He accused slaveholders of attempting to destroy the freedom of speech, freedom of the press, and almost every other freedom guaranteed by the Constitution. He compared the advanced development of northern states with the backward development of southern states, attributing this difference to slavery. And he included considerable personal invective, calling his chief accuser, Thomas

Marshall, an alcoholic unfit to follow in his illustrious uncle's footsteps. Of his other main accuser, Henry Wise of Virginia, who had killed a man in a duel, Adams said he had entered Congress "with his hands and face dripping with the blood of murder."[33]

On and on Adams spoke, hour after hour, day after day, to the avid interest of the nation. According to one account, as the days progressed, "he became more and more aroused, and drawing one arrow after another from his well-stored quiver, he sent them with unerring aim into the flesh of his victim, with no other apparent object than to see him writhe under the infliction." Newspapers throughout the North, even those that were proslavery, increasingly sided with Adams. His opponents became progressively more dispirited and realized that their attempt to get rid of Adams had been a big mistake, especially when Adams announced that, even if he were expelled, he would immediately run for reelection and would therefore be right back. On day six, Adams indicated that he had another week's worth of arguments in his own defense but that, if his colleagues wished to withdraw their motion of censure, he would agree to stop. They immediately agreed to do so.[34]

The 1842 victory of John Quincy Adams over the proslavery forces trying to expel him from Congress was viewed as a significant turning point by the abolitionists. Theodore Weld wrote to his wife: "This is the first victory over the slaveholders *in a body* ever yet achieved since the foundation of the *government,* and from this time their downfall *takes its date.*" Joshua Giddings told his family: "We have triumphed, the north has for once triumphed. . . . I am confident that the slavepower *is now broken.*" Charles Torrey sounded a similar note in his dispatch to the *New York Evangelist*: "The defeat of the slaveholders, in a fight of their own seeking . . . mortifies them very much. The tone of the greater portion of the Northern, and many of the best Southern papers convinces them that the reign of their despotism is over. . . . A few more similar defeats would kill slavery, and they know it." Even William Lloyd Garrison, who abhorred anything political, wrote enthusiastically about the "tremendous excitement in Congress" that had produced "a signal victor for the cause of liberty and its advocates." Abolitionists increasingly viewed slaveholders as standing at the edge of an abyss. Even as he wrote his dispatches for the *New York Evangelist,* Torrey was busily developing other plans for pushing them over the edge.[35]

But the southern members of Congress were not finished yet. If they could not have the scalp of the most hated John Quincy Adams for their trophy room, they would settle for the next most hated—Joshua Giddings. Their opportunity came six weeks after Adams's censure had been withdrawn during a congressional debate about the *Creole.* The *Creole* was an American ship that in early November 1841 had sailed form Virginia with 135 slaves aboard, bound for New Orleans. Once at sea, the slaves had seized control of the ship, killed one of the slaveowners, and sailed to the Bahamas, a British territory, where they declared themselves to be free. The United States demanded that the British return the slaves, but they refused, and some members of Congress threatened to go to war.

The abolitionists seized the opportunity to emphasize how the slaves were increasingly freeing themselves. On March 21, Joshua Giddings took the floor of the House and delivered an impassioned speech, written with Weld's assistance, on the *Creole* affair. Southerners, he said, had always claimed that slavery was a state, not a national, issue, and so it should be. Since that was the case, said Giddings, then "when a ship belonging to the citizens of any State of this Union leaves the waters and territory of such State and enters upon the high seas, the persons on board cease to be subject to the slave laws of such State." For southerners, this was an outrageous statement, implying that slaves could become free merely by sailing out to sea. If enacted, the provision would make it virtually impossible to recover runaway slaves.[36]

Southern congressmen immediately introduced a motion to censure Giddings for conduct "altogether unwarranted . . . and deserving the severe condemnation of the people of this country, and of this body in particular." Not wishing to repeat the mistake they had made with Adams, they then instituted a series of parliamentary maneuvers to block any opportunity Giddings had to defend himself. The motion for censure carried by a vote of 125 to 69; the vote reflected how much Giddings was disliked not only by southern members of Congress but also by some northern members of his own Whig Party, who viewed him as threatening the fragile party alliance by repeatedly introducing the abolition issue. So censured, Giddings submitted his letter of resignation and stopped to shake the hand of teary-eyed John Quincy Adams on his way out of the chamber.[37]

Giddings, of course, was not finished. He immediately declared himself a candidate for reelection in the special election for his seat. The Whig Party, both in Ohio and nationally, did everything it could to undermine Giddings's candidacy, despite his being a Whig, declaring that he was not a team player and would not follow party leaders. The electorate of northern Ohio, however, were staunch abolitionists and reelected Giddings with a huge majority, larger "than that of any other representative in the present or any other Congress" up to that time. Six weeks after having been expelled, Giddings returned to Congress triumphant, as Torrey happily reported in a letter to Amos Phelps. When he was formally reintroduced to the House of Representatives, Giddings reported that "many looked up with smiling faces, while others appeared to be perfectly dumbfounded." To prove that Giddings had lost none of his abolitionist fervor during the brief hiatus, he soon rose in Congress and essentially repeated the speech that had led to his ouster. Torrey, in his dispatch to the *New York Evangelist,* noted that "a few testy slaveholders interrupted him," but the speech was delivered "with a logical and legal force that made a powerful impression."[38]

The congressional victories of Adams and Giddings in 1842 have been regarded by some historians as a turning point in the fight against slavery. According to one: "Giddings' immunity [from further censure], it was found, also applied to his antislavery colleagues; and their freedom to denounce slavery on the floor of the House was never again put in serious jeopardy. The Southern conspiracy of silence on slavery was broken." Slavery had finally become an issue for open national debate. Moreover, according to historian James McPherson, Giddings's victory had even more far-reaching political consequences. He had openly defied the leaders of his own party and yet had been overwhelmingly reelected. His victory "over party regularity contained the seeds of the [Whig] party's demise little more than a decade later," and the rise of the Republican Party in its place.[39]

* * *

Throughout the spring of 1842, Charles Torrey continued his work as a congressional reporter, filing weekly columns. He wrote extensively about the *Creole* and other abolitionist issues and about non-abolitionist issues such as the tariff debate; the annexation of Texas; reapportionment (Congress *reduced* its total membership from 242 to 224); international copyright laws; a request from the District of Columbia that Congress buy streetlights for the city (Torrey noted that Washington's "citizens seem to think they have a right to *free forage* in the U.S. Treasury"); and even the fact that President Tyler "is a profane swearer, and often interlards his conversation with oaths," a trait that Torrey thought merited "severe rebuke."[40]

Increasingly, it became evident that Torrey was disgusted with Congress and not much interested in its workings:

> *March 17, 1842.* The doings of the past week have been of so little importance, that I will not follow the daily routine of their stupidity, but present them under different heads as they occur to me.
>
> *March 24, 1842.* The past week has been almost wholly wasted in both Houses, in the manufacture of partizan speeches for "home consumption."

Torrey had only one interest—the abolition of slavery—and it had taken possession of his soul. His editor on the *Boston Daily Mail* described this obsession: "He was employed to write the Washington correspondence of this paper in the winter of 1842. . . . Our understanding with him was, that he should confine himself to congressional proceeding, and matters of general interest at Washington; but his heart was so full of his loved subject, the abolition of slavery, that it would 'shine out' in spite of him. But he never complained when we applied the pruning knife to his letters." In fact, by the spring of 1842, Torrey was quietly trading his reporter's job for one that was much more exciting.[41]

5

AGGRESSIVE ABOLITIONISM

It is unclear when Charles Torrey first formulated his plans to assist slaves to escape their bondage, but he had been considering it for many months. His experience with John Torrance, who failed in his attempt to free himself, showed Torrey that slaves often needed assistance if they were to be successful. The mutinies of slaves aboard the *Amistad* and, more recently, the *Creole,* also demonstrated the success of self-liberation, but in both cases abolitionists had been instrumental in preserving the slaves' liberty. Torrey's four days in the Annapolis jail, in company with thirteen men, women, and children being sold back into slavery, also affected him profoundly.

For Torrey, aggressive abolitionism must have seemed like an idea whose time had come. Two days after he was released from the Annapolis jail, at an antislavery convention in upstate New York attended by fifteen hundred people, Gerrit Smith had given a historic speech "To the Slaves of the U. States of America," the first time any white abolitionist had publicly issued a call to the slaves. According to historian Stanley Harrold, Smith's speech "stirred furious debate among abolitionists and between abolitionists and nonabolitionists" and "gained an immediate and sustained notoriety."[1]

Smith opened his speech with references to the successful slave uprisings on the *Amistad* and *Creole,* uprisings that, according to Harrold, "were central to the sense of crisis among abolitionists" at that time. Smith cited these uprisings as bold moves but urged slaves and abolitionists to be even bolder, "continually rising higher and higher in their bold and righteous claims." The abolitionist, said Smith, not only must "enter into and maintain all practicable communications with the slave" but also "has a perfect moral right to go into the South, and use his intelligence to promote the escape of ignorant and imbruted slaves from their prison-house."[2] Such action was precisely what Torrey had in mind.

Smith urged the slaves not to rise up in violent and bloody revolt. Rather, he called "on every slave, who has the reasonable prospect of being able to run away from slavery, to make the experiment." In doing so, Smith said it was legitimate for the slaves to take with them "the horse, the boat, the food, the clothing, which you require . . . so far as is essential to your escape" Slaves should do this "and feel no more compunction for the justifiable appropriation than does the drowning man for possessing himself of the plank, that floats in his way." Slave escapes were to be the trend of the future. "We rejoice with all our hearts, in the rapid multiplication of escapes from the house of bondage—there are now a thousand a year; a rate more than five times as great, as that before the anti-slavery effort. . . . The principles of abolition have already struck their root deep in the genial soil of the free states of our Union; and even at the South, abolitionists are multiplying rapidly."[3]

Word of Gerrit Smith's speech reached Washington shortly after Charles Torrey had returned from Annapolis. South Carolina Senator John C. Calhoun, who had argued that slaveholding was "a positive good," denounced Smith's speech on the Senate floor. Theodore Weld said that the speech was causing "a mighty stir," and Joshua Leavitt praised Smith for addressing the slaves directly: "It is a shame that we have never done it before." Torrey's paper, the *New York Evangelist,* exulted that the "boldness and explicitness" of Smith's words "has already excited considerable remark."[4]

Even as Smith's speech was circulating in Washington, Charles Torrey was being visited at his boardinghouse by a free black named Thomas Smallwood. Smallwood was twelve years Torrey's senior and had grown up as a slave in Prince George's County, Maryland. As a young man, he had been sold to a minister who had taught him to read and write. At age thirty, Smallwood had purchased his freedom, become a shoemaker, married, and settled in Washington with a job at the Navy Yard. Smallwood's wife did the washing at Ms. Padgett's boarding house, where Torrey was living. Hearing about Torrey's incarceration in Annapolis for attempting to report on the antislavery convention, Smallwood recalled that "immediately after his acquittal and return to Washington . . . through the agency of my wife . . . I sought and obtained an interview with him." "At our first interview," Smallwood continued, "he informed me of a scheme he had in view." The "scheme" consisted of taking large wagonloads of slaves north; this would save on costs, since it cost little more to rent a wagon and team of horses that could carry fifteen slaves than it did to carry three slaves. Torrey probably had in mind the thirteen members of the black families in the Annapolis jail, where he may have conceived of this specific plan. It was to be an Underground Railroad that ran in only one direction: north.[5]

In 1842, the idea of an Underground Railroad was not new. Slaves had been escaping from their masters since colonial days, and there had always been many individuals, especially Quakers, who were willing to act as station agents and provide the runaway slaves with food and shelter. When George Washington had a slave run away in 1786, he had complained about Quakers and others "who would rather facilitate the escape of slaves than apprehend them when runaways." Some northern cities, including Philadelphia and New York, had committees organized by whites, free blacks, or both to provide shelter to runaway slaves and to prevent free blacks from being kidnapped and sold back into slavery. The New York Committee of Vigilance, for example, reported in 1837 that "it had protected a total of 335 persons from slavery" in the first two years of its existence.[6]

The best known station agents on the Underground Railroad in the early 1840s were Levi Coffin, Thomas Garrett, and John Rankin. Coffin began sheltering runaway slaves at his home in southern Indiana in 1826. He later moved to Cincinnati, where he was widely referred to as the "president" of the Underground Railroad and credited with giving "safe harbor to over three thousand runaway slaves." Thomas Garrett, an iron merchant in Wilmington, Delaware, began sheltering runaway slaves as early as 1813, and during half a century "he left a record of more than twenty-seven hundred slaves he had assisted to escape." In 1860 the Maryland legislature even offered a reward of $10,000 ($240,000) "for anyone able to arrest Garrett on the grounds of slave stealing." Garrett responded that "$10,000 was not enough and that for $20,000 he would turn himself in." John Rankin sheltered runaway slaves in his home in Ripley, Ohio, throughout the 1830s. He regarded slavery as "a never failing fountain of the grossest immorality, and one of the deepest sources of human misery; it hangs like the mantle of night over our republic, and shrouds its rising glories." Although his home was attacked several times by supporters of slavery, Rankin fought back: "Now I desire all men to know that I am not to be deterred from what I believe to be my duty by fire and sword. I also wish all to know that I feel it my duty to defend my HOME to the very uttermost, and that it is as much a duty to shoot the midnight assassin in his attacks as it is to pray."[7]

The plan proposed by Charles Torrey in 1842 was substantially different from the activities of Coffin, Garrett, Rankin, and other station masters at that time. These men did not encourage or incite slaves to run away but rather served the runaways' needs once they had done so. According to Larry Gara's book on the subject, "Thomas Garrett would render assistance to fugitives who came to him voluntarily" but regarded going to southern states and encouraging slaves to abscond as a "reckless undertaking, involving too much risk, and probably doing more harm than good." Levi Coffin also thought "it was no part of his business in the South 'to interfere with their laws or their slaves'" and specifically admonished one man who was doing so to "quit his dangerous work." These sentiments were consistent with those of most abolitionists, who "were unwilling, for the most part, to involve themselves more deeply in danger by abducting slaves from thralldom." William Lloyd Garrison and some of his supporters opposed spending any abolitionist funds to assist runaway slaves, as Coffin, Garrett, and Rankin were doing, believing that the goal for abolitionists should be "to end slavery, not to help a few former slaves." Such efforts, they argued, were "wasteful of energies better devoted to agitation in the North for general emancipation." Despite Garrison's personal beliefs, many of his supporters, especially those in Philadelphia, were very active in supporting runaway slaves.[8]

Torrey's plan included both encouraging slaves to abscond and then also transporting them to freedom. Torrey and Smallwood would not merely be station masters but also would solicit the passengers for the train, issue the tickets, and be the engineers who would run the train along the Underground Railroad. There was precedent for what they proposed to do, but it was relatively sparse.

For example, in 1838, John Mahan had been charged with guiding slaves from Kentucky to Ohio. In 1839, three black sailors in New York had been accused of helping slaves to escape. The same year, Leonard Grimes, a free black in Washington, was convicted of having helped a slave family in Virginia to escape, and he was sentenced to two years in the state prison. And in 1841, Alanson Work, James Burr, and George Thompson had been sentenced to twelve years in prison for helping slaves escape from Missouri to Illinois.[9]

Torrey's plan to encourage slaves to run away was part of a broader strategy. Since the District of Columbia was both the center of the federal government and the center of the slave trade, and since the federal government had jurisdiction over the District, then the District was "the Achilles heal of the entire institution" of slavery. The existence of slavery in the nation's capital, said Torrey, was "a sort of symbol and proof of its control over the government of the country." If large numbers of slaves could be induced to run away from Washington and the surrounding regions of Maryland and Virginia, then keeping slaves in that region would become increasingly less secure and attractive. As Stanley Harrold explained in *Subversives: Antislavery Community in Washington, D.C., 1828–1865*: "Since their [Torrey and Smallwood's] ultimate objective was to destroy masters' confidence that they could continue to hold slaves in the Chesapeake, the two men played on the masters' fears of aggressive abolitionism." Torrey thus argued: "I regard it as important to make more vigorous assaults than ever, upon slavery in this District."[10]

Torrey and Smallwood implemented their plan in a highly organized but necessarily secretive fashion. Torrey did not even tell Amos Phelps the details of what he was doing, merely hinting in a letter than he had "been accumulating no small amount of valuable knowledge on subjects very foreign from a minister's duties and studies, but on topics on which I feel the deepest interest and in the discussion of which my mind has been absorbed for a long time past." He said that this new activity was his "preference for other forms of serving God and my fellow men."[11]

Torrey and Smallwood identified slaves who wished to be free until they had accumulated a group of at least twelve, and sometimes as many as twenty, to send together. In some cases, the slaves were hidden at the boarding house by Ms. Padgett, who was an active participant, or at Smallwood's house, while awaiting transportation. The slaves were mostly recruited from the black churches frequented by Torrey and Smallwood. In at least two instances, slaves were referred to Torrey by the congressmen living at Ms. Sprigg's boarding house. For example, John Douglass, a slave of a Georgetown master who worked as a waiter at the boarding house, "had nursed [Congressman] Gates through an illness and when . . . his master threatened to sell him to a trader, Gates directed him to Torrey, who 'told him how to get off.'" It is certain that Congressmen Giddings, Gates, and Slade were aware of Torrey's activities, and Joshua Leavitt and other members of the Washington abolitionist group may have been as well. An August 1842 letter from Joshua Giddings to his son commented on the recent epidemic of slave disappearances, including entire families at once, and sarcastically speculated that "there is a *Subterranean rail road* by which they travel *underground*." A letter by Seth Gates refers to "Smallwood of the navy yard" and Torrey in the context of slave disappearances. Families in danger of being split up and sold were given priority, as were slaves who could contribute some funds toward the rental of the wagon and horses needed for the trip. "Constantly changing secret meeting places where potential escapees could rendezvous with their guides" were utilized, and travel was usually done at night.[12]

The first group of slaves identified by Torrey to be taken north included a couple and their children owned by George Badger, a Whig Party leader who had been appointed as secretary of the Navy by President Tyler. This illustrated Torrey's plan to select slaves from politically high-profile families, including southern congressmen, whenever possible so as to produce a bigger effect. This initial group of slaves was collected and sent north in March of 1842. Thereafter, groups left every three to four weeks, depending on the number of slaves collected and the availability of funds to rent a wagon and horses. The ultimate destination for most was Albany, from which the freed slaves could either settle in upstate New York or New England or continue to Canada. As early as April 26, 1842, Abel Brown, a minister in Albany, was soliciting funds from the Eastern New York Anti-Slavery Society to support Torrey's efforts, noting that

"Mr. Torrey had also been instrumental in supplying the Committee with this species of merchandize, for transportation or disposal in the free States, as might best serve their convenience." An additional solicitation for money followed the next month "to aid no less than *fourteen* of these our brethren and sisters to Canada, to save them from the miseries consequent upon a life of the severest bondage." In June 1842, Brown wrote to "Very dear Bro." Torrey, informing him of his efforts to raise $300 ($6,700) for him. "You cannot work for nothing," Brown said, "and [you] run all the risk." By November 1842, Smallwood claimed that "the Washington branch of the underground railroad had helped 150 escapees since the previous March."[13]

On several occasions, Torrey personally guided groups of slaves north. His initial trip, in August 1842 with fifteen men, women, and children, almost ended in disaster. Nobody could be found who would rent him a wagon and horses, so he had to raise the money and purchase them for $118 ($2,600). When the appointed rendezvous time arrived, fifteen people were there, but the wagon was not yet ready, so the people had to be hidden. Meanwhile, "a terrible uproar" ensued when the masters discovered their slaves gone. "A general pursuit was instituted on all the roads leading North, but all to no purpose, for the people were yet in the City." After Torrey finally procured the wagon, he also headed north, unaware that his pursuers were actually ahead of him. But his wagon broke down, causing Torrey to pull off the road just as the pursuers were returning and unknowingly passed them by. Smallwood "saw the hand of God in this," and Torrey was able to proceed north to Albany, where he put the fifteen slaves on a canal boat for Canada.[14]

Pursuit by slaveowners was just one of the many dangers associated with the business. Slaves represented wealth; an able-bodied male field hand was worth approximately $1,000 ($22,000) at a Washington slave auction in 1842 and even more in Charleston or New Orleans, with women and children selling for considerably less. The total value of the first 150 slaves driven north by Torrey and Smallwood was estimated by Smallwood to be approximately $75,000 ($1,675,000). Slaveowners regarded people like Torrey and Smallwood as "vile fiends" and "worse than thieves, robbers, or murderers," and they would not hesitate to kill them if caught.[15]

Another danger was slave catchers. Some of these were professionals, such as the eighteen men employed by the Washington police and known as the Washington Auxiliary Guard. Torrey publicly described these men as "human monsters . . . so loathsome in their corruption, that everyone in Washington, who has the least pretensions to decency, shrinks from the sight of them as men shrink from contact with the plague spot." These men often used dogs to track runaway slaves and "knew how to block potential escape routes." Rewards for slave catchers could be substantial; in Maryland in 1842, rewards were often $100 ($2,200) or more, and "by 1850, the average reward was approaching two hundred dollars [$5,200]; if one were willing to return a fugitive from Pennsylvania, he might collect a payment of five hundred dollars [$12,900]." Especially dangerous were criminal gangs who operated as slave catchers. The best known was the notorious Cannon gang, which kidnapped free blacks in Maryland, Delaware, and Pennsylvania and sold them south. They also operated what they advertised to be safe houses for runaway slaves; when the slaves stopped, they were tied up and returned to their owners for the rewards. When the gang was finally brought to justice in 1829, the leader, Patty Cannon, confessed to having murdered eleven people, including her husband and one of her children. Other criminal slave-catcher gangs, such as the Gap gang in central Pennsylvania, continued to operate in the 1840s.[16]

To get wagonloads of slaves safely to the North, Torrey and Smallwood utilized a network of safe houses where the slaves could be fed and hidden during the day. According to Smallwood, the trip from Washington to the Pennsylvania border usually took two and a half days. The first night's trip was thirty-seven miles, which took them to the Baltimore area. The main road, the Washington and Baltimore Turnpike, which had been chartered in 1812, was often watched by slave catchers, so back roads were used. Sandy Spring, a Quaker community between Washington and Baltimore, had several homes that regularly sheltered escaping slaves. The Gilpin home in Mount Airy was also used. Baltimore had a large population of free blacks, many of whom were willing to offer shelter. Torrey and Smallwood relied especially on Jacob Gibbs, a free black who was said to lead "an underground operation similar to the one in Washington." In

1875 Henry Wilson, in his *History of the Rise and Fall of Slave Power in America,* identified Gibbs as "Mr. Torrey's chief assistant in his efforts," although it is possible that Wilson was confusing Gibbs with Thomas Smallwood.[17]

From Baltimore to Pennsylvania, there were several possible routes, but the one usually taken by Torrey and Smallwood was a northeastern route through Harford County. It utilized the road that ran past the large Gough plantation at Perry Hall to the village of Bel Air, the seat of Harford County. From there, one could take the Peachbottom Road to the Susquehanna River at the point where the river crossed the Pennsylvania state line. This route had two important advantages. Harford County included five congregations of Quakers as well as over 2,500 free blacks, many of whom "lived in rural settings and had ideal locations for hiding fugitives." In addition, this route crossed the Gunpowder River and Deer Creek, both useful for resting and watering horses when they were being driven all night. The Susquehanna could then be crossed on the Maryland side at Conowingo, on the seven-span covered bridge that had been built in 1820, or on the Pennsylvania side at Peachbottom; free blacks were available at both locations to ferry passengers across. Alternatively, if these areas were being watched, the escaping slaves could follow the western shore of the river on the Mason-Dixon trail north to Wrightsville, to a safe house run by Samuel Mifflin. The bridge over the Susquehanna River from Wrightsville to Columbia was at that time the longest covered bridge in the world and charged 6 cents ($1.30) per pedestrian. The bridge was often patrolled by slave catchers, so Mifflin usually arranged crossings by boat.[18]

Once in Pennsylvania, the slaves were comparatively safe. As Henry Wilson noted in his 1875 history of slavery: "To no section of the land did they [the slaves] flee for succor and safety as they did to Eastern Pennsylvania; nowhere were there so many whose ears quick to catch the footfall of the weary and fainting fugitive.... The counties of Delaware, Chester, Lancaster, York, and Adams were studded with stations of the 'Underground Railroad,' where faithful men and women stood ready to act as agents and conductors, to help forward the fleeing chattels."[19]

When using the river crossing at Peachbottom to cross into

Pennsylvania, slaves were taken to Drumore Township to the homes of either John Russell or Joseph Smith. According to a later account: "During the height of Rev. Charles T. Torrey's campaign, a party of twenty-two fugitives was brought to John N. Russell's house about twelve o'clock at night. Their pilot, a colored man, threw a pebble against the window of friend Russell's sleeping-room, which aroused him and his wife. They came down, prepared a meal for them at the 'witching hour,' tumbled them into a four-horse covered wagon, and took them to the next station." From Drumore township, slaves were taken to Bart township to the homes of Jacob Bushoong, Caleb and Joseph Hood, or Thomas Whitson. "One night, in the spring of 1843, eight fugitives came to their [the Hood] house at one time, brought by Joseph Smith of Drumore. . . . One party of fugitives told the Hoods of having been brought from Baltimore to a place on the Susquehanna by Rev. Charles T. Torrey." Thomas Whitson was a well-known abolitionist, having attended the organizing meeting of the American Anti-Slavery Society in 1833. From Bart township, the slaves were passed along to safe houses in Christiana, Sadsbury, and eventually Philadelphia.[20]

Although Torrey, Smallwood, and those helping them usually accompanied their charges safely across the Pennsylvania state line and Susquehanna River, they then relied on an organized network of Quakers and free blacks to get them to Philadelphia. Occasionally, however, Smallwood or Torrey would himself guide the slaves all the way to Philadelphia. For example, on September 3, 1842, Caleb Cope, a Quaker who lived in Chester County near Philadelphia, made the following entry, exactly as written, in his diary. He had been awakened, he noted, by a stranger knocking on his door:

> he had with him 15 fugatives from Washington in the District of Columbia and they were on their rode to Canida and if they could get a little food for themselves and horses (they were in a 2 horse waggon) they would thank us and hoped the Lord would bless us for it I asked him his name he said it was Charles T. Torrey and that he hat [sic] started last first-Day night from Wash I told him we would accommodate them as well as we could So I went down and opened the door and

there came in 7 men 5 women an 3 children fine harty looking people and well dressed we gave them some bread and
meet and let them sleep on the floor till morning when we
gave them some breakfast and they started from here between
7 and 8 Oclock it appears that he had perswaded them to run
away from their Masters.[21]

Philadelphia was the major stopping point on the road between
Washington and Albany on the Underground Railroad operated by
Torrey and Smallwood. It was a city with two faces. On one side,
Pennsylvania in 1780 had been the first state to abolish slavery, and
by 1810 Philadelphia had an active Abolition Society, with Benjamin
Franklin as president. By 1840 the city had over fifteen thousand free
blacks, constituting "America's largest northern urban black population," approximately 10 percent of the total population, and was a
major destination for slaves fleeing north. A small number of blacks,
such as sailmaker James Forten, had become successful businessmen, so that "a survey published in 1845 listed six Afro-Americans
among the city's several dozen wealthiest people."[22]

Philadelphia's other face was described by Frederick Douglass
as "mean, contemptible and barbarous." The city had "huge textile
mills" that were dependent on cotton from the South, and its "man-
ufacturers, bankers, and merchants" emphasized their ties to the
South. "Everything Southern was exalted and worshipped," according to a journalist at that time. The white and black communities in
Philadelphia were thus rigidly segregated. Anti-black and anti-abolitionist sentiment was frequently in evidence, most prominently during riots in 1829, 1834, 1835, and 1838, the last of which resulted in the
destruction of Pennsylvania Hall during an antislavery convention.[23]

Philadelphia's abolitionist community divided following the 1839
schism, with some continuing to follow William Lloyd Garrison and
moral suasion, while others aligned themselves with the Liberty
Party and political abolitionism. Among the latter group, James J. G.
Bias and Charles D. Cleveland became Torrey's associates and close
friends.

Bias had been born a slave in Maryland. His owner was a physician, "whose carriage he drove, and from whom he obtained some

knowledge of the medical art and practice." When he became free, Bias moved to Philadelphia and initially made a living by "leeching, bleeding, and extracting teeth." He then "opened a shop, in which he sold all kinds of medicinal herbs, drugs, and stationery." Once the shop was established, Bias "entered one of the medical schools of Philadelphia . . . from which he graduated, and after which he obtained quite an extensive and lucrative practice." Bias was one of the leaders of Philadelphia's black community. He was a founding member of the Association for Moral and Mental Improvement and the temperance society and was also a lay preacher in the African Methodist Episcopal (AME) Church.[24]

Bias was one of Philadelphia's most active abolitionists. In 1838 he founded the Philadelphia Vigilance Society to assist runaway slaves, and "in 1850 he chaired a meeting of black Philadelphians opposed to the Fugitive Slave Law." According to AME Bishop Daniel Payne's later account, Bias "was also a zealous and heroic member of the 'Under-ground Railroad Association,' and many times periled his life to aid the escape of fugitives from the South." In this he was assisted by his wife, Eliza, who had also been a slave. "Gladly did she second all the movements of her husband in hiding and forwarding in her home and from her home troops of flying slaves, conducted to her home by the martyred Torry [sic]." According to another source, Bias's "home and bed were always available to slaves directed to him by the white abolitionist, Charles Torrey. In addition to providing sleeping accommodations for his runaway charges, it was not unusual for Bias to give his overnight guests a quick medical checkup." When Torrey was in Philadelphia, he usually stayed at the Bias home.[25]

Torrey's other associate in Philadelphia who assisted in efforts to free slaves was Charles D. Cleveland. A native of Salem, Massachusetts, where Torrey had been employed as a minister, Cleveland had been educated at Dartmouth College. In 1834 he moved to Philadelphia to open C. D. Cleveland's School for Young Ladies. At that time, Cleveland had no special interest in slavery. However, two years later, while visiting Cincinnati, he observed a proslavery riot directed against James Birney's abolitionist newspaper. Thereafter, according to Cleveland's son, "he was incessantly busy in personal rescue of the slave."[26]

In 1840 Cleveland helped establish the Liberty Party in Pennsylvania, and it may be at that time that Torrey met him. In one speech Cleveland noted that, since the slave states were "inferior in morals . . . inferior in mental attainments . . . inferior in intelligence . . . inferior, in short, in everything that constitutes the . . . true greatness of a nation—it is wrong, it is unjust, it is absurd, that they should have an influence in all the departments of government so entirely disproportionate to our own." Cleveland was also a well-known scholar and editor of a paper called the *American Intelligencer.* He used his talents to write books such as *A Compendium of English Literature* and also reprinted a large edition of J. J. Gurney's *Letters from the West Indies,* which described the positive results of the abolition of slavery that had taken place in 1833.[27]

Cleveland was a strong supporter of Charles Torrey's efforts. Since he had access to "those of his own class," he was able to raise funds to support Torrey's efforts, and "beat lustily and incessantly at all the parts of the iron image of wrong sitting stolidly here with close-shut eyes." For his abolitionist efforts, he suffered "the slow martyrdom of social scorn" from many of his professional peers. After Torrey's second arrest, Cleveland was one of the most active workers in efforts to bring about his pardon and release.[28]

It is thus clear that Charles Torrey and Thomas Smallwood had a well-organized and effective biracial network for conveying large groups of slaves from Washington to freedom in the North. Torrey himself referred to it using the term "underground railroad." The origin of this term is obscure. An oft-quoted 1899 article in the *New York Times* attributed it to an 1831 event in Kentucky when a slaveowner, trying to follow his runaway slave, concluded that he "must have gone off on an underground railroad." In *The Liberty Line,* a study of the Underground Railroad, Larry Gara claimed that the first use of the term was in a Chicago newspaper on December 23, 1842. Irrespective of its origin, the term was being widely used in newspapers by the mid-1840s.[29]

What role did Torrey play in the development of the Underground

Railroad? A memorial published in the *Emancipator* shortly after his death in 1846 called Torrey "the originator of the 'underground railroad,'" but that exaggerates his contribution. A British book, *The Anti-Slavery Cause in America and Its Martyrs*, published in 1863, included the following:

> It was during this [Annapolis] incarceration that he [Torrey] had a quiet time to reduce to a system the time-honored institution of the "Underground Railroad." The escape of slaves had been aided wisely and faithfully from the earliest days; but the *name* was given after a regular plan had been arranged of handing on the poor fugitive from one benevolent and trustworthy agent at *stations on the line* to another so the chain was completed from the slave states to Canada. After Mr. Torrey's liberation, he proceeded to carry out in detail the outline he had formed, and so successful was he, that before many weeks were over, the line was completed from the slave states to Canada.

Similarly, Wilbur Siebert's history of the Underground Railroad published in 1898 claimed that "the first well-established line of the U.G.R.R. had its southern terminus in Washington, D.C., and extended in a pretty direct route to Albany, N.Y. . . . Mr. T., his agent in Washington City, was a very active and efficient man; the Superintendent at Albany was in daily communication by mail with him." Thus, in the nineteenth century, there appeared to be some appreciation among historians that Charles Torrey had made a contribution to this mode of helping slaves to gain freedom.[30]

As an engineer on the Underground Railroad, Torrey finally had a job he enjoyed, despite its dangers. The trouble, however, was that it was not a paying job, and his reporter's salary was insufficient for the needs of his family. Letters to his wife during 1842 are replete with financial woes; one suspects that these were exacerbated by Torrey's use of his limited funds to help rent wagons and horses for trips north. In April he wrote to Amos Phelps complaining of his pecuniary problems and asking if Phelps knew of any well-paying job.[31]

During the summer of 1842, as increasing numbers of wagonloads of slaves were spirited away from Washington, word began to circulate among Washington slaveholders that these disappearances were associated with Charles Torrey. In October, Dr. William Gunnell "swore out an arrest warrant for Torrey, charging him in the escape of a slave." Smallwood later confirmed that one of Gunnell's slaves and her two children had, in fact, been taken north by Torrey two months earlier. Everything considered, Torrey decided that it was probably a propitious time to leave Washington, find a better-paying job, and coordinate the Underground Railroad from its terminus at Albany.[32]

6

THE SECOND ARREST

In October 1842, Charles Torrey moved from Washington to Albany, New York, where his family joined him, the first time he had lived with them in almost a year. He had accepted a position as editor of the *Tocsin of Liberty,* an abolitionist weekly whose name was subsequently changed to the *Albany Patriot.* The paper had been started by Edwin W. Goodwin, a well-known portrait painter and staunch abolitionist. Goodwin's fiery editorials against slaveholders and active membership in the Albany Vigilance Committee had elicited belligerent reactions from local slavery supporters. Two months before Torrey arrived, for example, Goodwin had been "brutally assaulted in the street." In addition, Goodwin's newspaper office had been attacked because of his efforts to free a slave who had been brought to New York State by her owner, at which time the slave had technically become free.[1]

Torrey's main abolitionist collaborator in Albany was Abel Brown, a Baptist minister three years his senior. Torrey had known Brown since 1839, when Brown had been a pastor in Northampton, in western Massachusetts, and an agent for the Massachusetts Abolition Society. Like Torrey, Brown disliked Garrison, whom he referred to as that "pestilent fellow." Like Torrey, Brown also was deeply religious, chronically short of money, and a dedicated and aggressive abolitionist. As early as 1836, he had been arrested in Baltimore on charges of helping slaves escape but had been released for lack of evidence. In 1838 he had worked in western Pennsylvania as an agent for the Western Anti-Slavery Society and had described the opposition: "I have been in close action with the enemy. Friday, Saturday and Sunday was one continued row. A mob drove me from my house on Friday night. Saturday night I could not get to the house unless through showers of stones, and Sunday the house was found nailed up. . . . It is hardly safe for me to walk in the street after dark." Later in 1838, it is reported, "an attempt was made . . . to throw him into the [Ohio] river, by twelve men assembled for the purpose of thus taking his life," but "he stood fearless before them, looking them directly in the eye and talking to them of the 'judgment to come.'" "My spirit cannot rest," Brown wrote, "so long as my brethren are crushed by the iron hoof of oppression. . . . The slaves must be free. Yes, they will be free or *death* will overwhelm the nation."[2]

Abel Brown had moved to the Albany area in May 1841, as the pastor of a church at Sand Lake, "a thoroughly abolitionized community" east of Albany. In April 1842 he organized the Eastern New York Anti-Slavery Society with the support of Gerrit Smith and aggressively promoted the antislavery cause, in Albany and in other towns in upstate New York. An excerpt from Brown's 1842 diary illustrates his wide-ranging activities:

> *June 3.* Wrote and prepared letters for the Am. [American] and Foreign A.S. [Anti-Slavery] Soc'y—aided Fugitives. Watched Kidnappers, etc.
>
> *June 4.* Went to Troy to watch a constable from Baltimore [who was trying to recapture a runaway slave], and aid the friends in Troy in knowing and watching him.
>
> *June 10.* Spent most of the week in aiding runaways, and in sending off Circulars—Soliciting money and finding solicitors [to defend the runaway slaves]. Went to Sand Lake, and made arrangements to send a certain person there.

Some of the money being raised by Abel Brown was sent to Torrey and Smallwood in Washington to support their operation. Brown was an enthusiastic support of their activities and was convinced that only aggressive action would put an end to slavery. Brown's activities, like Goodwin's, elicited predictable reactions from proslavery advocates in Albany. According to a memoir published by Abel Brown's wife, on one occasion when a mob gathered to oppose Brown's activities, "a friend who mingled with the mob as they passed up Albany street, says *their plan and design was to knock Mr. B. down and then trample him to death.*"[3]

Torrey's departure from Washington in October of 1842 left Smallwood in charge. By that time, according to a narrative written by Smallwood nine years later, "suspicion had already pointed to me," so he had to be very careful. He continued:

> I was the sole proprietor of the so-called underground railroad in that section, it having been started without the assistance of any earthly being save Torry [sic], myself, my wife, and the Lady with whom he [Torrey] boarded. Torry having gone North, the burden and responsibility of consequences rested entirely on me, therefore I had to watch every moment with an eagle's eye. I generally went out on the suburbs of the city previous to the night intended for their departure and selected the place at which they were to assemble, never selecting the same place a second time, nor were more than two allowed to come in company to the place selected, and that in different directions, according to the advice of Mr. Torry.

An example of such a meeting place used by Smallwood was "the shore of the eastern branch of the Potamic [sic], opposite to Washington."[4]

At the Albany end of the line, slaves sent north by Smallwood were well cared for by Abel Brown and, when he arrived, Torrey. Tom Calarco, in his book describing the Underground Railroad in eastern New York, claimed that, "during the early 1840s when Abel Brown and Charles Torrey were working the line, there apparently were two separate vigilance committees [in Albany] assisting runaways. . . . It is doubtful there were any more pro-active conductors than Torrey and Brown." The 1842 annual report of the Albany Vigilance Committee claimed that "no less than 340 fugitives had been aided to a place of safety by the Committee, at an expense of more than $1,000 [$20,000]." Such efforts were described in the memoir written by Brown's wife:

> Early in the year '42, Mr. Brown engaged in labors for the slave in Albany; a city, which from its location on the banks of the Hudson, was the constant resort of fugitive slaves, when traveling in the direction of the North Star, to seek shelter under the wing of Queen Victoria's dominion, or happily, perchance, to find an Asylum in the nominally free States. To effect this,

and also to render their flight effectual, and speed them on their course to the goal of freedom, it was found necessary that a systematic train of operations be devised, by Committees formed for the specific purpose of aiding those who thus sought the protection of friends in a strange land.[5]

According to Wilbur Siebert's history of the Underground Railroad, the main routes out of Albany ran directly north to Canada, or west to Syracuse and Rochester and then across Lake Ontario. "These routes," claimed Siebert, "appear to have been used at an early date." A route through central New York that was used later by Harriet Tubman was not prominent in the early 1840s. At Sand Lake, the village where Abel Brown was serving as a minister, there was a company that sent sand to a glassmaking company in Durhamville in central New York, and it is alleged that the Albany Vigilance Committee "transported slaves in empty barrels between the locations." From Durhamville, the slaves could be taken to the nearby Erie Canal to continue west to Rochester or Buffalo, or they could be taken north to Lake Ontario.[6]

Slaves who wished to continue north from Albany used a well-defined network of safe houses to reach the Canadian border. The first stop was usually Greenwich, then known as Union Village or Quaker Union. In 1836 Theodore Weld had given an antislavery lecture there, and the following year a group of abolitionists had founded the Free Church, creating "a major hub of Abolition and the Underground Railroad." Nine abolitionist families lived within a block of each other. Continuing north, the slaves came to Chestertown, said to have been "the most abolitionized community in the [Warren] county." The leading abolitionist was Quaker Joseph Leggett, who was friends with Abel Brown and Gerrit Smith. Judge Tyrrell was also part of the Chestertown network; during a remodeling of his house many years later, a hidden room was discovered in the cellar that contained "a cot, a dresser, a washstand, a water pitcher, a candle, a folded sheet, a blanket, and a bible." Further north, near Keeseville, lived Samuel Keese and other Quakers who provided assistance to the fugitives. When one of them, Stephen Smith, dictated his memoirs in 1887, he reported that he had spent $1,000 ($22,300) "of his own money in providing food, clothing, and other necessities to the runaways." The final safe house on this route was the home of Noadiah Moore in the village of Champlain, very close to the Canadian border. "Moore took the freedom-seekers across the border to Lacolle, where he owned mills and was able to help them find work."[7]

Traveling to slave states, persuading slaves to run away, transporting them north, and helping them reach Canada were aggressive abolitionist activities that were regarded as both outrageous and criminal from the slaveholders' point of view. During 1842 and 1843, however, Charles Torrey, Edwin Goodwin, Abel Brown, and Thomas Smallwood did all these things and carried their scheme yet one step further. Using the *Albany Patriot,* they began publishing the names of the slaves they had assisted to run away and also published the names of their owners, usually ridiculing them in the process. Sometimes, they even sent a copy of the newspaper to the slaveowner whose slaves had been taken. Virtually all other participants in the Underground Railroad were making great efforts to keep their activities secret, but these abolitionists were publicly advertising theirs. The articles in the *Albany Patriot* were sometimes unsigned, sometimes signed by Abel Brown, and sometimes signed by "Samivel Weller," the Cockney valet in Charles Dickens's immensely popular *Pickwick Papers,* which had appeared in monthly installments in 1836 and 1837. Thomas Smallwood, despite not having had a formal education, had become very fond of English literature and later acknowledged that he was "Samivel Weller." In 1843 Charles Torrey also used this name for some of his published letters.[8]

Such letters appeared in their abolitionist paper as early as June of 1842:

Albany, June 20th, 1842.

Dear Sir: —The vigilance committee are up to their elbows in work, and are desirous to have you inform a few of those men who have lately lost *property consisting* of articles of merchandize (falsely so called) in the shape, and having the minds and sympathies of *human beings,* that we are always on hand, and ready to ship cargoes on the shortest notice, and ensure a safe passage over the *"Great Ontario."* Please inform the following persons, that their property arrived safe, (though some of it was badly worn) and has been forwarded and arrived safe in Canada.

Cheney Hutton is hereby informed that two very large men, the one a market man and teamster, the other a first rate field hand, came up on the "Peoples Line." . . . They confessed that they were runaways and their countenances proved that they were guilty of being as black as a slaveholders heart. They did not appear to be ashamed of what they had done, but a gentleman present said, he was ashamed for them that they had not done one thing more, and that was, to have driven along the market wagon well loaded, as part payment for the robbery of about 30 years service. Friend Hutton may as well give up the chase, —for Benjamin and Phillip, will hereafter sell their own poultry, raise their own corn and own their bodies, and let Cheney Hutton do his own marketing or pay for doing it, as honest men do.

Abel Brown, Forwarding Merchant, Albany

Thus, Brown was even encouraging runaway slaves to steal goods from their owners as they left. Other letters followed:

Dr. Robert Dausey, Mount Pleasant, Baltimore Co., Md. will doubtless be pleased to learn that Richard arrived about two weeks since . . . destitute of money but in good spirits.

Please also inform Robert Gilmore of Baltimore, that he need not give himself further trouble about his very intelligent and noble slaves, Marianna, Polly, Elisabeth Castle, and her fine little girl, for they have got safe over the great Ontario, where such men as his honor, would not look very well placing their feet for the purpose of kidnapping.

Tell him also that his slave John Weston left here more than a week since, at full speed, in a fine carriage drawn by fleet horses, and report says, there were not less than six well loaded pistols in the hands of John and his associates. The carriage was driven by as fine looking and noble hearted a son of the South, as I ever saw. The kidnappers who came on from Baltimore after John, have great reason to be thankful that they were outwitted and did not overtake the carriage, for most surely they would have met a *hard* reception. John said he would die sooner than go back. I am quite sure that Marianna, Elisabeth, John, and the little girl, have had a joyful thanksgiving in the other land. (I hope Robert will not envy them their happiness.)

Inform Dr. Steward, that *Mary Ann* had some fears when here, that he would catch her, but that the kindness of *friends* dried up her tears, and she too went over that awful lake, that smiles on slaves, and frowns on slaveholders.

Some of the letters also mocked slave catchers who had been sent to capture the runaway slaves:

Mr. Editor: *Certain gentlemen,* who take such a deep interest in the welfare of Miss Leah Brown, lately held in servile bondage by Mrs. McDonald, are hereby informed that Leah has no wish to return to the embrace of the family who have robbed herself and mother, and her brothers and sisters, of their inalienable rights, from their earliest infancy. Also that she is beyond the *reach* of those men who have lately offered *one hundred dollars* for her delivery, to the woman who formerly held her as a slave. She earnestly hopes, that Mrs. McD. will treat her mother and sisters kindly, and not sell them to Georgia.

On occasion, the letters even mocked the police, such as one directed at the Baltimore police that called them "poor puppies" for failing to catch the runaway slaves. Others sarcastically claimed a reward for telling the slaveholders what had happened to their slaves:

Tell Mrs. Widow Margaret A. Culver, that the reward of $100 [$2,200] which she offered for her slave Levi, put us on the watch, and sure enough, he came pat upon us and handed out his bill of lading.

We told him that the kidnappers of this city, were looking out. . . . We trust she will send us forthwith, $25.00 [$560], as a reward for telling her where he may be found. We think he is now about half way over the *Great Ontario,* on the steamboat *Freedom,* or at least Levi calls her Freedom.

Occasional letters accused slaveholders by name of grossly abusing their slaves, or even killing them:

> Mr. Wm. Howard, Oracoke, North Carolina. It gives me great pleasure to inform you that the four noble men that sailed away in a boat from your town, are safe, and well satisfied with their situation. They passed through this city last week, on their way to Canada. . . . The back of one was most cruelly scarred; all had been beaten severely. The scars on the heads of two of them, which you made with a cane, were quite visible. . . . The boat can be found on a beach, somewhere between your town and New York city.

> There is one Mr. Woodford, living far below Baltimore, whom we wish you to inform at as early a day as possible, respecting that women, Eliza Wilson, whom he pounded with sticks of wood, whom he stripped naked again and again, and whipped with the cat and nine tails, until her body was completely lacerated, whom he then washed with salt brine, to make the smart worse, whose eyes he also filled with salt and water, whose neck and head my own eyes saw covered with scars, caused by blows from him and his agents, whose back the women say is one complete scar, having been whipped several different times, until it was completely cut to pieces; whose head bears the mark of heavy clubs, in different places, whom he ever treated as a brute, a beast of burden, and whom he has robbed of the Bible and of education, from her earliest infancy; whom he made to work on the field, and submitted to be treated like the brutes that perish.

> Tell him that he had better repent of his awful crimes, for God's vengeance is out against him, and he will certainly feel even more than he has poured upon the innocent head, of perhaps his own daughter. But she is now beyond his reach. We want money to aid in sending another on the *same road.*

> One day last week eight noble persons arrived, all panting

for liberty. . . . A certain knave in New-Orleans owned two of them, and another who intended to have come with them, and who laid the plan for their escape, was whipped to death by Joseph Wolcott. That same murderer has sent his sons to a northern college, where they have been educated, and are now following the business of their ungodly father. . . . But thank indulgent Heaven, Sarah and her little girl of four years old are safe, and her unborn child will, we trust, never feel the curse of slavery. May God have mercy upon the man who killed its father.

In what was a massive understatement, Thomas Smallwood claimed that such "letters were a great annoyance to the slaveholders."[9]

During 1842 and 1843, therefore, Charles Torrey and his colleagues carried aggressive abolitionism to a new level. They not only encouraged slaves to run away and helped them to do so but also ridiculed the slaveowners in the process. In addition, they encouraged slaves to take from their masters whatever they needed to run away, as Gerrit Smith had recommended in his January 1842 address to the slaves. In 1843 Abel Brown gleefully informed Smith that the "doctrine advocated in the [his] address to the slave has gone into extensive practice," noting that some runaway slaves were citing Smith's address to justify their actions. Not surprisingly, it was at this time that "certain gentlemen in Baltimore" offered a reward of $1,500 ($33,500) "for the apprehension of Brown, Torrey and E. W. Goodwin." Ridiculing the offer, the three responded that they would gladly go to Baltimore "for half that sum provided the money was only deposited in a good bank . . . as they were in great need of funds, to help the poor fugitives."[10]

By 1843, therefore, Charles Torrey and his colleagues were becoming increasingly aggressive. Perhaps foreshadowing what he believed was coming, Torrey in 1842 predicted that "50,000 colored troops, including 15,000 *fugitives from slavery,* from every Southern State, with the war cry of freedom for their fellow sufferers on their lips . . . aided by 100 or 200,000 white troops, would sweep over the South, without even the possibility of serious resistance."[11]

The Washington-to-Albany branch of the Underground Railroad

continued to run smoothly for several months after Torrey moved to Albany, but it was an expensive and dangerous business. Abel Brown described it:

> FUGITIVES. "The cry is still they come."—Two, yesterday morning, and two this morning. . . . Will our friends send in funds to the Treasurer of the Eastern New York Anti-Slavery Society, to defray the expense of forwarding them on? Money! Money! Friends. The two fugitives last mentioned, we are informed, were followed to New York by their master—both master and slaves arriving at the same time—he on one boat and they on another. Happily, some colored hands on one of our North River towboats secreted them on board, and they arrived in this city in safety this morning.

Fundraising was an endless task and not without risks. During a public lecture by Abel Brown in Auburn late in 1842, "a riotous scene occurred" in which a proslavery mob was determined "to assault the speaker. . . . Several attempts were made by the mob to assault Mr. Brown. . . . Some assaults were made by canes, but I am not aware that any blood was shed."[12]

One person who was especially helpful in fundraising for Charles Torrey and Abel Brown was Lewis Washington, who had been one of the first slaves freed by Torrey. He was an excellent speaker, and "though unaccustomed to our northern winters, he traveled in connection with Mr. Brown—often through snows impassable, by any mode of conveyance except on foot." According to one source, "audiences were moved by Lewis' stories of the four decades he had spent in slavery." A newspaper announcement of one Abel Brown antislavery lecture promised singing by Abel Brown's wife but "if not, the native eloquence of Louis [sic] Washington . . . [will] go far to compensate for the want of music."[13]

By the spring of 1843, however, problems were emerging on this Underground Railroad line. Because of the large number of slaves disappearing from Washington, another reward of $2,000 ($46,200) was offered by authorities for information leading to the capture of the perpetrators. Smallwood had to rely on other free blacks to help conceal the fugitive slaves awaiting transportation north, and one

of these men betrayed him. Smallwood knew he had major problems when he discovered that "fugitives had been taken by Williams, the slave trader, soon after they had been concealed." In addition, Smallwood was arguing with Abraham Cole, the leader of one
of the black churches, whom Smallwood had publicly accused of not
doing enough to help the slaves. Consequently, according to Smallwood, "his friends strove to do me all the injury they could by making use of the most disreputable means to accomplish their object.
. . . They would try underhandedly to point me out to the slaveholders as being the man who was aiding in the escape of their slaves."
Smallwood realized that he had become a marked man: "The cloud
of treachery began to thicken, and get blacker and blacker over me.
. . . Washington was no longer a place of safety for me."[14]

Smallwood left Washington on June 30, 1843, stopping in Philadelphia and Albany to discuss the situation with Torrey, Brown, and
others with whom he was working. He next went to Canada to look
for a place to live, then returned to Washington in September to collect his family and belongings. On the night before he was scheduled to leave with his family, his house was surrounded by police
with a search warrant. According to Smallwood: "I had another slave
woman concealed in my house. . . . To get her out of the house unper-
ceived was a matter of great importance. However, that was speedily accomplished by some females, who took her through a back door
into the garden, and concealed her in some corn." On the morning of
October 3, Smallwood put his family on a steamboat for Baltimore,
intending to sell his furniture and meet them there the following
day. He learned, however, that a warrant had been issued for his arrest, so he did not return to his house, hiding all day and walking to
Baltimore that night using back roads. He arrived in Toronto with
his family on October 14.[15]

The loss of Thomas Smallwood's efforts in Washington was a
major setback for Charles Torrey's plan to abscond with hundreds of
slaves, thus destabilizing slaveholding in the nation's capital. With
Smallwood's departure, there was nobody left there to recruit the
runaways and coordinate their departures. Torrey himself could not
return, since a reward had been offered for his capture. In addition,
he was involved in editing the *Albany Patriot,* supporting his family,

and helping to plan the nominating convention of the Liberty Party, scheduled to take place in Buffalo in late August. Uncertain what to do, Torrey traveled to Peterboro in July 1843 to consult with Gerrit Smith. As a man with a plan to abolish slavery coming to talk with Gerrit Smith in 1843, Torrey foreshadowed by fifteen years another man with a plan to abolish slavery who would also come to talk with Gerrit Smith in 1858; his name was John Brown.[16]

Torrey had met Smith at Liberty Party and other abolitionist meetings and had been the recipient of Smith's largesse while organizing the Liberty Party in Massachusetts but had never previously visited Smith's home. And what a home it was, known as the Mansion House, with twenty-eight rooms and a rosewood dining table that seated twenty. It dominated the hamlet of Peterboro, a village near Syracuse that consisted of a green with a few shops, two inns, and two churches. Smith's father had built the house with money he had made in partnership with John Jacob Astor in the fur-trading business. From the business, Smith's father had accumulated almost a million acres of land and had thus become one of the wealthiest men in New York State.[17]

In 1843, when Torrey visited, Gerrit Smith's home was a cynosure of abolitionist activity. The house was a major stop on the Underground Railroad, and at any given time one or more slaves, some of whom may have been carried north on Torrey's Washington-to-Albany line, were likely to be staying. Other houseguests were numerous, including Elizabeth Cady, who was Gerrit Smith's cousin, and her husband, Henry Stanton, whom Torrey knew from their shared challenge to William Lloyd Garrison. Elizabeth Cady had met Stanton at Peterboro in 1839, when he had come to deliver abolitionist lectures in nearby towns. In her memoirs, she recalled such occasions: "Two carriage-loads of ladies and gentlemen drove off every morning, sometimes ten miles, to one of these conventions, returning late at night. I shall never forget those charming drives over the hills in Madison County, the bright autumnal days, and the bewitching moonlight nights. The enthusiasm of the people in these great meetings, the thrilling oratory, and lucid arguments of the speakers, all conspired to make these days memorable as among the most charming in my life."

Elizabeth Cady described Gerrit Smith as "a man of fine presence. . . . his hospitalities were generous to an extreme, and dispensed to all classes of society. . . . There never was such an atmosphere of love and peace, of freedom and good cheer, in any other home I visited. . . . To go anywhere else, after a visit there, was like coming down from the divine heights into the valley of humiliation." A decade later, Elizabeth Cady Stanton and Gerrit Smith's daughter, Elizabeth Smith Miller, would play major roles in reforming women's dress and initiating the women's suffrage movement.[18]

Gerrit Smith's dedication to the abolition of slavery had personal roots. His father had owned slaves before New York State passed legislation in 1799 making slaveholding illegal. As a boy, Gerrit and his brother were made by their father to do manual labor on the estate, often working alongside the remaining slaves, who had not yet reached their twenty-eighth birthday, as specified by the 1799 Act of Emancipation. According to a biographer, "it was an experience he never forgot; it made his understanding of slavery not something abstract and conceptual but palpable and real, and it eventually helped him to empathize and identify with slaves and the poor." Thus, Gerrit Smith not only offered a station stop on the Underground Railroad, he also purchased the freedom of slaves; gave away land to free blacks; supported legal efforts to abolish slavery by political means, such as the Liberty Party, and supported illegal efforts to free slaves, such as the work of Charles Torrey and, later, John Brown. Torrey greatly admired Gerrit Smith for all these things and also for Smith's January 1842 address "To the Slaves in the U. States of America."[19]

After leaving Peterboro, Charles Torrey traveled west to Buffalo, where he and Abel Brown "held meetings in the city." The National Convention of Colored Citizens was meeting there at that time. It was at this meeting that Henry Highland Garnet made a memorable speech urging slaves to rise up and free themselves. Garnet had been born a slave in Maryland but as a child had escaped with his family to New York. He had been well educated and strongly influenced by Gerrit Smith. In his speech, Garnet praised Denmark Veazie, Nat Turner, Joseph Cinque of the *Amistad,* and Madison Washington of the *Creole* as "noble men" and urged others to do likewise:

Brethren, it is wrong for your lordly oppressors to keep you in slavery, as it was for the man thief to steal our ancestors from the coast of Africa. . . . Brethren, the time has come when you must act for yourselves. . . . Think of your wretched sisters, loving virtue and purity, as they are driven into concubinage, and exposed to the unbridled lusts of incarnate devils. . . . *To such degradation it is sinful in the extreme for you to make voluntary submission. . . . Neither God, nor angels, or just men command you to suffer for a single moment. Therefore it is your solemn and imperative duty to use every means, both moral, intellectual, and physical, that promise success. . . .* You had far better all die—*die immediately,* than live slaves, and entail your wretchedness upon your posterity. . . . Let it no longer be a debatable question, whether it is better to choose *liberty* or *death.* . . . Let your motto be *resistance, resistance, resistance*—No oppressed people have ever secured their liberty without resistance.[20]

Charles Torrey, Abel Brown, and Gerrit Smith were pleased with Garnet's call for aggressive action. One who was not pleased was Frederick Douglass, who publicly criticized Garnet's call for physical resistance by slaves. Douglass was at the Buffalo convention as a representative of William Lloyd Garrison, with whom he had not yet had a falling out. Garrison supported the right of slaves to run away but, following pacifist principles, opposed any use of force in doing so. Douglass was one of five Garrisonians, including Abby Kelley, who had come to Buffalo to try to persuade delegates to the National Convention of Colored Citizens, and the Liberty Party convention that was to follow, that moral suasion was the true path to the abolition of slavery. Garrison also recommended that the North should secede from union with the South, a position he had announced in 1842. He continued to oppose any political action, and especially the Liberty Party, which he said had been "conceived in sin" and was "the most dangerous foe with which genuine anti-slavery had to contend." According to one of his biographers, Garrison believed that the true "object of the Liberty Party . . . was not the abolition of slavery but the overthrow of William Lloyd Garrison."[21]

At the Liberty Party convention, which followed the Convention of Colored Citizens in Buffalo, Garrison's representatives had little success. According to one account, "some six or seven thousand people were present, assembled in and around the great Oberlin tent, transported from Cleaveland [sic], expressly for the occasion." Liberty Party delegates represented twelve states, with the largest number coming from Massachusetts, Ohio, Pennsylvania, and New York, where the party was best organized. Owen Lovejoy, a younger brother of abolitionist martyr Elijah Lovejoy, reported that "the utmost harmony prevailed throughout the meeting. . . . The spirit of God hovered over us." A dedicated abolitionist, Lovejoy had vowed on the body of his dead brother to "never forsake the cause that had been sprinkled with my brother's blood." Lovejoy later became a member of Congress and a good friend of Abraham Lincoln.[22]

James G. Birney was again nominated as the party's presidential candidate for the 1844 election. The party platform consisted of "21 planks based almost entirely on the slavery question," including a prohibition of slavery in Texas, California, Oregon, and any other new territory added to the Union. The platform also decreed that it was not the duty of the government "to maintain slavery by military force," thus implicitly sanctioning slave revolts. In a passage that evoked the image of Nat Turner, the platform asserted that "when freemen unsheath the sword it should be to strike for *Liberty*, not despotism." William Lloyd Garrison's pacifism was clearly not on the Liberty Party's agenda.[23]

Charles Torrey was one of the organizers of the Liberty Party convention, and on the second day he introduced the following motion: "Resolved: That the Liberty Party cordially opens its doors to receive members of the 'Old,' 'New,' or no 'organizations'—all men who are ready to labor for the slave, and the restoration to all men of their Heaven-derived and unforfeited rights, and we recognize as true abolitionists all who are opposed to slavery, and refuse to support it, its defenders or apologists." This was Torrey's attempt to reach out to Garrison's remaining followers and encourage them to join the political abolitionist movement. Garrison's position had considerably weakened; the remnants of the American Anti-Slavery Society was "transacting only a small fraction of its former business." Even the original Massachusetts society had lost many members and was restricting its activities to attempts to racially integrate the Boston public schools and to integrate travel on trains and steamships. Garrison's reaction to his increasing marginalization was to elevate his invective directed at Torrey and his colleagues, calling the clerics "a brotherhood of thieves" and the church "steeped in blood and pollution." These, said Garrison, were the "haughty, corrupt, implacable and pious foes of the anti-slavery movement." In a letter to his wife, Garrison advocated "blowing up the priesthood, church, worship, sabbath, etc."[24]

Following the Buffalo convention, Torrey and Abel Brown returned to Albany, stopping en route to hold antislavery rallies and raise money for their activities. As Brown reported to his wife: "We had a glorious meeting of three days continuance at Canastota. The large house was filled to overwhelming day and night, and the interest was intense. We had one discussion which lasted twelve hours." Brown also said that, at one meeting, "Torrey gave a great war speech upon another resolution," but it was voted down. When they arrived in Albany, Torrey, Brown, and Goodwin "lectured on the steps of the Capitol."[25]

At this point in his life, however, Charles Torrey had moved beyond conventions and rallies, resolutions and speeches. He had seen the faces of slaves as he took them across the line from Maryland to Pennsylvania, a free state. He had listened to the hopes of their children and felt the hands of the slaves as they pressed their effusive thanks upon him, often with tears in their eyes. Such experiences are intoxicating. Once one has tasted such fruits, it is no longer possible to be satisfied with mere words.

While in Buffalo, Torrey had journeyed to Toronto to visit Thomas Smallwood, who had settled there with his family and was planning to open a sawmill. Shortly after returning to Albany, Torrey received a letter from Smallwood saying that he had been solicited by four former slaves, three of whom had been carried to freedom by Torrey and Smallwood, whose wives and children were still in Washington. Smallwood suggested raising funds to send "to a certain friend in Washington, desiring him to send the above mentioned families to Philadelphia." According to Smallwood, however, Torrey proposed instead "that we should try and obtain a team [of horses] and proceed to Washington, and bring away as many slaves as we could."[26]

At this time, Torrey "closed his labors in Albany." His wife and children returned to Medway, Massachusetts, to live with her family. There had been suggestions of marital discord as early as 1841, when Torrey wrote to his wife: "Mary, can we not love one another with freshness and purity, and tenderness of our first affection? I was thinking of it much the other night . . . and thinking over how much holier and happier we might be, if we had more *forbearing* tenderness for each other." But by the autumn of 1843, the marriage had, for all intents and purposes, ended. Torrey would thereafter be accused of having abandoned his family.[27]

Torrey and Smallwood set about collecting funds to support their new venture. They received $30 ($670) from James Baker, another slave they had previously freed, on the condition that they include his still enslaved wife and child in the wagonload they proposed to free. In November they started south, proceeding at a leisurely pace. They spent two days in Philadelphia, where they reestablished contact with James Bias, Charles Cleveland, and others who had assisted their previous operations. They went to Wilmington for a day, where they stayed with Thomas Garrett, whose house was a major Underground Railroad station. They then returned to Kennett Square, just south of Philadelphia, where they were loaned horses and a wagon by abolitionists and drove across southeastern Pennsylvania to stay at "a tavern near Mason's and Dixon's line." Their route and deliberate pace suggests that they were probably reestablishing the line they had previously used for running slaves northward.[28]

Thomas Smallwood had made arrangements to use the suburban Washington home of John Bush, a free black friend, as the meeting point for the slaves. At sundown, as Torrey was loading the fourteen slaves into the wagon and Smallwood was harnessing the horses, white men were spotted on the hillside overlooking the Bush home. Torrey went to investigate and, according to Smallwood, "soon returned to me trembling, and saying they were constables and requested me to try and get the people out of the wagon." But it was too late. Smallwood and Torrey ran, and "after getting about a quarter of a mile from the place I heard the clanking of the chains, and shrieks of the poor souls, but we could afford them no help, they were in the claws of the lions." The police had apparently been tipped off, which was not surprising, given the local notoriety of Smallwood and Torrey and the substantial reward being offered for their capture.[29]

Remarkably, both Smallwood and Torrey escaped. Smallwood proceeded all night on foot to Baltimore, then by a circuitous route back to Toronto. He was aware, he said, that if he had been captured and convicted, he would have been "sent to the Penitentiary for fourteen years." Torrey remained in Washington for three or four days "to make arrangements with Mr. Hall, a lawyer, for the defense of our friend, John Bush, from whose premises we were routed, and the people taken, for which he was arrested." Torrey then returned to Philadelphia, where he stayed with James Bias and attempted to raise funds to pay for the horses and wagon that he had been loaned but that had been confiscated by the police.[30]

Charles Torrey's life seemed to be coming apart. The failure of his recent attempt to free more slaves was "the cause of heavy loss, as it is of mental suffering," he wrote to Gerrit Smith. He had narrowly escaped being caught in the act, for which arrest and imprisonment would have been certain. His plan to take hundreds of slaves from Washington, thus undermining slaveholding in the nation's capital, was no longer feasible, given that the police were watching for him. Other abolitionists had grown wary of him, perceiving his reckless behavior as endangering them all. For example, when Torrey was given the horses and wagon in Kennett Square for his ill-fated trip, "it was done with extreme trepidation and reluctance by most of the anti-slavery people, as his plan of going among slaves and encouraging them to leave their masters was not in accord with the general views and wishes of abolitionists, and they endeavored to dissuade him from it. But he believed that by so doing, property in slaves would be rendered so insecure that it would hasten emancipation, or the introduction of hired or free labor. So confident was he that his views were correct, that no argument could move him."[31]

To understand Charles Torrey's subsequent behavior, it is necessary to consider his personal situation at this time. He had failed as a teacher, as a minister, and as a provider for his family. The one thing at which he had been successful was in rescuing large numbers of slaves, and this had become the most important thing in his life. This, therefore, was what he decided to continue doing, despite its obvious risks. Did depression play a role in this decision? Had his tuberculosis recurred? Was he seeking martyrdom? All of these are possible. He attempted to explain his motivation in a January 1844 letter to Gerrit Smith: "Do you ask: 'Why waste your time so, and run these risks?' I reply . . . *Private* causes of personal misery render me—perhaps *reckless*. In toil and excitement the misery one cannot relieve, may be forgotten. . . . And, for a time to come, I shall relieve a few *individual* cases of suffering, while, I hope, I am not unfitting myself for duty to the whole cause." Torrey's personal situation was also consistent with an interview he gave at this time to the *Boston Daily Mail,* in which the interviewer explained:

> We saw him a few months previous to his arrest, and he talked as freely of his plans of running the "underground railroad" as he termed it, as though it was attended by no danger, and coupled with no violation of the law. We earnestly but kindly remonstrated with him. We pointed out the dangers and difficulties of the experiment. We admonished him that he was violating what every citizen was bound to protect. We appealed in behalf of the wife he loved and the friends who love him. But it was all in vain. He was fearless of consequences and apparently ready and willing to become a martyr to the cause. It was with a heavy heart that we parted with him on that occasion; for we well feared what must be the consequence of his daring and reckless career. And when, a short time afterwards, we heard of his arrest, it occasioned a good deal more of sorrow than surprise.

Daniel A. Payne, the first black bishop of the African Methodist Episcopal Church and later a university president, also tried to warn Torrey: "I was personally acquainted with Torrey, and had repeatedly warned him not to come to Baltimore or Washington. Having learned of the plot against him, I made it known to his friend, Dr. J. J. G. Bias, of Philadelphia, where he always stopped, and wrote him myself, advising him not to come. The warnings were unheeded. The idea of liberty consumed him."[32]

Despite the warnings and obvious dangers, Torrey continued making trips from Philadelphia to Maryland and Virginia to rescue slaves. He avoided Washington, given his recent experience there, but instead focused his efforts on Baltimore and rural Virginia. Financing for these forays was furnished by his friends in Philadelphia and probably also by Gerrit Smith.

In early December, Torrey went by carriage through Gettysburg and Harpers Ferry to Winchester. Emily Webb, a former slave who had purchased her freedom, had approached Torrey in Philadelphia and asked his help in freeing her husband and five children, who were owned by Bushrod Taylor, a slave dealer, in Winchester. Taylor had already sold two of her other children south. It was later alleged in court proceedings that Torrey stayed at a hotel in Winchester on December 9 under the name of "C. Turner." With the assistance of John Fountain, a free black in Winchester, who made the arrangements, Torrey met John Webb and his five children at a previously appointed spot, and they immediately started north. According to Torrey's account, they reached Chambersburg, Pennsylvania, "in 23 hours from Winchester over more horrible roads than I ever had the misfortune to travel . . . a combination of mud and rocks." They were pursued by two slave catchers from Winchester and a sheriff from Maryland; the pursuers reached Chambersburg "only four hours after we left for Philadelphia." From there, the Webbs fled to Canada. Fountain was imprisoned for ten weeks "under suspicion of having aided Torrey."[33]

For the next six months, Torrey traveled widely and continued to transport slaves north. In his writings, he described being in Frederick, Hagerstown, and Cumberland, Maryland, as well as Leesburg, Middleburg, and Winchester, Virginia. In a letter to Gerrit Smith, he reported that he "brought 5 out of the . . . horrible Bastile" of slavery, presumably referring to the Webbs, and that he was "expecting soon to go for a man in Raleigh, N.C.; a woman in Staunton, Va., and a man in New Orleans with some others." The major limitation on his activities, Torrey claimed, was the funds needed to hire horses and carriages. He also spoke optimistically about the chances of abolishing slavery in Delaware, believing it could be done within the following year if sufficient funds were available. "I am more deeply impressed with the horrors of slavery than ever," he told Smith, "yet more full of hope of its very speedy overthrow."[34]

It was during early 1844 that Torrey began sending regular communications to be published in the *Albany Patriot*. The column was titled "Notes of Southern Travel by a Negro Stealer," and although not signed, its authorship was obvious. In one column, Torrey provided a detailed account of his abduction of the Webb family, emphasizing that Mrs. Webb's biological father was a former member of Congress from Maryland and that Mr. Webb's biological father was "one of the wealthiest men in Maryland." The theme of slaves being fathered by white slaveholders was sounded repeatedly:

> Just below Baltimore resides a wealthy planter, commonly called "Nigger Tom W——," from the notorious habits of the man. I saw him once, at Annapolis. He is a stout, fat man, with a shrewd, but sensual face.— He has large families of children by four colored women, and other children by his own daughters. They number about 50 in all.
>
> One of the most influential citizens of Baltimore, is a well known military man, Col. S——t. By a colored woman he had two daughters; and subsequently had children by each of these daughters. Not long since, he sold the mother, daughters and grandchildren, all, to the slave trader Hope H. Slatter, for the southern market.

As part of his escalation of aggression, Torrey also indicated that he had learned the names of three free black "stool pigeons" who had betrayed his operation in Washington, and he publicly demanded that the three "must be sent from Washington . . . on or before April 26 on peril of their *lives*."[35]

Perhaps sensing that the end of his activities was nearing, Torrey labored ceaselessly to free slaves during the spring of 1844. He worked out of the Philadelphia home of James Bias until mid-April, when he moved to a boarding house in Baltimore. Much of his time Torrey had to spend raising additional funds. For example, he is recorded as having been present at meetings of the Philadelphia Vigilance Committee on March 11 and March 20, 1844, the object of the second meeting "being to hear some propersition [*sic*] for Mr. Torry [*sic*]." There is no evidence that he returned to Albany or visited his family in Massachusetts during those months, and a subsequent letter Torrey sent to his friend Amos Phelps confirmed that Torrey and his wife were estranged at this time. Since he had no paying job, it also seems unlikely that he was contributing to their support, an accusation that would be made publicly after his arrest.[36]

During these months, Torrey also kept in touch with his friends in Washington and monitored political developments. He heard about the incident in 1843, when Representative Charles Dawson of Louisiana threw Joshua Giddings "into the desks on the House floor, and reached for the bowie knife concealed beneath his coat." Then in December, Giddings attempted to gain freedom for a free black man who was being held in the Washington jail because the man could not prove that he had been manumitted. Giddings introduced a motion in Congress to investigate the case. When a southern congressman objected, Giddings challenged "the gentleman to *prove* his [own] freedom."[37]

In May of 1844, while Torrey was living in a Baltimore rooming house and continuing to transport slaves to Pennsylvania, both the Whigs and the Democrats held their presidential nominating conventions in Baltimore. The Whigs nominated Henry Clay of Kentucky, and the party platform remained silent on the issue of slavery. Four weeks later, the Democrats nominated James Polk of Tennessee. Thus, both parties were being led by southerners. Immediately after Clay's nomination, the *Albany Patriot* publicly charged that Henry Clay had fathered several children with his female slaves; the column was signed by "Samivel Weller." Abel Brown then posted handbills around Albany alleging that Clay "was not only a gambler, but that he had won and lost *human beings* at the gaming table." Torrey also published a letter accusing South Carolina Senator John C. Calhoun, a fierce defender of slavery, of having sold the "beautiful and pious wife" of his coachman, both of whom were Calhoun's slaves, to a planter in Alabama as "a harlot" for $1,400 ($28,000); Calhoun publicly denied the allegation.[38]

The end came abruptly for Torrey, in June 1844. According to later court testimony, on May 26 Torrey had been observed transporting "a black boy and a yellow man" on the road to Pennsylvania. On

June 5 he had been seen driving a black woman north. On June 7 he had been observed by several persons driving three slaves belonging to William Heckrotte of Baltimore. Over the following days, Torrey had visited the Baltimore slave pen of Hope Slatter, a notorious slave dealer known for commissioning others to kidnap free blacks whom Slatter would then sell south as slaves. Torrey was attempting to negotiate the freedom of a runaway slave known as Big Ben, who had been kidnapped from Bucks County in suburban Philadelphia and was being held by Slatter for sale south. Torrey was trying to raise funds for his release and was negotiating the price with Slatter. Slatter, however, had been told that Torrey had been the person who had abducted John Webb and the Webb children from Bushrod Taylor in Winchester six months earlier. He therefore notified Taylor, who immediately filed a warrant for Torrey's arrest. On Monday evening, June 24, Torrey was arrested by the Baltimore police; he was reported to have been armed with two pistols at the time of his arrest.[39]

7

TRIAL

The Baltimore city jail to which Charles Torrey was taken on June 24, 1844, was on Madison Street, immediately adjacent to the Maryland Penitentiary. It was, coincidentally, the same jail in which William Lloyd Garrison had been incarcerated for seven weeks in 1830 for having libeled a ship owner in the abolitionist newspaper he was co-editing. The jail held approximately eighty men and women, among whom, according to Torrey, were slaves "confined for loving freedom too well" and "free colored persons, shut up in prison to compel them to prove their legal title to be free." The majority of prisoners were "thieves, murderers, pickpockets, swindlers, men who have brutally beaten their wives, . . . rowdies and loafers from the street-fights, harlots and bawds from the brothels, and a mixed multitude of like criminals."[1]

Torrey's initial reaction to being incarcerated was to view it as an opportunity to continue his abolitionist activities. He counseled slaves in jail on how to use the Underground Railroad, and consequently "several of the slaves Torrey met in jail later escaped northward." He also wrote letters, some of which were published, accusing the Baltimore police of illegally profiting from the slave trade. For example:

> It is very common here for the police and other slave hunting knaves, to play tricks on slave holders. I will give you a few samples. One police firm has in pay, over twenty colored spies here, besides others in Philadelphia and elsewhere. Their business is to inveigle slaves to run away, hide them up, and betray them.—When the master misses his slave, he soon advertises his $100 reward; often he applies to this very police firm for aid! In a few days they are ready, of course, to hand over the poor victim of their arts, and pocket the reward, besides getting praise as *very vigilant officers*![2]

Torrey's second reaction to his arrest was to view it as an opportunity to challenge the constitutional legitimacy of slaveholding in general. He had conceived of this strategy months earlier in regard to the arrest of John Bush, the free black man in Washington who had helped Torrey and Smallwood in their failed attempt to transport a wagonload of slaves north. In January 1844, Torrey had written to Gerrit Smith about the Bush case, recommending that it was "deeply important to carry it to the highest court, on the question of the constitutionality of slavery in the District of Columbia." Charges against Bush were subsequently dropped, but Torrey regarded his own case as a similar opportunity.[3]

It is apparent that Torrey discussed this legal strategy with friends and other abolitionists who supported it. As Torrey summarized: if "it is no crime for a slave to escape if he can, . . . therefore it *can* be no *crime* to help him." The *Pennsylvania Freeman* wrote that "there is a probability of the case being carried up to the Supreme Court." Joshua Leavitt, the editor of the *Emancipator,* editorialized strongly in support of this strategy, adding that "it was suggested by one of the most eminent statesmen and jurists now living, whose soundness of judgment the reader would hardly question on points like this." The "eminent statesman" was John Quincy Adams, whom Leavitt knew from having helped defend him during his congressional "trial." Adams apparently suggested that Torrey's best opportunity for successfully challenging slavery was to have the case appealed to the Supreme Court and thus tried before Chief Justice Roger Taney. Taney was a southerner who had manumitted his own slaves and had ruled for the release of the *Amistad* slaves two years earlier in the case defended by Adams. Thus, it would have been logical for Adams to have recommended that Torrey follow a similar judicial path. Torrey also had the *Amistad* case in mind, noting that, "without any exception worth naming, every case carried by the abolitionists into the State or Federal courts, has been ultimately decided *in favor* of freedom!" Whether Adams was asked to assist in Torrey's case if it was successfully appealed to the Supreme Court is not known.[4]

Torrey's arrest in Maryland had been based on charges that he had abducted slaves belonging to Bushrod Taylor in Virginia. The governor of Virginia had then sent a requisition to Maryland asking that Torrey be sent to Virginia for trial. The strategy for taking the case to the highest courts was outlined by Joshua Leavitt in the *Emancipator*:

> It is proposed, 1st, to take the Virginia requisition immediately, by the aid of eminent counsel, into the Circuit Court of the United States. A disputed requisition is *properly* cognisable only in the courts of the United States, not in a mere State court.
>
> The requisition may be resisted, there, on various grounds. (1.) No proof of the actual commission of any breach of law is made, to authorise it. (2.) Still less is any proof given of Mr. Torrey's complicity in any crime. (3.) Even if it were *proved* that he had aided ten thousand slaves to escape, such an act is neither "treason, felony, or other crime," in the view of the constitution of the United States, or of the common law; or even under the State constitutions of Maryland and Virginia. Consequently, it cannot be made the basis of a requisition by the governor of any State or another. It is, and *can be* no "*crime*" for a slave to flee from bondage; nor, consequently, can it be made a crime, by local statutes, to aid any slave in escaping. Therefore, Mr. Torrey is entitled to discharge, and to compensation for false imprisonment.

If the lower courts decided against Torrey, the case would "be appealed to the Supreme Court where, from precedents already established in several great trials, there is great reason to hope that a correct decision may be secured." Such a decision, Leavitt concluded, "will be a mighty weapon of law, justice and freedom, to break the bonds of all the victims of slavery in the border States, besides giving the system, everywhere, a deadly shock."[5]

During July and August 1844, Torrey worked enthusiastically with Leavitt and others to pursue this strategy. In a letter to the *Baltimore Sun*, Torrey raised several questions: "Is it [a] 'felony or other crime,' within the meaning of the constitution of the United States, to aid a slave to escape to a free state? . . . Has slavery any constitutional or legal existence in Maryland or Virginia? . . . Is it a crime at all, by the law of God, by the common law, or the constitutions of Maryland and Virginia, to help a man out of slavery?" Torrey himself would not be on trial, he claimed, but rather *the States of Maryland and Virginia will go to trial before the tribunal of mankind.*" He concluded with rhetorical flourish:

> Liberty may be taken away from me: my GOOD NAME cannot, until I have done something more to forfeit it than acts which nine tenths of the civilized world deem to be the bare performance of the duties imposed on us in common humanity and the Christian faith.
>
> I said, I make no appeal to public sympathy. Let *the guilty* do that! I shall give the eminent counsellors who plead my cause, in the courts, but one instruction: it is, that they make no admission, even by way of argument, that it *can be a crime* to aid one of God's children, formed in his image, to escape from slavery. The crime is, to make God's child a slave![6]

Charles Torrey's arrest received wide publicity in abolitionist newspapers and elicited letters of support from as far away as Scotland. He used this publicity to launch a vigorous public relations campaign, the goal of which was to present himself as a Christian martyr in order to elicit public sympathy and to raise funds for his defense. The need for funds was acute; it was initially estimated that at least $300 ($6,900) would be needed for his legal fees, but later it was said that $2,000 ($46,200) would be needed to gain a hearing before the federal Circuit Court. In a letter to the *Baltimore Sun,* published as a paid advertisement, Torrey described himself as "a man of blameless life and unspotted Christian character." He then proceeded to describe the "scores of public meetings in the Free States, numbering from one to eight thousand persons, each [of whom] have spoken of my imprisonment in terms like the following:

> *Resolved,* That we have heard with mingled feelings of indignation and sorrow of the arrest and imprisonment in Maryland, of a citizen of Massachusetts, Rev. Charles T. Torrey, through a requisition from the executive of Virginia, charging him with having carried out in practice the doctrine of the

Declaration of Independence, that *all men are created equal* and endowed by their Creator with an *inalienable right* to liberty.... We protest in the name of that declaration against this denial of its truths and violation of its principles, on the part of the authorities of Virginia and Maryland, in the case of our fellow-citizen, Mr. Torrey; and we call upon all who love liberty and hate oppression, to unite with us in indignant reprobation of a system which can only exist by making humanity a crime.[7]

Torrey's twofold legal and public relations strategy, however, encountered twofold problems. Legally, his efforts to get his case into federal court, based on the requisition from Virginia for his interstate transfer from Maryland, failed because Maryland refused the request. Instead, William Heckrotte of Baltimore, from whom Torrey had taken three slaves shortly before his arrest, filed charges against Torrey, and Maryland decided to try Torrey on those charges before sending him back to Virginia. Second, even if it had been possible to move the case to the federal courts, it was proving impossible to raise the $2,000 needed to get a federal court hearing. Stephen Pearl Andrews, Torrey's lawyer at the time, said that he had "endeavored for several weeks ... making every exertion in our power to that effect, but without success ... solely on account of the odium attached to the unpopular nature of the charge."[8]

"Odium" referred to the fact that Torrey's public relations campaign was failing. The majority of abolitionists did not agree with Torrey's actions, viewing them as reckless and imprudent. Lewis Tappan, for example, wrote following Torrey's arrest that "no abolitionist has a right to go into a Slave State with the avowed design of trampling upon its laws. If he does we are not bound to sustain him." Tappan's feelings were especially significant, since he and his brother were among Torrey's wealthiest potential contributors. A letter in the *Emancipator* similarly called Torrey's action "unwise and hurtful to the *general* cause of emancipation, ... and if Mr. T. is guilty of the charge alleged, he has acted in the matter *solely* upon his own responsibility, and in opposition to the views and feelings of his best friends and the friends of the slave."[9]

In addition to this general allegation of "imprudence," Torrey's efforts to present himself as "a man of blameless life and unspotted Christian character" encountered his old nemesis, William Lloyd Garrison, who, not surprisingly, failed to share that opinion. In an editorial in the *Liberator* following Torrey's arrest, Garrison wrote:

> Circumstances have occurred in the painful divisions which have taken place in the anti-slavery ranks, to impair my confidence in Mr. Torrey as a true-hearted abolitionist. Probably, of all the false friends who have lifted up their heels against me—of the host of enemies who have maliciously sought to destroy my influence in the anti-slavery cause, by covertly assailing and misrepresenting my religious sentiments—no one has surpassed him in the venom or subtlety of his attacks upon me, especially during his agency in behalf of the Massachusetts Abolition Society.

Garrison then added: "But I care nothing for the past. . . . I feel as ready to espouse his cause as though he were my bosom friend." It is very doubtful if anyone believed this. These doubts were substantiated in subsequent issues of the *Liberator*, such as one in which Garrison reported that $40 ($925) had been collected for Torrey in Hingham, "an excellent specimen of 'old organization' magnanimity, inasmuch as Mr. T. has been very hostile in spirit to those who have thus kindly remembered him in his prison cell."[10]

Despite his claims, Torrey had not led a "blameless life." He had offended many people in addition to Garrison, and he had neglected the needs of his family. Confined in a prison cell with little prospect of getting out, Torrey was regarded by his enemies as wounded prey. A letter in the *Emancipator* claimed that he "greatly mistook his calling . . . especially with the circumstances of his family." Torrey had abandoned, it said, "an amiable wife and two children, who are now thrown upon the cold charity of the world for their support, and who are now, with a circle of dear friends, in a state of deepest affliction and suffering on his account." The letter was simply signed "Norfolk," which is the name of the Massachusetts county in which Mary Torrey and her children were living with her family.[11]

Both proslavery and Garrisonian publications used Torrey's

incarceration as an opportunity to discredit him. A Philadelphia paper editorialized that, despite Torrey's apparent piety, "he is a wicked person, and had to flee from the East for lewd and licentious conduct towards the female members of the church he presided over." A Baltimore paper intimated that Torrey had had an improper relationship with his landlady's daughter. As described by Torrey himself:

> My kind landlady and the young ladies of her family, almost daily called on me, to give me a chance to breathe the fresh air, by walking a few minutes in the prison yard. . . . They were very kind to one almost a stranger. That was enough for malice to work upon. Suddenly the *young ladies* were excluded, with rude insults, from the jail yard. The reason assigned was, such gross lewdness in the sight of half a score of persons, constantly passing, as would imply in me and the lady, a degree of shameless degradation that not even rashness and drunkenness would excuse in common street walkers. . . . This shameless tale was trumpeted about the city. . . . It did me much injury in many worthy minds.

Other rumors circulating at this time, according to Torrey's published account, concerned his failing marriage and an allegation that his wife was seeking a divorce.[12]

By early September 1844, Charles Torrey's initial optimism regarding the outcome of his incarceration was waning. His lawyer had told him that chances were not good for getting his case into federal court and thus challenging the constitutionality of slaveholding. Fundraising to support his legal strategies was going much more slowly than hoped, largely because of a lack of sympathy by many abolitionists and the continued antipathy of Garrison's supporters. Torrey's public relations campaign had been undermined by rumors regarding his sexual indiscretions and his wife's possible wish for a divorce.[13]

Torrey's reaction to the accusations of "imprudence" was to aggressively defend himself. To Gerrit Smith, he wrote: "The question of my prudence I must adjourn to the Judgement Day. I *have* done, many things in the South, that prudent men *dared* not do, and probably shall again. . . . I am *bold* and *decided.* God made me so. He did not make me *cautious.* So that, while commonly successful by my boldness, when I *do* fail, half my acquaintances cry out, 'how *very* imprudent he is.'" And to Amos Phelps: "I have always been fully aware of the difference of opinion among my friends, in regard to my course: especially, my proceedings in the South. Some of them disapprove from ignorance of facts, others because men *will* differ in judgement. . . . I have neither the temper or education of one who will be called 'wise and prudent.'"[14]

Torrey dismissed the rumors regarding his landlady's daughter as baseless and, in a published account, attributed them to "a noted slave trader and two police men" who "have spared no falsehood to destroy the good name of the family in which I boarded." Given Torrey's rigid attitude toward sexual matters, the veracity of such rumors seems doubtful.[15]

The rumors regarding his wife's wish for a divorce were less easily dismissed, despite Torrey's attempts to do so. In a letter of July 28, 1844, from Torrey to Amos Phelps, marked "very private" and including instructions to "burn this private letter as soon as you have read it," Torrey indicated that he knew the identity of the writer of the "Norfolk" letter accusing him of not having supported his family. He suggested that the writer was none other than his father-in-law, Reverend Jacob Ide. As always for Torrey, the underlying problems included money, with Ide having brought suit against Torrey in March of 1844 for nonpayment of debts. This, said Torrey, "had been poisoning the peace of my house, nearly severed me from my family, and still more nearly driven me to insanity." Torrey denied to Phelps that he had not supported his family, telling him that he still owned $1,000 ($23,200) in Maine real estate that could be used, and that "the pecuniary wants of my wife and children are provided for, from Dec. 1, '43 to Dec. 1, '45." He did not say where this money was coming from; if true, the most likely source would have been Gerrit Smith, who almost certainly had been supporting Torrey's slave-stealing efforts in Washington. In any case, the fact that Torrey appears to have made no attempt to return to his family following his trip to Washington in November 1843 suggests that he was indeed having major marital problems.[16]

At this time, Charles Torrey attempted to break out of the Baltimore jail. He had considered the possibility for several weeks and had obtained the necessary tools. He had commissioned another prisoner who was being released to go to Philadelphia and obtain saws and chisels, probably from James Bias, and then bring them back to Baltimore and give them to Torrey's landlady. She then smuggled them into jail and "took them out of her bosom wrapped up in a piece of brown paper." The escape attempt almost succeeded but was betrayed at the last minute by a fellow prisoner in whom Torrey had confided. The result was that Torrey spent twelve days in irons and his trial date was moved forward from February 1845 to November 1844.[17]

It was a very depressing outcome for Torrey. Seated on the damp flooring of his jail cell, he labored to write a legible letter. The cell was "partly above ground" with "one grated window, opening to the yard." It was also, he wrote, "well supplied with rats and mice, red ants, and mosquitos." Ink had to be carried from a bottle on the floor to the paper on his lap, resulting in ubiquitous, unwelcome black splotches. But the letter had to be written, for Mary needed to hear the news directly from him.

Sept. 14, 1844

My Dearest Wife,—

I am in much affliction. When I wrote you last week, I was suffering from a fever, the effects of long and close confinement. Yesterday I made an attempt to escape, which was detected, or rather betrayed by a counterfeiter named Dryer [whose real name was later found to be Southmayd]; and myself and others put into the cells, in irons. . . . I deemed it my *duty* to try once to escape out of the hands of my enemies. But God knows best, and has ordered it otherwise.[18]

The "irons" in which he was placed consisted of a twenty-five-pound ball and chain riveted to his ankle, making it impossible for him to get to his feet without assistance from his stronger fellow prisoners, similarly ironed.[19]

Torrey remained in irons for twelve days. He wrote: "During those twelve days, my bed lay on the hard, damp floor. My linen became loathsome from filth. The air of the cell was constantly like a confined privy vault. . . . Seven of those twelve nights I slept *none,* from pain, and the utter prostration of the nervous system. The remaining nights, save one, I slept from one to four hours." On day eleven the jail physician, concerned about Torrey's deteriorating health, ordered him to be released from irons, but the guards refused to do so until the following day. Torrey was probably the most hated man in Maryland for having assisted almost four hundred slaves to escape. He had also mocked the slaveowners by naming them in his abolitionist newspaper and describing in detail how their slaves had fled to Canada. Torrey and his collaborators had publicly called the Baltimore police incompetent and "poor puppies." Now, in irons in the Baltimore jail, Torrey could expect no favors.[20]

The failed escape attempt was all the more disappointing because it had almost succeeded. According to the *Baltimore Sun,* "on examining the window one of the large upright iron bars was found cut at both the upper and lower points of its intersection with the cross bars nearly through, requiring but a little more labor to complete its removal, and to afford ample space for the egress of the prisoners." The work had been done with "a saw made from the mainspring of a watch" and "a small new gunsmith's saw" found concealed in Torrey's bed along with "four mortising chisels apparently quite new." The seriousness of the escape attempt also became clear when jail officials found a "handful of bullets and a small paper of powder" among Torrey's personal effects along with a letter he was carrying that alluded to "pistols" and "ladders." It was, noted the *Baltimore Sun,* fortunate that the escape had been foiled, "as it could scarcely by any possibility have otherwise eventuated without loss of life."[21]

The possibility of losing his life while trying to escape was not troublesome to Torrey, for he was losing his life anyway. Tuberculosis, which had afflicted him for nine years, was growing worse, with fevers and "intense pain, chiefly in the heart and brain." While chained, he made a will and wrote to his wife: "I do not feel that I have long to live."[22]

Torrey published an attempted justification for his attempted jail break, listing among other things his illness and his belief that he would not get a fair trial. But he realized that the escape attempt had been a mistake, since it made him appear to be guilty of a crime he had denied having committed and further weakened his support among other abolitionists. Even his closest friend, Amos Phelps, did not write to him for two months. Gerrit Smith, who had been sympathetic to Torrey's slave-freeing efforts and was the single biggest source of his fiscal support, deemed the escape attempt a great mistake. And Lewis Tappan, who was the other major donor to abolitionist causes, was so exasperated with Torrey that Torrey concluded Tappan probably hated him.[23]

The two months following his failed jailbreak, as he awaited trial, were dark days for Charles Torrey. He took some solace in the fact that other abolitionists appeared to be following his lead by aggressively freeing slaves. For example, in July 1844, Jonathan Walker, a Massachusetts sea captain, had been arrested off the coast of Florida with seven slaves he was taking to freedom in the British Bahamas. He was imprisoned, and his hand branded with the letters "S.S." for slave stealer, a branding that made him an abolitionist celebrity for the rest of his life. In September, Calvin Fairbank and Delia Webster had been arrested in Kentucky for helping three slaves escape to Ohio. One of the escaping slaves, Lewis Hayden, had been traded "for a pair of carriage horses" by his master; Hayden would later become a leading abolitionist in Boston. Fairbank, a former Oberlin student, had been assisting slaves to get to free states for seven years and was sentenced to fifteen years in prison. Noting these arrests, Torrey commented approvingly that "slave prisons were filling up."[24]

In mid-November, Torrey became more depressed when he learned that Abel Brown had died on November 8, one day prior to his thirty-fourth birthday. Brown had been giving abolitionist lectures throughout western New York State when he had become caught up in a snowstorm, ill with pneumonia, and then died from "dropsy of the brain" after an illness of three days. His death ensured that, even if Torrey was able to regain his freedom, it would be very difficult to reconstruct the Washington to Albany line that had been such a successful part of the Underground Railroad.[25]

For brief periods during his pre-trial period, Torrey entertained flickering hopes that he might be found not guilty. He was encouraged when he learned that Thomas Southmayd, the prisoner who had betrayed him and was scheduled to testify against him, had spent three years in prison for horse theft and thus might not be considered a credible witness. He was also encouraged when he was told that two witnesses had been bribed to testify against him; he wrote to Gerrit Smith in mid-November that "I am quite in hopes of an acquittal on the Maryland charges." Torrey's hopes also revived on rumors that William Heckrotte, the owner of the Maryland slaves Torrey was charged with stealing, might entertain an offer of a cash settlement of $4,000 ($92,500) in exchange for dropping the charges. Torrey probably hoped that Smith would offer to put up the money, but that apparently did not happen.[26]

The other possible source of such money was a "Torrey martyr fund," which was being collected by many people and sent to Lewis Tappan. In October, Torrey wrote Tappan asking that the funds be turned over to him to be used to get his case into federal court. Tappan had severely criticized Torrey for abducting slaves from southern states and for attempting to break out of jail. Relations between the two men had been cool since 1840, when Torrey had borrowed money from Tappan and then been very slow in paying it back. Tappan thus refused to send Torrey the money from the fund. Later it was revealed that Tappan had previously discussed the disposition of the funds with Dr. Ide, Torrey's father-in-law, and that they had agreed that the funds should go to Mary and the children for their support. According to a letter from Tappan to Amos Phelps, Torrey replied to Tappan's refusal to send him the money by writing "one of the most abusive letters I ever saw. It is a curiosity. Can he be a sane man?" After receiving another abusive letter from Torrey, Tappan wrote Phelps again: "I must believe that Torrey is insane."[27]

Torrey's letters to Lewis Tappan have apparently been destroyed, so it is not possible to assess the rationality of the writer. Torrey was desperate to get his case into federal court and to get out of jail, and he was apparently fighting with his wife and father-in-law as well. In such circumstances, it is understandable why he would have wanted the funds to be sent directly to him.

Since Tappan's letter regarding Torrey's alleged insanity has been quoted by some historians, it is worth considering the allegation.

It is clear that Torrey's tuberculosis had not only recurred at this time but had probably spread to his brain. In September he complained of being "brain fevered," having an "aching brain," and "intense pain, chiefly in the heart and brain." He was aware that his mind was "wandering strangely" and at one point said, "I am not quite crazy tonight." Such symptoms are consistent with a cerebral form of tuberculosis that has been rarely seen since the introduction of anti-tuberculosis drugs but was common in the nineteenth century. If Charles Torrey really was exhibiting irrational thinking in the last months of his life, cerebral tuberculosis must be considered as a possible explanation.[28]

As the days wound down toward his trial, Torrey wrote to many of his friends, thanking them for their support, financial and otherwise. He was especially grateful to Amos Phelps, of whom he said, "I love and trust more than *all* men living," and he asked Phelps to especially look after his son. As he turned thirty-one a week before his trial, he wrote that, since his conviction and imprisonment would "entirely prevent the trial before the Supreme Court," he therefore considered "that nearly every useful purpose of my imprisonment, to *the cause,* is lost." Similarly, he wrote to Amos Phelps: "I never had any very high esteem for Dr. All Talk or Esq. Resolution. And aside from what agitation I can make out of my *trial,* with a bold defense, I view my usefulness as about at an end: my life, indeed, for any really valuable ends, must close with my consignment to the Penitentiary." In closing, however, Torrey added with pride, "I have, I suppose, given freedom to more individual slaves than any white man now living in our country."[29]

Charles Torrey's trial opened on Friday, November 29, at the Baltimore Courthouse. A local newspaper predicted that it would "prove one of the most important and exciting trials ever had in this country." The proceedings had to compete for newspaper space with the heated campaigning for the presidential election, scheduled to be held the following week, on December 4. In attendance at the trial were Mary Torrey and her father, Dr. Ide. This was the first time Torrey had seen his wife in a year. To most friends, Torrey wrote how happy he was to see "my beloved wife." However, to his closest friend,

Amos Phelps, he wrote: "This week I am, or try to be, very happy in the society of my dear wife. She and her father will remain till all this is over, and I am safe in prison."[30]

For his trial, Torrey's friends hired Reverdy Johnson to defend him. A highly regarded Maryland lawyer and prominent Whig, Johnson was at that time aggressively lobbying the Maryland legislature to be appointed to the U.S. Senate. Three months later, he was appointed and four years later became the U.S. Attorney General. With Torrey's characteristic candor, he confessed to Johnson "that he had once aided one of that gentleman's slaves to escape." Charles Cleveland, Torrey's prominent supporter in Philadelphia, wrote on Torrey's behalf to Judge Nisbet, who was his wife's uncle and one of the three judges presiding over Torrey's trial.[31]

Twelve male jurors were impaneled for the three-day trial. George Richardson, Maryland state attorney, presented the prosecution's case over a day and a half. Torrey was charged with having enticed, persuaded, and assisted three slaves to escape from William Heckrotte, who operated a tavern at the corner of Charles and Camden Streets. The slaves were a woman, Hannah Gooseberry, and her teenage children, Judah and Stephen; all three disappeared on the evening of June 4.[32]

Mr. Richardson first put Mr. Heckrotte on the stand; he testified that one evening in late May he had seen a white man, whom he believed to be Mr. Torrey, talking to Judah Gooseberry next to his tavern. Next to testify was Nicholas Woodward, who said that on June 4 he had rented two horses with distinctive coloring and a carriage to Mr. Torrey. George Rigdon, who lived near Deer Creek, on the road between Baltimore and the Pennsylvania state line, was then sworn. He testified that on June 7, between 5 and 6 in the morning, he had crossed the Deer Creek bridge en route to his brother's house. He said he clearly saw Torrey and the slaves in question eating breakfast and also watering and feeding their horses at the edge of the creek. Several days later, Rigdon saw an ad in the newspaper for the runaway slaves, so Samuel Rigdon, his brother, wrote a letter for him to the authorities in Baltimore. Robert Rigdon was certain of his identification because the woman was missing a front tooth, just as was said of Hannah Gooseberry. George Amos, who lived near

Rigdon, also saw Torrey and the slaves going north, and Benjamin Amos saw Torrey returning. In addition, Samuel Rigdon testified that, at a place where Torrey and the slaves had stopped to eat, he had found "some fragments of Bologna sausages" and wrappers for crackers identical to the crackers served in Heckrotte's tavern. He also found some pieces of ribbon, which he "took home to a little daughter." A member of Mr. Heckrotte's household testified that the ribbon matched the ribbon that had been used to trim Judah Gooseberry's bonnet a few weeks previous. Three other men testified they had seen Torrey on this road on other days carrying black people in a carriage toward Pennsylvania.

The final evidence was given by Thomas Southmayd, the prisoner who had betrayed Torrey. He testified that Torrey had told him that he had indeed persuaded Mr. Heckrotte's slaves to run away and in addition had taken "eight or nine from one man" and "three slaves from one Mr. Patterson" and "that he had taken so many away from this State that he could not tell me how many he had taken." Southmayd also related details of Torrey's operation, such as that he used "a house at the back of Greenmount cemetery" as a meeting place for the slaves and that "Torrey had got them to Pennsylvania in the neighborhood of Peachbottom."

As Torrey's lawyer, Reverdy Johnson faced a daunting task. Not only was the evidence of Torrey's guilt overwhelming but, by having published in the *Albany Patriot* his columns "Notes of Southern Travel by a Negro Stealer," Torrey had publicly advertised his guilt even though the columns had not been signed. Johnson attempted to cast doubt on Heckrotte's identification of Torrey and brought in a character witness to cast aspersions on Thomas Southmayd's veracity. But mostly he talked in general terms for almost three hours, as described by the *Baltimore Sun,* with a "powerful, eloquent, noble vindication of his client . . . [a] magnificent exordium with which he held the immense multitude, which crowded to overflow the spacious court room, spell bound in breathless silence." He had agreed to defend Torrey, he said, because he was aware that Torrey's previous 1842 arrest in Annapolis had "left his name behind, and prejudice had fastened upon it as a fit subject for animadversion," so he wanted to be sure that Torrey received "a fair and impartial trial."

Johnson's defense "commenced with an allusion to the institution of slavery, and with a strong, though carefully guarded language, drew the distinction between its moral and legal existence. He referred to it as the dreaded cause of civil strife, its agitation the frequent cause of servile war. . . . As a mere subject of political economy, as a matter of dollars and cents, Maryland would be infinitely richer if the whole system of slavery could be brought rightfully to an end. *Rightfully* he said. To be done with the law, not against the law."

Johnson also reviewed Torrey's character. He is "not an ordinary culprit," he said, but rather "a graduate with honor in one of the first Universities in the land," and his life had been "devoted to the study of Heaven's law." Johnson also extolled Torrey's wife, whom he noted "is now within the sound of my voice." "In all the mental accomplishments with which woman can be endowed, in all the loveliness of moral character for which her sex in its greatest perfection is noted, she can compare, and compare well, with any other woman within the limits of our country. She has come here to witness the trial of this husband in whom all her affections are centered. She has come to be present at the probably adverse termination of this trial. She has come—if such be the law and the evidence—to see him the last time before he is incarcerated within the walls of a prison." After Johnson had thus essentially conceded Torrey's guilt, the court was adjourned late on Saturday afternoon until Monday, for the prosecutor's closing statement.

On Monday, "the hall of the court house was quite thronged . . . previous to the opening of the doors. . . . Within two minutes after the doors were opened, the court room was thronged in every part." The crowd was "composed of the most respectable of our fellow citizens," including "the Hon. Mr. Pratt, Governor elect of Maryland."

Mr. Richardson first advised the jury that they should decide the case "upon the law and the facts" only. The case was not about slavery, he said, but rather about the alleged theft of three slaves. "It is not for you to consider the relations of private life which may exist with regard to this prisoner; nor are you to investigate those feelings which may actuate him, as supposed to emanate from God." Even "though the disunion of this confederacy be the results of your verdict, you cannot sever yourself from the obligations which you have respectively assumed."

Richardson then reviewed in detail each piece of evidence that pointed to Torrey's guilt, after which he asked: "If evidence could be demanded for the conviction of any man, stronger than this, I am unable to determine what the strength of testimony is." In closing, he looked directly at Torrey and said: "Are not the laws of the land, and the magistrates by whom they are administered, to be respected? Am I to be told that the man who lives in the constant violation of the laws of the land, is doing his duty? Vain man! Who told you that God's ordinances are higher than the laws of man? Who made you the judge of your fellows? In this country, from the Supreme court down to the lowest tribunal, the institution in question has had sanction and protection."

Following the prosecutor's two-hour summation, the jury retired to deliberate. They returned in one hour and forty minutes and announced that they had found Torrey guilty on all counts.

8

PRISON AND DEATH

Charles Torrey fully expected the guilty verdict handed down by the jury members on December 2, 1844. In the weeks preceding his trial, he had thought about what more he might accomplish in whatever time remained to him and had focused on two goals: first, to justify his past actions, and second, to raise funds to pay his lawyer's fees, pursue additional legal options, and support his family. To achieve these goals, he sent a long letter to the *Boston Morning Chronicle* on December 3, the day after the trial ended.

The first part of Torrey's letter reviewed the trial and claimed that much of the testimony against him had been perjured, although there is no indication that this was the case. He made efforts to discredit the damaging testimony of Thomas Southmayd, the prisoner in whom Torrey had mistakenly confided and who had then testified against him. Torrey added, however, that he forgave those who had testified untruthfully against him. Although none who knew Torrey doubted his guilt, his claim that he had been convicted only because of perjured testimony was widely reported. For example, in a memorial published in the *Emancipator* after his death, it was said that "Mr. Torrey never saw those slaves [he was accused of stealing] nor did he know there were any such slaves, until some days after they had run away, when he accidentally met with them on their way to the North, and assisted them." Nine years later, William Goodell, in *Slavery and Anti-Slavery*, wrote that Torrey "was convicted, as he affirmed, on evidence of perjured witnesses, who testified that they saw what they did not see." By 1855, even accounts of the antislavery movement published in England included an allegation that Torrey "was found guilty on the perjured testimony of the witnesses suborned to establish the charge."[1]

Torrey attempted to raise funds in a variety of ways. First, he wrote a 255-page autobiography, penned between December 8 and 20, as he awaited sentencing. On the title page, it was noted that the book was "written during his incarceration in Baltimore Jail, after his conviction, and while awaiting his sentence," and that it was being "published for the benefit of his family." The book was thus a fund-raiser and appears to have been largely ignored. Titled *Home! Or the Pilgrim's Faith Revived* (1845), the book included an odd assortment of childhood memories, accounts of the sins of his youthful acquaintances, a jeremiad on the decline of formal religion, and admonitions on the importance of living a strict Christian life so as to be ready to enter heaven. In the preface, Torrey described the book's "plot" as "simply the decline of spiritual religion in a Puritan church and its revival." Throughout the book, he challenged readers to live their lives as Jesus did: "A parting word. Reader. Is this world *your Home*? Our Lord Jesus Christ, will one day come with ten thousands of his saints; are you so forming a character like His, that he 'will be admired *in you*, in that day?'" In the autobiography, Torrey implicitly said that he had done his best to meet this standard, and in his letter to the *Boston Morning Chronicle*, he made this explicit: "Do you ask, 'Have you any thing to *regret*, in what you have done, whether for individual slaves, or the *cause* of freedom?' *No*, from the bottom of my heart, NO! According to the light given me, and the degree of physical and mental powers I possessed, I have labored faithfully, and as wisely as I knew how."[2]

Torrey also attempted to raise funds by portraying himself as a man worthy of sympathy: "Years will probably elapse before I shall again see cheerful faces, and hear any of the happy voices of infancy, or the tones of my own dear children. Even *they*, if I *live*, will have forgotten their father's features, even if love preserves his memory. . . . Sometimes I am anxious about my own dear wife and children. But I leave them in God's hands, confident that he will be better than father and husband to them. To-night my wife parted from me—not to meet again, perhaps—I say, *probably*, while we live. God bless her!" And in what must have caused great amusement among his friends, Torrey presented himself in the newspaper as the great conciliator and peacemaker among the warring abolitionist factions:

> From this jail, I *entreat* the different classes of abolitionists
> to lay aside "all wrath, clamor, and evil speaking" of each
> other; to "*love* as brethren," if their differing judgments will

not always allow them to *labor* together. Let each in his own way, work for the slave, without finding fault with each other's plans, or suspecting each other's spirit or faithfulness. As to the "old" and "new" organizations, the Liberty party and the [Garrison] non-voting party, I solemnly declare my conviction that *one heart, one spirit, one object, one purpose* animates, not only the "leaders," but the entire mass of both parties, with no more individual exceptions than we find wherever human infirmity is connected with, and striving for, any good and noble end.

Remarkably, in his December 3, 1844, letter, Torrey even referred to William Lloyd Garrison as "that noble man—whom, with all his faults, we love and honor still." Four months earlier, Torrey had made a similar overture to Garrison, writing to one of Garrison's closest friends that "personally, I feel greatly indebted for the magnanimous part he [Garrison] has taken." Although some historians have interpreted such overtures as Torrey's having had a change of heart toward Garrison, it seems much more likely that they simply reflect the stark reality facing Torrey and the fact that he was now dependent on the fiscal generosity of *all* abolitionist factions.[3]

Torrey's friends at this time redoubled their efforts to raise funds for him. To make the "martyr fund" more attractive to donors, the fund was enlarged to include Jonathan Walker, Alanson Work, and other abolitionists who, like Torrey, had been sentenced to prison for abducting slaves. The *Emancipator* and other abolitionist newspapers ran appeals for donations, including one appeal from Torrey himself dated December 23, 1844. Typical of the positive responses was a letter from Nathaniel Colver, a Boston abolitionist who had been part of Torrey's breakaway abolitionist faction: "I believe that Walker, Torrey, Work, and others who are now suffering in southern prisons, are there for having done their duty. . . . They have imprisoned Torrey, but his spirit is yet abroad—it will cry, To the rescue! in the ears of all the good. It will haunt the guilty oppressor with ceaseless alarm. In the moaning of the night wind, it shall scream to his ear the yell to the onslaught. It shall rattle death groans from his very window shutters. . . . The families of these noble men must not suffer."[4]

Despite such appeals, the martyr fund increased slowly. Garrison and his supporters were not impressed by Torrey's disingenuous adulation and not inclined to support anything that might help get him out of prison. Garrison's supporters also viewed it as an opportunity to publicize Torrey's shortcomings, especially his failure as a husband and provider. For example: "Why did he not, when engaged in this low business of smuggling negroes, think of his lovely wife, on whom his conduct has inflicted a hundred deaths? If negro stealing was to be his business, he should not have dragged [an] innocent and delicate woman into the miseries which it entails." Torrey was, one letter said, "a piece of walking moral carrion."⁵

Ironically, the days immediately following Torrey's trial might have been among the happiest of his life. On December 3, the day following the trial, seventy-seven-year-old John Quincy Adams introduced a resolution in Congress to formally and permanently rescind the so-called gag rule that had effectively limited congressional discussion of slavery. The motion carried 108–80. The *New York Tribune* editorialized: "The Gag-Rule Abolished. Let every lover of freedom rejoice," and the abolitionists did so.⁶

On the following day, December 4, the presidential election was held; thereafter, the date for the election was permanently set for early November. The Democratic candidate, James Polk, narrowly defeated the Whig candidate, Henry Clay. The Liberty Party candidate, James Birney, received 68,000 votes, less than 3 percent of the total, but this was sufficient to tip the election in New York State, where Birney got 15,812 votes and Clay lost by only 5,082 votes. If Clay had won New York State, he would have become president. The Liberty Party, with its single-theme abolitionist platform, had effectively determined the outcome of the national election and had thereby become a political force, to the delight of the political abolitionists. Even Garrison, much to his chagrin, admitted that the Liberty Party had been the deciding factor. To make matters even worse for Garrison, the Liberty Party did especially well in Massachusetts, where it received over 8 percent of the vote. In Essex County the party received one-third of the vote, and in towns such as Amesbury, "Liberty office seekers got 46 percent of the vote in 1844." Since Torrey had played a major role in organizing the Liberty Party in

Massachusetts, and especially in Essex County, these victories must have been bittersweet as he sat in his jail cell, forcibly removed from the fray.[7]

On Friday, December 27, Charles Torrey was sentenced to six years in the Maryland Penitentiary, two years for each of his three indictments. On the following day, he was transferred across the street from the jail to the state prison and registered on the prison log as having been convicted of "enticing slaves to run away (3 indictments)." He was one of 265 male and female inmates in a prison that had been opened in 1811. It was, according to a later prison survey, "one of the best managed and most successful in the country both morally and financially." All prisoners worked, the majority in manufacturing cotton and woolen goods, and the prison was financially self-supporting. Considered by many to be a model prison, it was visited twice by prison reformer Dorothea Dix during Torrey's first six months there, although it is not known whether the two met. A. I. W. Jackson, reputed to having been harsh, was the warden when Torrey arrived, but six weeks later he was replaced by William Johnson, whom Torrey described as kind and considerate. The officers of the prison were also described by Torrey as "gentlemen," not like the "brutes and tyrants" who ran the jail.[8]

Torrey's brick cell was eight feet long and four feet wide with a four-inch window. It was equipped with only a bed, "water-can and bucket." He wore flannel prison clothing, including "a skull-cap of cotton cloth, of different colors." There were no candles or other lighting in the cells except the small window, so "from dark to daylight . . . we are in our cells without any lights." Torrey worked as a warper in the section for clothing manufacturing; "the warping machine is turned by a crank, which is kept in motion by one hand while the yarn is adjusted with the other." When not working, he was allowed to write letters and read, although all mail and books were censored by the warden. He also wrote letters for other prisoners, becoming "a sort of general amanuensis." To occupy his time, he planned "to acquire at least *one* new language a year," and he asked his wife to send him an Italian dictionary to begin."[9]

Torrey's initial months in prison were reasonably tolerable. His tuberculosis appeared to be in temporary remission, and he was able to work, write, read, and receive visitors. Joshua Leavitt, editor of the *Emancipator*, was especially attentive, as illustrated by what was probably the first letter Torrey received after being transferred to the prison:

Jan. 1, 1845

Dear Torrey,—I wish you a happy new year! "Strange saluta-tion," you say, for a poor prisoner, clad in sackcloth, fed on the coarsest food, cut off from society, and even from liter-ary delights, and bending his feeble frames to *hard labor* in a penitentiary. But why, my dear Charles, should you not have a happy new year? Let those be unhappy who have committed crime. Let those be unhappy who have no hope in our atoning, and interceding, and present Savior.... And may each return-ing new year's day, which brings nearer and nearer the over-throw of slavery, not only in Maryland, but throughout our country, make the remembrances sweeter and sweeter to your soul, that you have done what you could, to bring it about.

Gerrit Smith also maintained close contact, assuring Torrey "you are much in my thoughts" and "you need have no concern that your wife and children will not be provided for." He encouraged Torrey:

If, my dear brother, you are fully and sweetly resigned to all the Lord's will, then it is "well with you," and all these things that you are called to suffer are "light afflictions." So you have preached—so you have called on others to feel—and so, I trust, you now feel yourself. God is emphatically testing you. He is trying whether you will learn, in your own person, the re-duction to practice of your own preaching. God's grace is suffi-cient to make your cell, your toil, and all your privations, dear and precious to you. This you believed, before your confine-ment—and this, I hope, you are now experiencing the truth of.

Amos Phelps visited Torrey and also made efforts to secure writing jobs for Torrey's wife, who was an accomplished writer and in need of the funds. Torrey had recognized his wife's talents, calling her "second to no female writer of our country, in *prose*," and in a letter to her added: "It has been one of the dearest hopes of my life, that I might place you in a situation to devote your time freely to literary pursuits. . . . Little did I think *my prison* would be your only aid in your career."[10]

This letter, however, and the entire published correspondence between Charles Torrey and his wife must be viewed in a particular light. While Torrey was in jail awaiting trial, Joshua Leavitt and other friends had proposed collecting his letters and publishing them to raise additional funds. The letters between Torrey and his wife thus have a stilted quality, often saying things they thought they should say to elicit sympathy and support. Here, for example, are two letters from Torrey's wife:

> January 15, 1845: Our dear children often weep, when they speak of their dear father, and anxiously inquire "how long will it be before father will come home?" And when I present the motive of their father's approbation, as an incentive to good conduct, I find it one of the most powerful means to induce them to do well.

> February, no date, 1845: I wish sometimes that you could look into our room, and see Charles and Mary with your miniature. They take it and talk to it, carry it about, and really seem sometimes as though they thought you had returned. It is a great comfort, I assure you, to have it, and especially as it is such a good one.

At the time, the children were ages five and seven and had not seen their father in over two years. The intent to publish such letters was also made explicit by Torrey and his wife when they specified in some letters that certain parts should not be published. In fact, the plan to publish the letters was never carried out, although some of them were included in Lovejoy's *Memoir,* published after Torrey's death.[11]

Torrey's initial months in prison were alleviated somewhat by encomiums. David Ruggles, a prominent black New York abolitionist, noted that "some *soi-desant* friends of Mr. Torrey have said he was rash and imprudent. This charge is ever made against the faithful and true in the cause of humanity." Torrey, Ruggles said, was not imprudent but rather simply braver than other abolitionists. The *Albany Patriot* added that "one hundred like Torrey would do more to deliver the slaves speedily than all paper resolutions, speeches, presses, and votes."[12]

Torrey also followed with great interest the events in Congress, especially those involving his friend Joshua Giddings. On February 6, Giddings was, as usual, speaking against slavery when Representative Edward Black of Georgia "began screaming insults at Giddings, while delivering one of the most vicious and unprovoked personal attacks ever heard on the floor of the House." Black accused Giddings of being "interested in the horses which . . . Torrey lost when attempting to aid slaves to escape in Maryland." Giddings replied that "he knew nothing but what he had seen in the newspapers." Black, screaming loudly, told Giddings that he should "go home" to Ohio or he would "knock him down in his tracks." Giddings replied that "the people I represent did not send a coward here," adding, "I have never seen an infernal coward who did not talk loud."

Black, now enraged, advanced toward Giddings with cane upraised. Unperturbed, Giddings continued his antislavery remarks. Black was then joined by John Dawson, representative of Louisiana, who had assaulted Giddings previously and who reached in his pocket, loudly cocking his pistol, and said, "I'll shoot him, by God I'll shoot him!" Two other southern congressmen joined Black and Dawson, while four northern congressmen, at least one of them armed, took positions next to Giddings, who continued speaking. Black and the other slaveholders, realizing "the awkwardness of their position, quietly returned to their seats" and, after Giddings finished, "the business of the legislation was then resumed."[13]

Another event that Torrey found of great interest occurred in July 1845, when a group of Maryland slaves armed themselves and started marching north. They were met by armed men in Gaithersburg, just north of Washington. There followed "a pitched battle in which several slaves were killed" and the "slave rebellion" broken. Some leaders were imprisoned and others sold south, but the damage had been done. A Baltimore newspaper lamented that "slave property in Maryland is becoming utterly worthless. . . . In a few years more, Maryland will be numbered among the free states." This, of course, was exactly the result Torrey had hoped to bring about by his activities.[14]

Sitting in prison, Torrey also received news from Amos Phelps and other friends concerning the activities of William Lloyd Garrison and his followers. During 1845, Garrison was continuing to edit the *Liberator* and give speeches to abolitionist groups. Freeing individual slaves and electing abolitionist officials would accomplish nothing, Garrison said, until a moral revolution changed the hearts of slaveholders. It would be better, Garrison said, for the North and South to simply split into separate countries. Torrey was especially amused when he heard in 1845 that Abby Kelley, his old adversary, had married Stephen Foster, another Garrison supporter who was adamantly anti-clerical. Like Kelley, Foster "undertook a personal campaign of church disruption. . . . he would often cap his charges with the well-honed accusation that by allowing thousands of slave women to be held in concubinage, the church was worse than any brothel." The result was that "Foster had been ejected from twenty-four churches, twice from the second story, and jailed four times." Torrey and Phelps agreed that Abby Kelley and Stephen Foster were a perfect match.[15]

Beginning in mid-1845, the lights began to dim for Charles Torrey. His tuberculosis returned in force, involving his brain, and he was moved to the prison hospital. In a September letter to his wife, he said that for three months

> I have not been, for two days at a time, free from excruciating pain in the head, with occasional severe pains in the heart, accompanied by general weakness in the system. You will not think it very strange therefore, that I have not been able to write a connected letter for many weeks past, at least, for five or six. Other causes, before that, delayed my doing so. My mental energy, and sanity, have been much affected by such long continued pain in the brain; so that very often, for three months past, I have been obliged to struggle to repress the impulse to utter insane ravings, and even wicked follies which my whole soul abhors. Most of the time I have very little

control over my thoughts. If a painful idea takes possession of the mind, it is as if a rough iron was drawn over the brain, for whole hours, and even days at a time. . . . Last Sabbath I tried to write, but my efforts produced bad English and nonsense. To-day, a state of nervous excitement *only* short of absolute insanity, enables me to write easier, so far, though, for the week past, my mind has been generally more crazed and unsettled than before. I know at times, I exhibit a pitiable degree of weakness and imbecility to those around me.

A visitor at this time described Torrey as "pale, emaciated and sick. . . . his eyes are dim, his voice hoarse, his spirits depressed, and to me he appeared as one not long to be held by the massive walls of iron and granite that now surround him." Torrey acknowledged "that I shall die here," because of "the seeds of disease sown in my feeble frame."[16]

By this time, Torrey had given up hope of being released from prison. He reflected on his life: "Playmates of my childhood! where are ye now? One lies in the fathomless depths of old ocean. . . . Some are toiling for wealth and honor in the crowded marts of the cities and villages. . . . Many live in honor and usefulness. Some have been laid in the grave of shame. . . . Happy boys we were then; little dreaming of the future that might await us; what opinions of morals, politics, religion we would cherish; what labors and toils for ourselves or others we should perform or endure." He was indeed enduring, and remembering the many "labors and toils" that had led him from the sylvan settings of Scituate to his immuration in a Maryland prison.[17]

By this time, Torrey also recognized that he would die a martyr's death. He had previously claimed to be "one who is so little disposed to be a martyr," yet also noted, "I find the road to Jesus shorter from the prison floor." To his wife, he wrote: "If I am to suffer, it is a great consolation to know, that it will not be in vain; that Providence will use even my sufferings to overthrow, more speedily, the accursed system that enslaves and degrades so many millions of the poor of our land." Having been raised in a strict Puritan tradition, the concept of martyrdom was familiar to Torrey. John Foxe's *Book of Martyrs* "came second only to the English Bible in influence upon the

Puritan spirit. . . . All the Puritans read it, imbibing the values of the author as spiritual mother's milk." There, for example, was a picture of William Tyndale being burned at the stake for having translated the Bible into English. Charles Torrey had not actively sought Martyrdom as such, although he had found her attractive. Rather, by his impetuous actions he had courted her sister, Disaster, aware that Martyrdom sometimes kept her sister company.[18]

Ever since Torrey's sentencing, his friends, family, and lawyer, Asa Child, had discussed ways to get him pardoned by the governor of Maryland. An initial plan was to have Torrey recant and say that he had been wrong to induce slaves to run away from their owners. This plan was firmly rejected by Torrey: "I am *not poor* enough yet, though a penniless prisoner, to sell my cherished principles for liberty. . . . How can I assent to doctrines to which my heart, my conscience, and my matured judgment . . . led me to reject as opposed to the Bible and to right reason? . . . Shall I, for the sake of escaping a prison for the short remnant of my life, do an act so basely selfish as to sign what I believe Christ abhors? . . . It is better to die in prison, with the peace of God in our hearts, than to live in freedom, with a polluted conscience." A second plan was to have Torrey promise, if granted a pardon, that he would "*never go into those States for that purpose again.*" This Torrey agreed to, telling his wife that "so far as my return to the South, with reference to aiding slaves to escape, I have no hesitation in saying, that I have no purpose, plan, wish or intention to do so, in case of my release from that imprisonment to which perjury consigned me."[19]

Despite their marital problems, Mary Torrey continued to strongly support her husband's principles and public stand. One week following his sentencing, she wrote a detailed exegesis, later published, on why the laws of God should take precedence over the laws of men: "Who will say it is a crime, if the laws of the South had not made it so, to render assistance to a poor creature, who implores your aid to prevent his being sold to the far South, from wife and children, or become the victim of his master's ungoverned passions? . . . But those *laws*, I repeat, I would analyze with the dissecting knife of truth, till their true nature and obligation were felt, as they will be felt in the light of eternity." And she fully endorsed her husband's refusal to say that he had been wrong as a condition for a pardon: "I am not willing my husband should humble himself before the States of Maryland and Virginia. They have injured, insulted and abused him long enough. They have tried to destroy his character, and now [that] they have not been able to do it, they mean to compel him to do it himself, by forfeiting his integrity in order to be free."[20]

The problem with *any* plan for having Charles Torrey pardoned, however, was that the governor, Thomas Pratt, would have to agree to it. Pratt was a native Marylander, the son of a slaveholding family, who had been educated at Georgetown University and Princeton University (then known as the College of New Jersey) and then studied law. In 1838 he had been elected to the Maryland Senate, and in 1844, at age forty, he had been elected governor by a narrow margin of 548 votes. In the days between the election and assuming office, Pratt had attended the final day of Charles Torrey's trial, so he had a firsthand understanding of the charges against him.[21]

The impediments to Governor Pratt's granting of a pardon were many. He was a staunch proslavery southerner who would support secession of the South at the beginning of the Civil War. His son would fight for the Confederacy. Pratt's most serious political problem when he had become governor was a disagreement between Maryland and Pennsylvania over that state's refusal to return fugitive slaves, and Pratt later estimated "that not less than $80,000 [$1.6 million] worth of slaves was lost every year by citizens" of Maryland. But the most serious problem was that Torrey was probably the most hated man in Maryland; not only had he stolen slaves, but he had publicly taunted and ridiculed the slaveowners. Torrey himself acknowledged "that the feeling, in certain quarters, is *exceedingly* bitter against me." For a politically ambitious man like Pratt—he would later become a U.S. senator—granting a pardon to Torrey was not likely to enhance his political future.[22]

As Torrey's health declined in the autumn of 1845, efforts to obtain a pardon intensified. Prominent in these efforts were his wife; father-in-law; Amos Phelps; Joshua Leavitt; and Charles Cleveland, Torrey's friend in Philadelphia. Torrey's lawyer, Asa Child, was intermittently hopeful for a pardon and encouraged such efforts, but Mary and her father decided that Child was incompetent, suggesting to Phelps that he be fired. Mary also submitted a petition to Governor Pratt asking for a pardon "as a wife, whose heart bleeds with sorrow for one she loves." She admitted that her husband "assisted two slaves who had previously run away . . . although my husband did not know to whom they belonged at the time," and she guaranteed that "my husband will never [again] visit your State for that purpose." Mary got forty people to sign the petition, including two Massachusetts ex-governors, the Massachusetts Speaker of the House and president of the Senate, "and many other gentlemen of high standing for character, talents, integrity and judgment."[23]

During the period of most intense negotiations for Torrey's release, between December 1845 and March 1846, Amos Phelps made three trips to Baltimore, variously accompanied by poet and abolitionist John Greenleaf Whittier, Charles Cleveland, and Torrey's father-in-law. One issue being negotiated was how much money Heckrotte would require as compensation for his stolen slaves in order to recommend a pardon to Governor Pratt; the final figure was $3,200 to $3,300 ($76,800 to $79,200). Another issue was what would happen to the outstanding slave-stealing charges against Torrey in Virginia if Maryland pardoned him. Finally, there was the issue of Governor Pratt, whose friends hinted that he might consider a pardon but who himself said nothing. For a brief period in December 1845, it appeared that a pardon might be feasible, and Torrey wrote excitedly to his wife that "the preliminary arrangements for my release have all been made as successfully as could be desired. . . . There is no great reason to doubt a favorable result." However, he advised her that, "if released, I shall be compelled to travel slowly; at least, to rest a couple of days each in Philadelphia, New York, and New Haven, or Albany. . . . I have business, chiefly legal in each place." Even on what was essentially his death bed, Charles Torrey's priorities were clear, despite his not having seen his children or elderly grandmother in more than two years.[24]

However, it soon became clear that obtaining a pardon for Torrey would be impossible. During their visit to Baltimore in early March

1846, Amos Phelps and Reverend Ide met with Heckrotte and Governor Pratt. Heckrotte had lost interest in any payment from Torrey's friends because he had been told that the Maryland Legislature would reimburse him for his loss. Governor Pratt, according to Ide, "coolly deferred the whole subject until April," when he said he would present the issue to a grand jury for their opinion. When Ide returned to the prison to tell his son-in-law what Governor Pratt had said, Torrey "burst into tears." It seems probable that Governor Pratt never intended to pardon Torrey. According to one account, "the Governor told his father-in-law (Dr. Ide) that '*he could with more safety pardon two murderers*'" than pardon Torrey.[25]

The curtain had risen on Charles Torrey's last act. He lay in the prison hospital, "a large room occupied at present by ten patients." According to a visitor in April, he "could not hold up his head," "it was with extreme difficulty that he could talk," and "his countenance is ghastly in the extreme." All agreed that his life expectancy was a matter of weeks, and eulogies and recriminations began to appear in the *Emancipator*:

> When his spirit, which has already plumed its wings for an immortal flight, and is even now fluttering in its cage, shall burst the bands of clay and wing its way from the midst of the prison walls and grated doors of the lonely cell, attended by good angels to the Throne of the Eternal, Christ shall say unto him, "Forasmuch as ye did it unto one of the least of these my brethren, ye did it unto me." "Enter thou into the joy of the Lord."
>
> And now should Mr. Torrey die in prison, as most probable he must, in the skirts of whose garments will be found his blood?—Where rests the responsibility of American slavery, there will be found the dark stain. Should he die, his blood like that of Abel, will cry for vengeance, not only from the prison of Baltimore, but from the primary assemblies of the people, from our ballot-boxes, from our senate chambers and halls of legislation, from the Congress of these United States, and from the pulpit too; —every freeman and every Christian who

has not done all in his power to abolish this system of abominations, must plead guilty to the charge of Charles T. Torrey's murder!

Governor Pratt was publicly consigned by Torrey's supporters "to posterity side by side with Nero, Caligula, Herod, Pilate, Judas Iscariot, and such other moral monsters as have from time to time . . . cursed humanity with their presence."[26]

Mrs. Ide, Mary's mother, wrote Torrey a final letter. "My Dear Son," she said, "If you have truly made your peace with God, death must be to you the gate of glory." Mary was said to be in poor health and unable to travel, but then at the last minute she was said to feel a little better and "anxious to see her husband while he is alive and to have a private interview with him." Time, however, usurped any such plans.[27]

Insofar as Charles Torrey was aware of news from the outside world in his final days, it would not have increased his desire to live. Responding primarily to the wishes of the slave-owning states in the South to extend their reach, Congress had annexed the territory of Texas in 1845. Mexico had warned that it would resist this illegal land grab, and by April 1846 skirmishes had begun between Mexican and American troops along the Rio Grande. As Torrey lay dying, newspapers reported that war was imminent. Word of a major battle reached Washington on May 9, hours before Torrey's death, and that evening President James Polk's cabinet adopted war measures. Abolitionists regarded the war as a major setback in their efforts to prevent the spread of slavery.

During Charles Torrey's final days, he was visited regularly by Porter Snow, a Baltimore friend of Reverend Ide's. On Friday, May 8, Snow visited Torrey for the last time and described him as follows:

> On Friday morning the Warden told me that he had suffered a hemorrhage the night before, and was very low. The physician remarked that he could not live more than a day or two. I then asked him for the last time how he felt in view of his nearness to the eternal world, and he repeated to me several passages of scripture that were a comfort to him in these, his last hours. He spoke of the mercy and kindness of his Savior, and of the

beauty of the passage—"sick and in prison, and ye visited me." For a few moments he was delirious, and when I prayed with him his reason seemed to return, and he added a fervent amen at the conclusion. I then bade him farewell, and was obliged to leave the city the next day, so that I never saw him again. He died on Saturday, at 3 o'clock.

Appropriate to the setting, it was the deputy warden of the prison who sat with Torrey during his final hours. This was described by the deputy warden to W. C. Bradley, who then forwarded the information to Amos Phelps:

> The deputy warden was with him to the last, and seemed quite attached to him. He said that Torrey was perfectly conscious to the "last breath," though unable to speak. He sat four hours by his bed-side, wetting his lips with an acid water, and ministering as far as possible to his comfort; for which he repeatedly expressed his gratitude in signs and looks that much affected him. His exit was perfectly calm and peaceful. He died without a groan or struggle; and with every indication of a happy state of mind. *He* [the deputy warden] had no doubt as to his piety; nor had any officer in the institution.

As a Baltimore newspaper noted: "Charles T. Torrey is at last gone, freed from prison without the aid of the governor."[28]

Arrangements for Charles Torrey's funeral were well underway prior to his death. Embalming was uncommon at the time, but by injecting arsenic into the arteries, a body could be reasonably well preserved for several days. This was done to Torrey's body by an anatomist at the Baltimore Dental College. The body was put into a zinc-lined, cherry casket with a small glass window in the top for viewing, then shipped by train to Boston.[29]

In Boston, a "Committee of Arrangements for the Funeral of the Rev. C. T. Torrey" had been organized on May 2 by Torrey's supporters, including Amos Phelps, Samuel Sewall, and Joseph Lovejoy, another younger brother of the martyr Elijah Lovejoy. In a spirit of postmortem ecumenism, they invited William Lloyd Garrison to be a member of the committee, but he declined for what he said were "various reasons." The committee decided that the spacious and historic Park Street Church would be the most appropriate place for the funeral, and this was so announced in the *Liberator* on Friday, May 15. It was a Congregational church in which Torrey, as a Congregational minister, had preached in 1837. In addition, Torrey's brother-in-law, Emmons Ide, not only was a member of the church's congregation but also served on various church committees.[30]

Permission to hold Torrey's funeral in the Park Street Church had been given by a church official, probably William T. Eustis, who was then chairman of the church board. The date was set for Monday, May 18, and notices were sent out. Then a remarkable thing happened. On Saturday evening, May 16, less than two days before the scheduled service, permission to use the church was rescinded. In what was described as "a curt note," the church board "sent a messenger to one of the committee of arrangements, who roused him out of sleep in his bed at 10 o'clock on Saturday night, to tell him that Park Street Church could not be let for Mr. Torrey's funeral." William Goodell, in his 1853 book on the antislavery movement, called this refusal "the most fiend-like expression of hatred against Torrey," adding that "the corpse of the martyred Torrey was denied, what would *not* have been denied to the worst of malefactors—the decencies of a temporary resting-place in the house of prayer during the accustomed religious exercises of such an occasion."[31]

Nobody who knew the history of the abolitionist schism in Massachusetts doubted for a minute who was behind the decision to bar Torrey's corpse from the church. The Park Street Church had been the site of William Lloyd Garrison's first major antislavery speech on July 4, 1829, the place where he had labeled slavery a national sin and called for a moral revolution. Ever conscious of his place in history, Garrison, who was in Boston at the time, was not going to allow Torrey, whom he despised, to end his abolitionist career in the same church in which Garrison had begun his own.

Hurriedly, the venue for Torrey's funeral was changed to the Tremont Temple, a Baptist church one block from the Park Street Church. There, on Monday afternoon, May 18, "an immense crowd gathered, and long before 3 o'clock the building was thronged to the utmost." "All the avenues leading to the Temple were blocked with dense masses of human beings. Tremont Street, between Park and School Streets, was completely thronged with carriages." Torrey's coffin was placed on display in a downstairs room in the temple for three hours before the beginning of the service, with "a continuous stream entering at one door and passing out at the other." Among those looking through the glass to view Torrey's face was six-year-old Nathaniel Bowditch, whose father had brought him there to "teach him to swear eternal enmity to slavery." Less than two decades later, Nathaniel, fighting for the Union forces, "would be killed in Virginia, in a charge against Confederate cavalry."[32]

Among the three thousand persons at the funeral were "a large number of well-dressed and respectable looking colored people . . . [who] appeared much interested." "The entire platform was occupied by ministers of different denominations, and many more seated below for whom there was not room on the platform." Torrey's widow, two children, father-in-law, and grandmother who had raised him were all present. According to one observer: "When Mrs. Torrey, the wife of the deceased came in, with her two children, a beautiful boy and girl, the effect upon that immense audience was very great, tears glistened in many eyes, and bosoms swelled with strong emotions. As I looked upon that broken-hearted wife, and those fatherless children, clad in the weeds of mourning, I could but curse that system, from my very soul, which has robbed a wife of a husband, children of a father, and humanity of one of its most devoted friends." The $3,000 ($72,000) that had been donated to help free Charles Torrey had been given to his family for their support.[33]

Following opening prayers, Reverend Joseph Lovejoy gave the sermon. Lovejoy's brother had been the first prominent martyr of the abolitionist movement, and he spoke of Torrey as the second:

> His mortal remains lie indeed beneath you; but he has just begun to live. . . . While genius, energy and courage, robed in the milder virtues of piety and benevolence, shall be admired, the name of Torrey will be honored. . . . The life and death of Mr. Torrey will convince thousands, simply by drawing attention to the subject and securing its discussion—of the righteousness and expediency of direct efforts to assist the slaves,

individually, to their freedom. . . . Mr. Torrey has showed us again, that there is something worth dying for. . . . Slavery has *murdered* the young, vigorous, social, talented, and pious Torrey! Now, either shed no tear on that early grave, or write there the vow of Hannibal—*eternal war against slavery!*

Following the funeral, the family and many friends accompanied the body to the Mount Auburn Cemetery, adjacent to Cambridge. Opened in 1831, Mount Auburn was one of the first American garden cemeteries set "in an idyllic landscape of rolling hills, woodlands, ponds, and elaborate memorial statuary."[34]

After Torrey's body had been laid to rest, his friends and abolitionist supporters reconvened at Boston's Faneuil Hall for an evening memorial service that lasted until after 10 o'clock. Among the many speakers was Henry Stanton, who observed that "we have met to praise Torrey, not to bury him":

And who, it may be asked, was Charles T. Torrey, that we should praise him? Why should this assembly of Christian citizens meet in this hallowed hall, to honor one who was convicted as a felon, and died in the Penitentiary?

Let it be answered, that though he was convicted of having violated the laws of a republican state, he was not found guilty of violating any of the statutes of the Law giver of the Universe. . . . It is impossible to give any binding force to statutes which make one man the property of another. They are null and void from their own inherent injustice. . . .

What, then, was the act for which Torrey suffered and died? Stated in the simplest form and stripped of all extrinsic ornament, it was this:—He aided oppressed men peaceably to cast away their chains—he gave liberty to men unjustly held in bondage. . . . He has done something for liberty, and his name deserves a place in the calendar of its martyrs. Now that he is laid quietly and securely in his grave, we may safely publish those acts to the world which, while he lived, could be safely known only to the few. In a letter addressed to me while he was in prison awaiting his trial, he said, "If I am a guilty man, I am a very guilty one; for, I have aided nearly *four hundred* slaves to escape to freedom, the greater part of whom would, probably, but for my exertions have died in slavery."[35]

Stanton was followed by poet John Greenleaf Whittier, who had visited Torrey in prison and who closed his talk as follows: "The young, the beautiful, the brave! He is safe now from the malice of his enemies. Nothing can harm him more. His work for the poor and helpless was well and nobly done. In the wild woods of Canada, around many a happy fireside and holy family altar, his name is on the lips of God's poor. He put his soul in their soul's stead; he gave his life for those who had no claim on his love save that of human brotherhood." At the close of the evening, a poem, "On the Death of Charles Turner Torrey," was read. It had been written for the occasion by James Russell Lowell, a young lawyer and active abolitionist who was just emerging as one of America's best-known poets. It concluded as follows:

> Must it be thus forever? No!
>   The hand of God sows not in vain,
> Long sleeps the darkling seed below,
> The seasons come, and change, and go,
>   And all the fields are deep with grain.
>
> Although our brother lie asleep,
>   Man's heart still struggles, still aspires;
> His grave shall quiver yet, while deep
> Through the brave Bay State's pulses leap
>   Her ancient energies and fires.[36]

Charles Torrey's funeral continued seriatim for several weeks. Joseph Lovejoy traveled throughout Massachusetts, repeating his funeral address: North Brookfield, Worcester, Cambridgeport, Hallowell, Reading. Henry Stanton spoke at a memorial service in Lowell, and ministers in many other churches throughout New England dedicated a sermon to Torrey's accomplishments as a true Christian. Torrey commemoration events took place at Oberlin, Galesburg, and other abolitionist strongholds throughout the Northeast and Midwest. In Cincinnati, abolitionist Salmon P. Chase, who had participated in negotiations for Torrey's release and would later become a

U.S. senator and chief justice of the Supreme Court, "presided at a huge meeting" that "condemned Maryland's treatment" of Torrey and "sent a message of condolence to the widow." In upstate New York, a hymn written for the occasion was sung at Torrey commemoration services:

> Sons of the North—wake from your sleep!
>   Your cherished country save:
> Is that the boon your fathers won—
>   That cold New England grave? . . .
>
> Wake, then, and snatch that drooping flag,
>   And spread it o'er the slave—
> Go, link your interests with his own—
>   For thus speaks Torrey's grave.[37]

Tributes continued for months in many northern newspapers, especially those opposing slavery. The *Ohio Standard* noted that Torrey's "faith was verified in works; his sympathy in deeds of mercy." The *Christian Investigator* asked: "Who, among the thousands of his brethren was . . . more formidable or more forgiving? Who else could have conceived the ideas he translated into successful action?" The *New Jersey Freeman* predicted that Torrey "will continue to speak, in thunder tones, into the ears of slaveholders, until they loose their grasp upon their brother's throat." The *Liberty Standard* acknowledged that Torrey had been "imprudent" but "so was Luther, so was Jerome of Prague who was burnt to ashes, so was Lovejoy, so were other martyrs. Away with such quibbling casuistry!" And the *Western Christian* simply noted that for Torrey, like Lovejoy, "from every drop of blood shall spring up full-grown abolitionists."[38]

Tributes also poured in from England. On June 19, the day following Torrey's funeral, the British and Foreign Anti-Slavery Society passed a resolution on Torrey, saying that they "deeply sympathize with his afflicted widow and orphan children, in their irreparable loss." It also supported "the determination to use every legitimate means for breaking [the slaves'] fetters" and urged that slavery "be earnestly, constantly, and zealously resisted, by every friend of justice, humanity and freedom." The resolution was signed by Thomas

Clarkson, president of the society and dean of British abolitionists, and by John Scoble, secretary of the society. Elsewhere in England, Frederick Douglass "alluded with emotion" to Torrey's death during a public lecture, "observing that Mr. Torrey had nobly chosen to endanger his own liberty and life by extending a helping hand to his enslaved brethren . . . a deed on which Heaven looked down with benignity."[39]

Much of the tribute following Torrey's death came from the free black community. In Boston, a group of black leaders met at Zion Chapel on June 15 and pledged "to commemorate these deeds of Christian heroism, by the erection of a monument at Mount Auburn" over Torrey's grave. Their leader was William Nell, the black printer who had worked for Garrison but had then been fired by him. They formed the Torrey Monument Association and announced a fundraising rally for July 31. On that afternoon, "a brass band led a procession through the city to one of the churches, then on to Tremont Temple. Men carried banners which depicted a narrative of slavery against liberty. At Tremont Temple speakers addressed the citizens and all joined in a discussion of the Torrey story." Contributions to the monument fund accumulated more slowly than expected, however, because William Lloyd Garrison discouraged black Bostonians from contributing. In the *Liberator* on July 10, he had written: "We nevertheless think it more desirable to be active in procuring means to carry on the general cause for the deliverance of the living captive, than to build a monument to him who, being dead, needs no such expenditures on his behalf."[40]

The hatred of Garrison had followed Torrey even to his grave. One week prior to Garrison's publication of his *Liberator* letter, a related incident occurred in the fervently abolitionist Western Reserve section of Ohio. Abby Kelley, one of Garrison's staunchest supporters, attended a meeting of the ladies' anti-slavery society at which a collection was going to be taken for Torrey's widow and children. Just as the collection was about to be taken, "Mrs. Abby Kelley Foster arose, and in a most earnest and even violent manner, protested against contributing, because she said it was giving to the rich. . . . As there was not time to go into a discussion, she succeeded in defeating the collection." The *Emancipator,* which reported the incident, said that it was not aware of "an exhibition of a more hag-like spirit than this."[41]

Finally, by the fall of 1846, almost $500 ($12,000) had been collected for Torrey's memorial, and a ten-foot granite monument was erected over his grave. It had on one side the details of his life and on another a bronze relief of a female slave with her head bowed. The front was adorned with a bronze relief of Torrey and words from one of his letters:

> It is better to die
> in prison
> with the peace of God
> in our breasts,
> than to live in freedom
> with
> a polluted conscience.[42]

9
AFTERMATH

Charles Torrey's influence did not end with his death on May 9, 1846. Shortly after his body had been laid to rest in the Mount Auburn Cemetery, his spirit appeared to have been resurrected in the person of William L. Chaplin, one of Torrey's greatest admirers.

Born in 1796 in Groton, Massachusetts, the son of a Congregational minister, Chaplin had a distinguished pedigree that included a grandfather, William Prescott, who had commanded the American forces at the Battle of Bunker Hill. Chaplin received a Brahmin education at Andover Academy and Harvard College, after which he studied law. In the mid-1830s, Chaplin, like Torrey, became interested in the slavery issue, and in 1836 he gave up his law practice to become an organizing agent for the American Anti-Slavery Society. In this, he proved remarkably able, recruiting "more than 100 members in Auburn [New York] after just a single lecture." The following year he was made general agent for the New York State Anti-Slavery Society and in 1840 helped organize the Liberty Party. At that time he worked closely with Joshua Leavitt, Gerrit Smith, and Henry Stanton as well as Charles Torrey.[1]

Like Torrey, Chaplin was extremely empathetic to the suffering of slave families, referring to them as "fellow-men and fellow citizens crushed and dumb ... orphans more than motherless, made so by the infernal spirit of slavery." From the beginning "he endorsed the duty of abolitionists to help fugitive slaves reach safety in Canada." During 1842 and 1843, when Torrey and Thomas Smallwood were sending large numbers of slaves north, Chaplin was editor of the *American Citizen* newspaper in Rochester, and it is probable that he assisted slaves who had traveled on the Washington-to-Albany line and who subsequently obtained passage from Rochester across Lake Ontario to Canada.[2]

On December 24, 1844, shortly after Torrey's trial had ended,

Chaplin and Joshua Leavitt had visited Torrey in the Baltimore jail. Torrey had just published his letter in the *Boston Morning Chronicle* in which he had predicted that, "in 1850, the *law of liberty* shall be proclaimed from the capitol of Maryland. . . . Mark it well! 1850 is the *set time*!" Following his visit, Chaplin decided to move to Washington, ostensibly to act as a correspondent for the *Albany Patriot* but in reality to assume Torrey's mantle. Ten days following his visit, Chaplin wrote: "As I am a living man, I believe that one hundred men like Charles T. Torrey, in courage and devotion to his object, would do more to deliver the slave speedily, than all our paper resolutions, windy speeches, presses and *votes* into the bargain." Two years after Torrey's death, Chaplin exalted Torrey's status to the highest level: "Was not poor Torrey, in his dauntless efforts to burst the prison door and plunge into the deepest cell for the rescue of the forlorn captive, more Christ-like than any of us? . . . He *felt* and acted. . . . He laid his all on the alter [*sic*] of the great cause."³

According to Stanley Harrold's *The Abolitionists and the South, 1831–1861,* Chaplin lost no time in Washington in taking up where Torrey had left off. He "quickly began to attend black church services, to establish ties to black families, and to provide considerable support to black efforts directed at purchasing freedom and initiating freedom suits." Chaplin was aware that many northern abolitionist supporters were willing to donate funds to purchase the freedom of slaves, and he attempted to institutionalize these efforts by creating what he called a "Bureau of Humanity." Over one year, he raised about $6,000 ($150,000) to purchase the freedom of local slaves. Like Torrey, Chaplin believed that the District of Columbia was the key to abolishing slavery in the nation and that everything possible should be done there to undermine it. And, like Torrey, Gerrit Smith was his main financial benefactor.⁴

It is unclear, during his months in Washington, whether William Chaplin was also directly involved in helping slaves go north by way of the Underground Railroad, but it seems likely that he was. During 1848, however, his involvement in such activities became glaringly obvious. In February he approached Daniel Drayton, a ship's captain who sailed the eastern seaboard. The previous summer, Drayton had agreed to transport a slave and her five children from Washington to New Jersey, and this was probably why Chaplin approached him. Would he be willing, Chaplin asked, to transport some black families north? Drayton said that he would, for the right price.[5]

On the evening of April 13, 1848, seventy-seven black men, women, and children crowded into the hold of the ship, named the *Pearl*, at the foot of Seventh Street in southwest Washington. Included were slaves belonging to a South Carolina congressman, the secretary of the U.S. Treasury, and former President James Madison's widow. Many of the slaves were members of a black Methodist church, "a significant minority were light complected [and] all of them were representative of the *respectable* people of color who constituted the African-American component of Washington's biracial community." The *Pearl* pushed off but moved slowly down the Potomac because of the poor sailing conditions. Meanwhile, in Washington, a free black hackman, who had driven two of the slaves to the boat, went to the authorities, hoping for a reward. Several of the owners of the runaway slaves armed themselves and immediately set out in pursuit in a steamer belonging to one of them. They caught up with the *Pearl* shortly before it entered the Chesapeake Bay and forcibly returned it to Washington. Word of the event spread quickly, and a mob followed the procession to the jail. As they passed Gannon's slave market, its owner rushed at Daniel Drayton with a knife, but guards blocked the way. Other members of the crowd shouted: "Lynch them, lynch them!"[6]

It was widely rumored that the plan to free the slaves, the largest such attempt ever undertaken, had been conceived by William Chaplin and financed by Gerrit Smith; the authorities hoped to implicate them both. When Drayton's trial opened on July 27, the major question was whether he would tell what he knew. The prosecutor was slaveowner Philip Barton Key, son of Francis Scott Key. Massachusetts Congressman Horace Mann defended Drayton and argued, implausibly, "that the *Pearl* fugitives had spontaneously decided to escape on the same day, and had coincidentally managed to find their own way to the ship." Drayton was found guilty but, receiving promises that his family would be taken care of and all his fines paid, refused to implicate Chaplin or Smith. Drayton was initially sentenced to twenty years in prison, but on appeal this was reduced to a fine of $10,000 ($249,000), although he had to remain in prison until the fine was paid. After serving four years in prison, Drayton was pardoned by President Millard Fillmore in 1852.[7]

The episode of the *Pearl* was an important impetus to a further deterioration in relations between the North and South. A week after the failed attempt, Joshua Giddings announced to his congressional colleagues that the slaves who were trying to achieve freedom on the *Pearl* had the "same right to liberty as any Congressman ... [and] the right to free themselves by *any means* God has put in their power." According to James Brewer Stewart's biography of Giddings, he "had full knowledge of this risky enterprise [the *Pearl*] beforehand and was anxious for its success." His southern colleagues strongly suspected this fact and were enraged by his public defense of what they viewed as the largest ever attempt at slave stealing. Rep. Robert Toombs of Georgia "applauded mob action against Giddings," while Rep. William Haskell of Tennessee suggested Giddings "ought to swing as high as Haman." Senator John Calhoun of South Carolina called the stealing of slaves "the gravest and most vital of all questions to us and the whole Union." Senator Jefferson Davis of Mississippi added that, if the District of Columbia was to be made the center of the abolition struggle "from which civil war is to radiate here, let the conflict begin!" When Giddings returned to his boarding house, he "found several notes threatening his life under his boarding house door."[8]

William Chaplin was pleased with the outcome of the *Pearl*, despite its failure to free the slaves. He wrote excitedly to Gerrit Smith that "this attempt of the 77 [slaves] to 'conquer' their freedom is the grandest event for the cause of anti-slavery that has occurred in years. It is working great good here and elsewhere. If our Abolitionists will take hold we can drive slavery out of this District at once!" Joshua Giddings also regarded the *Pearl* episode as a victory, writing to his wife: "We have gained much by the contest. It has thrown forward the cause of freedom and we are more firm than we were before." In *The Rise of Aggressive Abolitionism*, Stanley Harrold argued that the *Pearl* incident was important in "convincing more Garrisonians, especially black Garrisonians, that assisted slave escapes must become an abolitionist priority." A prominent example of such changed thinking was Frederick Douglass, who, two months after the *Pearl* incident, attended his first Liberty Party convention and endorsed the policy that "'all men' had a duty to go south to help slaves escape." At this time, Douglass broke with William Lloyd Garrison, thus becoming one of Garrison's most prominent defectors to abandon moral suasion for activist political abolitionism.[9]

Much encouraged by the outcome of the *Pearl*, Chaplin redoubled his efforts. Perhaps, he thought, it really might be possible to abolish slavery in the District of Columbia and Maryland by 1850 and make Charles Torrey's prediction come true. He thus "increased his already impressive engagement with desperate African Americans in the city and its vicinity" and assisted "black people in court cases and efforts to purchase freedom." He also increased his efforts to help slaves escape, personally driving them to freedom in Pennsylvania, just as Torrey had done. Wisely, however, he did not use the same route Torrey had used but rather one further west, going through Frederick and Emmitsburg in Maryland to Adams County, Pennsylvania. His usual destination was a farm owned by abolitionist James McAllister, located on Rock Creek between Cumberland and Mt. Joy townships. A member of the McAllister family later estimated that Chaplin "brought about twenty fugitives to the farm." From McAllister's farm, the slaves were usually forwarded to Quaker William Wright at York Springs.[10]

For William Chaplin, as for Torrey, luck ran out. On August 8, 1850, Chaplin hired a closed carriage and horses and set out to carry two slaves from the District to Pennsylvania. One of the slaves belonged to Rep. Robert Toombs, the Georgia congressman who had publicly encouraged mob action against Joshua Giddings. The other slave belonged to Alexander Stephens, also a Georgia congressman, who would become vice-president of the Confederacy during the Civil War. Toombs and Stephens were regarded as the leaders of the southern Whigs in the House. Two slaves belonging to another southern congressman, William Colcock, had also absconded during the summer, a period of intense debate in Congress over the slavery issue. It had become obvious that somebody was intentionally trying to embarrass southern members of Congress by taking their slaves.[11]

John Goddard, the captain of the Washington Auxiliary Guard, believed he knew who that somebody was, and he was monitoring Chaplin's movements. Thus, Goddard and five members of his force, all armed, were waiting for Chaplin as he drove the carriage with the two slaves north from Washington on Brookeville Pike, now called Georgia Avenue. At the Maryland border, just south of what is now Silver Spring, Goddard's men stopped Chaplin's carriage by ramming a fence post into the spokes of a wheel. Next, "Chaplin drew a pistol from his coat and fired at a man who tried to seize the reins. The fugitives, who were also armed, then began blazing away from inside the carriage." According to contemporary accounts, "not less than twenty-seven shots were fired, and the fight continued for five or six minutes." The carriage was said to be "completely riddled with bullets, and one of the doors was much cut to pieces with a bowie-knife. . . . Stephens' man [slave] had escaped death only by the protection of a large, old-fashioned watch which he wore, which was deeply indented by a bullet." Both slaves and one of the police suffered superficial wounds, but the fact that nobody was killed reflected both the poor quality of the firearms and the aim of the participants. One slave temporarily got away but was captured the following day, and Chaplin and the other slave were arrested. Today, a historic plaque marks the site of the shootout.[12]

Chaplin was jailed and indicted on charges of attempted murder and multiple other counts, with bail set at $25,000 ($622,000). Despite this enormous sum, the abolitionists were not interested in having another prison martyr, so they raised the funds, the majority coming from Gerrit Smith. Chaplin was released from jail after five months and immediately went to New York, thereby forfeiting bail. It was December 1850, and Chaplin had done everything in his power to fulfill Charles Torrey's prediction. Still a bachelor at fifty-four, Chaplin then married a much younger woman, Theodosia Gilbert, an abolitionist and women's rights activist who helped run the Glen Haven Water Cure on Skaneateles Lake, not far from Gerrit Smith's home in upstate New York. The Water Cure was owned by James Jackson, the abolitionist editor of the *Albany Patriot,* and was a gathering place for abolitionists and other reformers, including Elizabeth Cady Stanton. Stanton and other women had held the first women's rights convention in nearby Seneca Falls two years earlier. Chaplin and his wife established a home on the lake and had two children before Theodosia died, probably in childbirth, four years after they were married.[13]

The summer of 1850, in fact, proved to be a watershed for the abolitionist movement in America. William Chaplin's attempt to shoot the Washington Auxiliary Guards and defend the slaves was symbolic of a new militancy and confident activism. Two years earlier, Quaker Thomas Garrett, a friend of Torrey's, had sounded this same note when he was convicted in Wilmington of sheltering runaway slaves and fined $5,400 ($134,500), virtually bankrupting him. After the verdict, Garrett announced to the court:

> I am called an abolitionist, once a name of reproach, but one I am ever proud to be considered worthy of being called. For the last twenty-five years I have been much engaged in the cause of this much injured race, but owing to a multiplicity of other engagements, I could not devote so much time and mind to their cause as I otherwise should have done. I am now placed in a situation in which I have not so much to claim my attention as formerly [*alluding to the loss of his worldly wealth, by having to sell his farm to meet the legal penalty and costs imposed on him*], and I now pledge myself, in the presence of this assembly, to use all lawful and honourable means to lessen the burdens of this oppressed people, and endeavour, according to ability furnished, to burst their chains asunder and set them free. . . . I now consider the penalty imposed may be regarded as a licence for the rest of my life; but be that as it may, if any of you know of any poor slave who needs assistance, send him to me; as I now publicly pledge myself to double my diligence, and never neglect an opportunity to assist a slave to freedom.[14]

In August of 1850 in upstate New York, this new spirit of militancy was writ large. Gerrit Smith invited a biracial group of 2,000 abolitionist supporters to a meeting in Cazenovia, near Peterboro. Frederick Douglass chaired the meeting, and resolutions praising Charles Torrey and William Chaplin were duly passed. Chaplin was supposed to have been at the meeting but was confined to jail. The *New York Tribune* reported that Chaplin, in fact, had intended to bring the slaves of the two southern congressmen to the Cazenovia meeting to have them speak and "give it *éclat*."[15]

The high point of the Cazenovia meeting was the presentation of Gerrit Smith's "Letter to the American Slaves," a sequel to his previous address, "To the Slaves in the U. States of America," that had been published in 1842. Smith, who almost certainly had financed the majority of Torrey's and Chaplin's activities, said: "For many years I have regarded the helping of slaves to liberty, especially at the great peril of the helper, as among the most beautiful expressions and among the most decisive evidences of disinterested benevolence and genuine piety." Smith's letter, which he read, advised slaves that they "are prisoners of war, in an enemy country," and "therefore, by all the rules of war, you have the fullest liberty to plunder, burn and kill, as you may have occasion to do to promote your escape." In order to effect their escape, Smith added, slaves should not hesitate to take their master's "fleetest" horse or to "break your master's locks, and take all their money." Smith also spoke of a coming "insurrection of the Southern slaves," at which time "the great mass of the colored men of the North . . . will be found by your side, with deep-stored and long-accumulated revenge in their hearts, and with death-dealing weapons in their hands." After some debate, those attending the Cazenovia meeting endorsed Smith's letter. Predictably, William Lloyd Garrison was horrified and dismissed the meeting as merely an assembly of "violent men."[16]

Even as Gerrit Smith was encouraging violent action by slaves, Congress was heatedly debating what to do about the increasing illegal freeing of slaves. In 1849, South Carolina Senator John Calhoun had described the problem as efforts by northerners to "entice, decoy, entrap, inveigle, and seduce slaves to escape from their masters, and to pass them secretly and rapidly" to Canada. A Richmond newspaper direly predicted that "the border states of Maryland and Delaware will, in ten years be denuded of their slaves." In January 1850, Senator Henry Clay proposed a series of resolutions to try to ameliorate the increasing tension between the North and South, and for the next nine months the resolutions were heatedly debated by

Clay and Senators John Calhoun, Daniel Webster, William Seward, Jefferson Davis, Salmon Chase, and others. The result was the "Compromise of 1850," including the Fugitive Slave Act, which provided federal enforcement mechanisms to assist slaveowners, allowing masters to pursue their runaway slaves in northern states and making it a federal offense for anyone to assist runaway slaves.[17]

The effect of the Fugitive Slave Act was the opposite of what Congress intended. Many northerners who had not previously considered themselves to be abolitionists felt sorry for runaway slaves and resented being told by Congress that they could be fined $1,000 ($25,900) or sentenced to six months in jail for helping them. Resentment was especially high after the publication of Harriet Beecher Stowe's enormously popular *Uncle Tom's Cabin*. It appeared in serial form in the *National Era* beginning in mid-1851 and was then published as a book in 1852; it sold 300,000 copies the first year. The book elicited much sympathy for slaves, especially for women, such as Cassy, the enslaved mistress of Simon Legree. In the book Cassy "tells Uncle Tom the long history of her sufferings at the hands of male slaveowners." The sexual exploitation of enslaved women had been a major issue for many abolitionists, including Charles Torrey and Amos Phelps, but following the publication of *Uncle Tom's Cabin* it was discussed much more publicly. For example, in 1860 Congressman Owen Lovejoy, brother of the martyr, gave a speech on the House floor, "The Barbarism of Slavery," in which he detailed "the offensive and brutal lusts of polygamy." The speech predictably elicited an "ensuing scuffle, with canes and pistols on the verge of use." A year later Harriet Jacobs published her *Incidents in the Life of a Slave Girl,* described as a "searing indictment of master's sexual exploitation of female slaves."[18]

Northern abolitionists were incensed by the Fugitive Slave Act and had no intention of following it. This became clear throughout the North and Midwest as white and black abolitionists increasingly often physically confronted slaveholders who ventured into free states to retrieve runaway slaves. Two highly publicized episodes occurred in September of 1851. The first took place in Syracuse, where a runaway slave named William Henry, known as Jerry, was arrested by deputy marshals under the Fugitive Slave Act. Word quickly circulated, and a group of Liberty Party members, including Gerrit Smith, crowded into the office of the federal commissioner, where Jerry's case was being adjudicated. Rather than awaiting a decision, they surrounded Jerry and rushed him out the door. He was immediately recaptured and taken to the police station, but "that evening an armed crowd besieged the station house and was able to spirit Jerry away" and send him safely to Canada. Fourteen white and twelve black men were indicted for taking part, but only one was found guilty; the rest were acquitted, or their trials ended in hung juries.[19]

The second episode took place in Christiana, Pennsylvania, when Maryland farmer Edward Gorsuch, his son, and some deputies arrived at the home of black farmer William Parker to claim Gorsuch's four runaway field hands, who were working for Parker. A signal was given by Parker, and other blacks quickly arrived from surrounding farms. Gorsuch continued to insist that he was going to reclaim his slaves, the slaves disagreed, shots were fired, and Gorsuch lay dead, with his son wounded. Parker and the slaves fled to Canada, sheltered en route by Frederick Douglass in Rochester. According to one account, "President Millard Fillmore and his Secretary of State, Daniel Webster, immediately saw that the murder of Gorsuch would be seen by the whole South as proof that the federal government could not be counted on to enforce the new Fugitive Slave Law." Federal officials therefore insisted on aggressive legal action, resulting in the indictment and trial of several men. A jury found them all not guilty, suggesting to many that the Fugitive Slave Act was, in fact, not enforceable.[20]

The writing was on the wall and seemed to have been written in blood. Even William Lloyd Garrison's most devout followers were gradually abandoning their nonpolitical and pacifist position as aggressive abolitionism appeared to be moving toward a violent denouement. Angelina Grimké Weld concluded that "we are compelled to choose between two evils, and all that we can do is to take the *least,* and baptize liberty in blood if it must be so." Parker Pillsbury said "he hoped to see the time come when Boston should run with blood from Beacon Hill to the foot of Broad Street." Even Wendell Phillips, Garrison's most prominent supporter, applauded the fact that "every five minutes gave birth to a black baby. . . . its baby hand would one day hold the dagger which should reach the master's heart."[21]

Sitting at his home in North Elba, in the mountains of northern New York, fifty-year-old John Brown followed these events with great interest. Abolitionist developments had been a passionate interest for him all his life. His father, Owen Brown, had helped organize the Western Reserve Anti-Slavery Society in Ohio in 1833 and had also been a board member of Oberlin College, founded as an anti-slavery institute. According to a biographer of John Brown, "Owen and John Brown were active workers for the Underground Railroad, ready at all times to hide Fugitives and help them on their way north." Later, at his farm in Ohio, John Brown constructed "a hiding place for fugitives beneath a haymow in his barn." In later years Brown acknowledged: "I have been connected with that business [the Underground Railroad] as *commonly conducted* from my boyhood and *never* let an opportunity slip."[22]

John Brown and Charles Torrey had a lot in common. Both had come from a New England Puritan tradition that revered martyrs. Both were deeply religious; as a young man Brown had "avidly read the Bible" and tried to commit its "entire contents" to memory. Both had been deeply moved by the martyr death of Elijah Lovejoy in 1837; at a memorial service for Lovejoy, Brown had stood up and proclaimed: "Here, before God, in the presence of these witnesses, from this time, I consecrate my life to the destruction of slavery." Most important, both Brown and Torrey were inclined to use aggressive action to bring about the abolition of slavery. Both men also shared important friendships with Joshua Giddings and Gerrit Smith.[23]

In 1847, one year after Torrey's death, John Brown told Frederick Douglass about a plan he had to liberate the slaves. The ultimate purpose of the plan, said Brown, was "to destroy the money value of slave property; and that can only be done by rendering slave property insecure." Brown went on to outline his plan of positioning small groups of armed men in the mountains of Virginia to attract slaves to join them. Gradually, they would enlarge their area of influence until they had freed all the slaves. Brown acknowledged that he "was not averse to the shedding of blood," adding that "even if the worst came, he could but be killed, and he had no better use for his life than to lay it down in the cause of the slave." Douglass believed that the "plan as it then lay in his mind had much to commend it," but he declined Brown's invitation to become part of it. To others, John Brown compared his plan to the working of the Underground Railroad: "Rail Road business on a *somewhat extended* scale is the *identical* object for which I am trying to get means."[24]

One year later, in April 1848, John Brown met Gerrit Smith when he approached him about land in upstate New York that Smith had offered to give away to blacks if they would homestead it. Brown said that, if given some land, he could help teach the blacks how to farm it. Gerrit Smith accepted his offer, selling him 244 acres at a very inexpensive price, and this was the beginning of their friendship. Thus, when Gerrit Smith issued his "Letter to the American Slaves" in August 1850, with its call for slave insurrections, John Brown was certain he had found a man who would understand his own plans.[25]

On January 15, 1851, John Brown wrote a document entitled *Words of Advice* in response to the Fugitive Slave Act. It was intended for black fugitive slaves living in Springfield, Massachusetts, where Brown was then residing. According to one Brown biographer, "it is a crucial document in John Brown's life, one of the best things he ever wrote." Brown opened with the words: "Nothing so charms the American people as personal bravery." He then recounted his own heroes: "Cinques [*sic*], of everlasting memory, on Board the 'Amistad.' . . . Have you seen the Branded Hand [Jonathan Walker]? Do you remember the names of Lovejoy and Torrey?" This was followed by specific advice to the fugitive slaves on how to defend themselves against kidnappers, slave catchers, or other threats:

> Should one of your number be arrested, you must collect together as quickly as possible, so as to outnumber your adversaries who are taking an active part against you. Let no able-bodied man appear on the ground unequipped, or with his weapons exposed to view: let that be understood beforehand. Your plans must be known only to yourself, and with the understanding that all traitors must die, wherever caught and proven to be guilty. . . . *Do not delay one moment after you are*

ready; you will lose all your resolution if you do. Let the first blow be the signal for all to engage; and when engaged do not do your work by halves, but make clean work with your enemies. . . . A lasso might possibly be applied to a slave catcher for once with good effect. Hold on to your weapons, and never be persuaded to leave them, part with them, or have them far away from you. *Stand by one another and by your friends, while a drop of blood remains; and be hanged, if you must, but tell no tales out of school. Make no confession.*

The document was signed, in Brown's handwriting, by forty-four fugitive slaves.[26]

John Brown was a patient man. He had been waiting since 1837 to ascertain how he might fulfill his pledge to bring about "the destruction of slavery." Finally in 1855 events appeared to offer an opportunity. Since 1820, under the Missouri Compromise, new states being admitted to the Union had to be evenly balanced between slave and non-slave states. Passage of the Kansas-Nebraska Act in May 1854 rescinded the Missouri Compromise by allowing residents of the Kansas and Nebraska territories to determine the status of slavery by ballot. Proslavery immigrants from Missouri and Arkansas and antislavery immigrants from northern states poured into Kansas, which was widely perceived to be the bellwether for the future of slavery; as Kansas went, so would Nebraska, Utah, and New Mexico. By 1855, five of Brown's sons had settled in Kansas, and Brown joined them, bringing guns donated by Gerrit Smith and his abolitionist friends. At Pottawatomie Creek, Brown killed five proslavery men, and in other fights they distinguished themselves, despite the loss of one son. John Brown became a national figure, a symbol of those willing to fight and even give their lives to end slavery. On a return trip to Kansas, Brown and his followers made a raid into Missouri, freeing eleven slaves.

Brown's notoriety brought him increasing donations, and in 1858 he began serious preparations for the plan he had discussed with Frederick Douglass ten years earlier. Gerrit Smith contributed $700 ($17,400) and was an enthusiastic supporter, saying: "If I were asked to point out . . . the man in all this world I think most truly a

Christian, I would point to John Brown." Smith then wrote excitedly to Joshua Giddings, hinting that "the slave will be delivered by the shedding of blood—and the signs are multiplying that his deliverance is at hand." Giddings needed few hints; he had met Brown "on a number of occasions," had entertained him in his home, contributed money to him, and given him "a letter of introduction to potential funders."[27]

John Brown's financial backers also included five Bostonians— Samuel Gridley Howe, George Stearns, Thomas Higginson, Franklin Sanborn, and Theodore Parker—who, with Smith, constituted the so-called "secret six." Even Wendell Phillips contributed "to purchase rifles and pikes," despite his pacifist beliefs; Phillips later confided to a friend that he had been aware Brown "was working in such ways." At an 1857 meeting in Theodore Parker's home, John Brown met William Lloyd Garrison. The two disagreed "vehemently about the morality of nonresistance, and of Garrisonianism in general." Whenever Garrison invoked the pacifism of Jesus, "Brown countered with blood prophecies from Jeremiah." Brown later dismissed Garrison and his followers, saying, "These men are all talk; what is needed is action—action!"[28]

On October 16, 1859, John Brown made his raid on Harpers Ferry, Virginia, to capture the federal arsenal so he could arm the slaves. The raid itself was a disaster, with all of Brown's small raiding party killed or captured. Garrison called Brown's actions "misguided, wild, and apparently insane" and "utterly lacking in common sense." Wendell Phillips, by contrast, regarded Brown as a hero and even proposed "a wild plan to free Brown by kidnapping the governor of Virginia and then working out an exchange of prisoners." Phillips publicly argued that Brown had "twice as much right to hang [Virginia's] Governor Wise as Governor Wise has to hang him."[29]

John Brown died a martyr. At his trial, prior to sentencing, he declared: "I say I am yet too young to understand that God is any respecter of persons. I believe that to have interfered as I have done, as I have always freely admitted I have done, in behalf of His despised poor, is no wrong, but right. Now, if it is deemed necessary that I should forfeit my life for the furtherance of the ends of justice, and mingle my blood further with the blood of my children and with the blood of millions in this slave country, whose rights are disregarded by wicked, cruel, and unjust enactments, I say let it be done." And on the day of his execution, he handed a statement to a jail guard that read: "I John Brown am now quite certain that the crimes of this *guilty* land: *will* never be purged *away*; but with blood. I had *as I now think; vainly* flattered myself that without *very much* bloodshed; it might be done."[30]

Charles Torrey, if he had lived, would have greatly admired John Brown. Although they never met, their lives, and deaths, bore many similar features. Torrey would have also been pleased that, on the eve of the Civil War, Governor Harris of Tennessee acknowledged the effectiveness of aggressive abolitionist activities in undermining slavery: "It [the North] has run off slave property by means of the 'under-ground railroad' worth millions of dollars, and thus made the tenure by which slaves are held in the border States so precarious as to materially impair their value." That was precisely what Charles Torrey had hoped to achieve; it had just taken longer than he had planned.[31]

For four bloody years, Union troops sang "John Brown's body lies a-mouldering in his grave" as they marched into battle against the Confederates. Among those who fought for the Union was Charles Torrey Jr., who enlisted on October 7, 1861; he was involved in fighting in the battles of Roanoke Island and New Bern in North Carolina and later worked as a clerk in the offices of the U.S. surgeon general. Also fighting for the Union was George Garrison, third son of William Lloyd Garrison; his other sons were conscientious objectors. By the end of the war, more than 600,000 young men lay a-mouldering in their graves. In the intervening four years, as many as a half-million slaves freed themselves by running away. Others gradually gained their freedom in a series of governmental actions, culminating on January 1, 1863, in President Abraham Lincoln's Emancipation Proclamation. All slaves living in the secessionist states were declared to be "then, thenceforward, and forever free."[32]

Word of the Emancipation Proclamation reached Boston that evening. William Lloyd Garrison was in attendance at the Music Hall when Beethoven's Fifth Symphony was interrupted for the announcement. The audience thereupon "gave nine ringing cheers for

Lincoln and three for Garrison and the abolitionists." Garrison was ecstatic and immediately expropriated Lincoln's proclamation as his own, the logical consequence of the revolution he had started thirty-two years earlier. The man who had refused to vote and who had ridiculed the political efforts of other abolitionists embraced Lincoln and his politics enthusiastically. The man who had preached nonresistance, a paragon of pacifism, and who had opposed all aggressive efforts of abolitionists now urged "the conflict to go on, until liberty shall become universal." When Garrison's pacifist supporters pointed out the contradictions of his position, he replied: "This is not the best period for an abstract ethical discussion of the question of Non-Resistance."[33]

President Lincoln needed William Lloyd Garrison's support, and any other support he could muster, for in 1863 he was being severely challenged politically. Garrison campaigned for Lincoln's reelection, and when he went to Washington in June 1964, Lincoln received him cordially at the White House. As the war drew to a close in April 1865, Garrison was invited to be an official guest at a flag-raising ceremony at Fort Sumter, where the first shots of the war had been fired four years earlier. The day following the ceremony, thousands of freed slaves gathered outside the Charleston Citadel, "and when Garrison appeared the freed people and their white supporters seized him joyfully and bore him around the square." He was then escorted to a black church, where he was introduced by a newly freed slave. Pointing to his two daughters, the man said: "Now, Sir, through your labors and those of your noble co-agitators, these are mine. No man can take them from me. Accept these flowers as a token of our gratitude and love . . . as a simple offering from those for whom you have done so much." Garrison, age sixty, was pleased to accept the flowers and any other accolade people wished to offer. The nation needed a symbol of abolitionism, a hero, and Garrison, who had rung the initial abolition bell in 1831 and provided leadership for the first decade, was more than willing to oblige.[34]

10

ASSESSMENT

What can be said regarding the life and abolitionist career of Charles Torrey? When he died at age thirty-two, he had been an abolitionist for eleven years, from 1835 to 1846, with one of those years having been spent recuperating from tuberculosis and two years spent in prison. By contrast, the careers of such abolitionists as William Lloyd Garrison, Wendell Phillips, Joshua Leavitt, and Henry Stanton lasted forty years or longer.

Charles Torrey's most important contribution was in helping to establish political and then aggressive and radical abolitionism as alternative strategies for achieving emancipation. These were tactical alternatives to Garrison's moral suasion, and many abolitionists favored different options at different times. Nor were they mutually exclusive; as John Stauffer made clear in *The Black Hearts of Men,* although the radical abolitionists "never abandoned moral suasion—the principle on which abolitionism had originally been based—they insisted on coupling it with 'efficient action' to give it teeth." In the view of the aggressive and radical abolitionists, Garrison's moral suasion by itself was not sufficient to get the job done. Garrison had set a goal but had provided his followers with no realistic means for achieving that goal; as historian Bruce Laurie described it, Garrison had "led his followers into something of a moral dead end." Charles Torrey, along with Amos Phelps and Alanson St. Clair in Massachusetts and Henry Stanton, Joshua Leavitt, and Elizur Wright in New York, challenged Garrison, leading to the schism of the antislavery organization and the emergence of these tactical options.[1]

The new organization that emerged focused on political means for ending slavery. One year later the Liberty Party, which incorporated the new organization, was born. Charles Torrey played a role in its birth, along with Alvan Stewart, Myron Holley, James Birney, Joshua Leavitt, Elizur Wright, Gerrit Smith, and others. Torrey then labored for almost two years to establish the Liberty Party as a political force in Massachusetts. According to Reinhard Johnson's history, the Liberty Party "became the major vehicle for abolition sentiment in the state by the mid-1840s," and its votes forced the gubernatorial elections of 1842, 1843, and 1845 "to be decided in the state legislature."[2]

Not satisfied with the pace of change, Charles Torrey moved on to aggressive abolitionism by going into the slave states and persuading slaves to run away. A few men had done so previously, such as John Mahan in Kentucky; Alanson Work, James Burr, and George Thompson in Missouri; and Leonard Grimes, a free black, in Virginia. Torrey, however, set up a system with the intent of liberating hundreds of slaves from the District of Columbia, focusing especially on slaves owned by southern members of Congress and other important officials. Torrey's ultimate goal was to make slaveholding unstable in Washington and thus hasten its abolition in the nation's capital. In these efforts, Torrey received much support from free blacks such as Thomas Smallwood and James Bias as well as from white colleagues such as Abel Brown, Charles Cleveland, Joshua Leavitt, Joshua Giddings, and Gerrit Smith. In the later months of these efforts, Torrey elevated his level of aggression still further by publicly naming the slaves being taken and by ridiculing their masters. When he was finally arrested, the two pistols being carried by Torrey suggest the radical direction in which his aggressive abolitionism was headed.

In demonstrating such aggressive methods, Charles Torrey presaged John Brown by almost two decades. As noted by Stanley Harrold: "As Torrey and Smallwood engaged in clandestine subversive activities, they *both* embraced an aggressive masculinity foreshadowing that of John Brown." Thus, it is not surprising that John Brown regarded Torrey as one of his models. In this regard, Torrey's martyrdom lies temporally midway between those of Elijah Lovejoy and John Brown. In *On Freedom's Altar,* Hazel Wolf contended that "after Elijah Lovejoy's death abolitionism had moved toward a new climax," and "Torrey's death brought that climax to the second decade of the militant antislavery crusade."[3]

In assessing Charles Torrey's contribution to the increasingly

aggressive abolitionist movement, his motivation was also histor-
ically noteworthy. Torrey freely acknowledged that he was breaking state, and even federal, laws by enticing slaves to run away from
their masters. At his trial and elsewhere, Torrey argued that state
and federal laws should be transcended by the law of God. As historian David Reynolds noted: "By liberating slaves, Torrey was breaking a state law but obeying the natural law of human equality announced in the Declaration of Independence. He was a traitor to
human law but a patriot to a higher law." Five years following Torrey's death, the preeminence of God's law became a common theme
in Harriet Beecher Stowe's *Uncle Tom's Cabin* and in a sermon given
by her brother, Charles Beecher, titled "The Duty of Disobedience to
Wicked Laws."[4]

In addition to helping move the abolitionist movement to a politically active and ultimately aggressive form, Charles Torrey made
two other important contributions. One was to organize and utilize
one line of the Underground Railroad. As previously noted, aspects
of the Underground Railroad had existed since the early 1800s, especially in Ohio and Pennsylvania. The line set up by Torrey, Smallwood, and their associates stretched from Washington to Albany
and thus preceded the line through central New York State used by
Harriet Tubman a decade later. Torrey's claim to have liberated almost four hundred slaves on the Underground Railroad does not appear to be exaggerated, since he was often carrying in a wagon fifteen or more slaves at one time. Similarly, Harriet Tubman, utilizing
a method similar to Torrey's, is said to have led "at least seventy African Americans out of slavery in Maryland, and indirectly enable
perhaps fifty others to escape to freedom on their own." According
to Fergus Bordewich's history of the Underground Railroad, "by provoking fear and anger in the south, and prompting the enactment of
draconian legislation that eroded the rights of *white* Americans, the
Underground Railroad was a direct contributing cause of the Civil
War."[5]

The final contribution of Charles Torrey was in being one of
the first white men to work closely with free blacks in a coopera-
tive effort. He went to their churches, stayed in their homes, and
jointly plotted with them the escape of slaves. As observed by Fergus

Bordewich, it was through the Underground Railroad that "blacks and whites discovered each other for the first time as allies in a common struggle, learning to rely on each other not as master on slave, or child on parent, but as fellow soldiers in a war that most Americans did not yet even know had begun."[6] Taken together, these three contributions are impressive accomplishments for a man who lived less than thirty-three years. They would appear to justify Torrey's self-assessment, written to Amos Phelps in July 1844, shortly after his final arrest: "When the 'secret history' of the cause of reform in our country shall be written, I have some confidence that it will not be found that I have been useless."[7]

Given these contributions of Charles Torrey to the abolition of slavery in the United States, why is he virtually unknown today? The majority of twentieth-century histories of the abolitionist movement did not even mention him. A few historians have noted his contribution, principally in regard to his having been a martyr. For example, Hazel Wolf, in *On Freedom's Altar: The Martyr Complex in the Abolition Movement* (1952), cited Torrey as an example of this complex. And James Brewer Stewart, in *Holy Warriors: The Abolitionists and American Slavery* (1976), attributed Torrey's abolitionist actions to "a pathological desire for martyrdom."[8]

A few other twentieth-century historians recognized Charles Torrey's contribution to the abolition of slavery. In *The Bold Brahmins: New England's War against Slavery (1831–1863)*, published in 1961, Lawrence Lader wrote: "Torrey assaulted slavery directly and violently. He had invaded the South on frequent trips, a pattern soon followed by others like the former slave, Harriet Tubman. He had conducted a one-man campaign among the border states, mingling with slaves and plotting their escape. It was dangerous enough for a New England abolitionist on the "Underground Railroad" to hide a fleeing slave in his cellar. But here was a far more radical weapon that brought the struggle to the plantation itself."

Also in 1961, in *The Liberty Line,* Larry Gara quoted nineteenth-century British sources crediting Torrey with being "the organizer of the underground railroad." In *Crusade against Slavery: Friends, Foes, and Reforms 1820–1860,* published in 1986, Louis Filler called Torrey the "father of the underground railroad" and said he had "first conceived the idea of a prearranged route for underground rail-road activities" while lodged in the Annapolis jail in 1842. However, the historian who has done the most to bring Torrey's contribution to public attention has been Stanley Harrold. Initially in an article "On the Borders of Slavery and Race: Charles T. Torrey and the Underground Railroad," published in 2000, and then in a chapter in his 2003 book *Subversives: Antislavery Community in Washington, D.C., 1828–1865,* Harrold recounted Torrey's activities and contributions more extensively than other historians had done.[9]

To understand why Charles Torrey has been neglected by most historians, it is necessary to review events in the second half of the nineteenth century. In the years immediately following Torrey's death in 1846, his contributions were recognized and chronicled. In 1847 Joseph Lovejoy, a brother of martyr Elijah Lovejoy, published a *Memoir of Rev. Charles T. Torrey,* which sold for $1 ($23) and was intended to raise funds for Torrey's widow and children. It consisted mostly of Torrey's writings and letters, all of which had been approved for publication by Mrs. Torrey. Since it was intended to elicit sympathy and appeal to a wide audience, the book included virtually no mention of Torrey's role in challenging William Lloyd Garrison and precipitation of the schism. Thus, it is of limited historical use and has been largely neglected.[10]

In 1849 Catherine Brown published a *Memoir of Rev. Abel Brown,* her deceased husband, and two years later Thomas Smallwood published *A Narrative of Thomas Smallwood, (Colored Man).* Both books provided extensive accounts of the Washington-to-Albany Underground Railroad. In England, Louis A. Chamerovzow, who had become the secretary of the British and Foreign Anti-Slavery Society, cited Torrey as the founder of the "underground railroad to Freedom." Elizur Wigham, writing in Edinburgh, credited Torrey with having been the first to pass the "poor fugitive from one benevolent and trustworthy agent at *stations on the line* to another, so the chain was completed from the slave states to Canada." In 1898 Wilbur Siebert also gave Torrey some recognition, devoting two pages to him in *The Underground Railroad from Slavery to Freedom.*[11]

Regarding Torrey's broader contribution to the abolitionist movement, recognition was initially achieved in 1853 in William

Goodell's *Slavery and Anti-Slavery: A History of the Great Struggle in Both Hemispheres.* Goodell, who had been a friend of Torrey's, described him as "a man of genius as well as of rare courage," and concluded that "few men have made a deeper impression upon society in so brief a life." Then, in 1875, Henry Wilson, who would serve as vice-president in Ulysses Grant's second administration, published a four-volume *History of the Rise and Fall of Slave Power in America.* In it, he provided a detailed but more nuanced picture of Charles Torrey, including references to his "mercurial temperament" and his neglect of his family. Ultimately, however, Wilson was sympathetic:

> It is easy now, as it was then, to criticise and charge him [Torrey] with imprudence, unfounded enthusiasm, and an improper estimate of the relative claims of his family and the slave. Doubtless he was imprudent. That he was too enthusiastic may be admitted, when his purpose is born in mind,—to "celebrate the emancipation of the slaves in Maryland in ten years." That a cooler and more calculating judgment would have led him to hesitate before subjecting his family to the contingencies resulting from his decision is probable. But these were errors of judgment, "leaning to virtue's side." In the light of eternity, above the interests, the friendships, and conventionalisms of earth, at Heaven's chancery, when this act shall be tested by the standards of the great law of love, another estimate will be made. That solemn promise, then written down, will be deemed a worthier record than that of many a prudent man, who, at a safe distance, left the slave to suffer and perish.[12]

Henry Wilson's history represented the high-water mark for recognition of Charles Torrey's contribution, after which he underwent an eclipse. The major reason for this is that the history of the abolitionist movement in the latter half of the nineteenth century was written largely by William Lloyd Garrison's supporters, most of whom were still alive. Torrey and his supporters, however, were mostly deceased. The discrepancy in longevity between the two groups is striking, even though the average age of the two groups was approximately the same. Garrison himself lived until 1879, as did Angelina Grimké; Lydia Maria Child until 1880; Stephen Foster, 1881; Wendell Phillips, 1884; Maria Weston Chapman, 1885; Abigail Kelley Foster, 1887; and Parker Pillsbury, 1898. By contrast Myron Holley (1841) and Abel Brown (1844) preceded Torrey's 1846 death, which was followed by the deaths of Amos Phelps and Orange Scott in 1847, Alvan Stewart in 1849, James Birney in 1857, and James Bias in 1860. Thus, by 1860, many of the people most familiar with Charles Torrey's contributions were dead.

Two other men who were familiar with Torrey's work and lived longer were not about to write accounts of their involvement with the abolitionist movement. One was Joshua Giddings, who lived until 1864. Following John Brown's raid on Harpers Ferry, the *New York Herald* claimed that Giddings had foreknowledge of Brown's plan. A southern newspaper offered $5,000 ($120,000) for Giddings's head and $10,000 ($240,000) for the "entire man." Giddings was summoned to testify before a congressional committee set up to investigate Brown's raid. He denied everything and issued a press release saying, "Brown never consulted me in regard to his Virginia expedition, or any other expedition, or any matter whatever." Similarly, Gerrit Smith, who lived until 1874, was publicly tied to John Brown's raid by the *New York Herald* and was terrified of being indicted. He was noted by a reporter to be extremely upset and, one week after Brown's raid, was admitted to the New York State Lunatic Asylum in Utica. There he remained for two months, being excused from testifying before the congressional investigating committee because of his condition. For the rest of his life, Smith continued to be involved in social causes but, understandably, almost never spoke or wrote about his involvement with Charles Torrey or John Brown.[13]

Three other abolitionists who worked closely with Torrey and lived longer were Joshua Leavitt, who died in 1873, Elizur Wright (1885), and Henry Stanton (1887). Leavitt had been one of Torrey's closest friends; according to Leavitt's biographer, he "considered writing a history of the antislavery struggle, . . . but he never completed it." Garrison, hearing of Leavitt's intention, told a friend that such a history would be "a very jaundiced one." Elizur Wright dropped out of the abolitionist movement altogether in the 1850s. A mathematician by training, he later became an expert on life insurance and served as state commissioner of insurance for Massachusetts. Henry Stanton wrote a rather episodic book, *Random Recollections,* at age eighty-one. Remarkably, despite Stanton's deep involvement in the schism of 1839, neither these events nor Torrey was even mentioned.[14]

In telling Garrison's side of the story, two books were especially important in relegating Charles Torrey to the dustbin of history. The first was William Still's 1871 book *The Underground Railroad.* Still, whose parents had been slaves, moved to Philadelphia as a young man and in 1850, four years after Torrey's death, became active with the Philadelphia Vigilance Committee. He assisted slaves who arrived from the South during the 1850s, including Harriet Tubman, and made notes about their experiences. He was a devout follower of William Lloyd Garrison, hosting a reception for Garrison at his home in 1865. In 1871 Still published his notes as an 812-page book with praise from Garrison: "It is a book for every household." A competent businessman, Still skillfully promoted his book through two more editions in 1879 and 1893; according to Larry Gara's *The Liberty Line,* "no other underground railroad book was so well advertised or systematically promoted," and it became an essential starting point for future historians."[15]

Still included in his book "portraits and sketches" of twenty-three individuals who had made important contributions to the abolitionist movement. A fourteen-page hagiography of Garrison identified him as "the leader of the movement for immediate emancipation" and the man who "has made slavery hateful, and . . . made freedom possible in America": "His sweet temper, his modesty, his unfailing cheerfulness, his rarely mistaken judgment of men and measures; his blameless and happy domestic life, and his hospitality; his warm sympathy with all forms of human suffering—these and other qualities which cannot be enumerated here, will doubtless receive the just judgment of posterity." Still's book was published eight years before Garrison's death and became "perhaps the most widely read" of all the early books on the Underground Railroad. In the 812 pages, Charles Torrey was not mentioned once.[16]

The other book that established Charles Torrey as a marginal figure in the abolitionist movement was the four-volume biography

William Lloyd Garrison, written by two of Garrison's sons, Wendell and Frank. Garrison himself had agreed in 1866 to write an autobiography and had even taken a $5,000 ($75,000) advance for doing so, but later decided not to write it and returned the advance. Ever conscious of his place in history, he may have decided that his story could be told more effectively by others, especially by his two sons, who shared his pacifist views. The book was well underway before Garrison's death and was eventually published in four volumes in 1894. Torrey was mentioned twenty-seven times in the 1,811 pages, mostly in the chapter "Contest for Leadership." He was portrayed in the biography as merely one of a group of "priestly conspirators" and referred to twice as an "old enemy" and one of Garrison's "bitter enemies." Torrey's 1845 praise of Garrison, written from his prison cell in an attempt to raise funds, was depicted as genuine. No mention was made of Torrey's death or the denial of the use of the Park Street Church for his funeral.[17]

The minimization of Torrey's role by Garrison's sons was also illustrated by a collection of abolitionist photographs assembled by one of the sons "to accompany his biography of William Lloyd Garrison." The collection was subsequently given to the Massachusetts Historical Society and is listed as "A Catalogue of Portraits of American Abolitionists and of Their Allies and Opponents in the United States and in Great Britain and Ireland, 1831–1865." Over four hundred abolitionists were included in the collection, including a few of Garrison's enemies, such as Amos Phelps. Torrey, however, is nowhere to be found, relegated to the status of non-person by Garrison's son.[18]

Other biographies of William Lloyd Garrison have also marginalized Charles Torrey. An 1881 book, *William Lloyd Garrison and His Times,* written by Garrison's friend Oliver Johnson, did not mention Torrey. Nor did an 1891 biography, *William Lloyd Garrison: The Abolitionist,* written by Archibald Grimké, a half-brother of the Grimké sisters. More recent biographies of Garrison have also minimized Torrey's importance. Those by John Chapman (1974) and Nick Fauchald (2004) did not mention Torrey at all, and those by John Thomas (1963) and James Brewer Stewart (1992) each mentioned him once in passing. In Henry Mayer's ambitious *All on Fire: William Lloyd*

Garrison and the Abolition of Slavery (1998), Torrey received four brief mentions and was called "mean-spirited." None of these biographies described the role Torrey played in bringing about the schism of the Garrison and anti-Garrison forces or Garrison's hatred of Torrey, which persisted even after Torrey's death.[19]

Published recollections by Garrison supporters in the last half of the nineteenth century also mostly ignored Torrey. In Samuel May's *Some Recollections of Our Antislavery Conflicts,* published in 1869, the author recalled talking to Garrison for the first time and having his soul . . . baptized in his spirit. . . . The impression which [Garrison's words] . . . made upon my soul has never been effaced." Torrey is not mentioned in the book.[20]

Parker Pillsbury's 1883 book, *Acts of Anti-Slavery Apostles,* was the last history written by those who had been involved in the 1839 schism. Pillsbury claimed that Garrison embodied all "the Christian virtues and graces" and compared his followers, of which he was one, to the first Christian apostles. He extensively recounted endless battles between Garrison's old organization, for which Pillsbury labored, and the new organization, which he described as having "lapsed entirely into the political vortex" and "endangered the good name of anti-slavery." The abolition of slavery, Pillsbury argued, had been effected by moral suasion, "a divine ministry of freedom, humanity and holiness" and a "moral, peaceful and religious agitation for the rights of humanity." Garrison's followers were portrayed in stark contrast to "the flawed men who supported abolitionist political action." According to historian Julie Roy Jeffrey, Pillsbury's book left no doubt that moral suasion "had done the real work of emancipation, although exactly how they had done so was unclear."[21]

In addition to such Garrison-centered biographies and histories, the reputation of Charles Torrey has also suffered because of personality traits attributed to him. The most serious such allegation was that he was insane, an allegation based primarily on a letter sent by his wife to Amos Phelps following Torrey's death. In the letter, Mary Torrey said that her husband had been "partially insane upon some subjects," which was apparently an attempt to explain how strongly he felt about some issues and to explain the intemperate letters being evaluated by Joseph Lovejoy for use in the *Memoir,* in preparation at that time. There is no evidence whatever that Charles Torrey was ever insane in a clinical sense, including the fact that his tuberculosis had most certainly spread to his brain. However, the allegation of insanity has occasionally been accepted as genuine, as by Aileen Kraditor in *Means and Ends in American Abolitionism.* After discussing Torrey's views, she concluded: "Perhaps, however, Torrey's views should be discounted, in view of a letter to Phelps from Torrey's widow . . . in which she states that her husband had been 'partially insane upon some subjects.'"[22]

More common have been characterizations of Torrey as having been "irascible" and "contentious and uncooperative." Several historians have cited Theodore Weld's 1842 letter to his wife, Angeline Grimké, in which he described Torrey as "an exceedingly vain, trifling man with no wisdom or stability." What the historians usually fail to add is that Angelina was a devout follower of Garrison and strongly disliked Torrey for having opposed making women's rights part of the abolitionist agenda. It is true that Torrey could appear "irascible," especially to those who did not share his views, but he could also be warm and caring, as is illustrated by his correspondence with his close friend Amos Phelps. Furthermore, many of the unpleasant character traits attributed to Torrey were found in equal measure in Garrison and several other leading abolitionists. The abolitionist movement produced many heroic figures, but few heroic personalities.[23]

Without question, William Lloyd Garrison deserves a place of honor among American abolitionists. As the editor of the *Liberator* and organizer of the New England Anti-Slavery Society, he was the leader for the first decade of the movement. However, in the second and third decades political and aggressive forms of abolitionism emerged, at which time it has been said that "only about one-tenth of the antislavery men paid any attention to Garrison."[24]

Nonetheless, since the end of the Civil War, Garrison has been the icon of the American antislavery movement. According to Julie Roy Jeffrey, "Garrison was lavishly praised, and other abolitionists and their work received brief, usually positive mentions." Garrison was depicted as the "moral inspiration" for the movement, and the later divisions and discords were little mentioned. As an 1890 history described it, "all acted in harmony against the pro-slavery idea." The *Personal Reminiscences* of abolitionist Aaron Powell, published in 1899, even gave Garrison credit for making "Lincoln later a possibility."[25]

Reunions were held, such as the 1875 centennial anniversary of the Pennsylvania Abolition Society. The reunion was organized by William Still and included almost exclusively Garrison's followers— Abby Kelley Foster, Lucretia Mott, Charles Burleigh, Robert Purvis. A letter from Garrison was also read. These abolitionists were, after all, the last abolitionists standing. Torrey, Phelps, Birney, Giddings, Leavitt, Smith, and virtually all the others who had led political abolitionism were dead and in the process of being relatively forgotten.

POSTSCRIPT

Charles Torrey's wife, Mary, continued to live in West Medway, Massachusetts, after her husband's death. Her house, just west of her parents' house on Main Street, was built for her in 1850 by the Massachusetts Abolitionist Society, and it still stands. She lived through the Civil War, in which her son fought, and saw the liberation of slaves and fulfillment of her husband's dream. She died on November 6, 1869, age fifty-two.

Charles Henry Torrey, their son, was discharged from the Union forces on September 30, 1865, and thereafter lived and worked in Manhattan. In 1882, on his forty-fifth birthday, he married Emma Deebach. Five years later, he married Mary Ardella Persinger. No record has been found of any children. He died in Manhattan on January 17, 1897, age fifty-nine.

Mary Emmons Torrey, their daughter, married Albert Bryant in 1865 at age twenty-five. Bryant was an 1862 graduate of Amherst College and had attended Princeton and Andover Theological seminaries. Like her mother, Mary married her husband within one week of his ordination. Bryant served as a missionary in Turkey for three years, held pastorates in several Massachusetts towns and in Lead City, South Dakota, and died in Scituate, Massachusetts, in 1904. Mary died on April 6, 1897, age fifty-seven.

Mary and Albert Bryant had three sons and a daughter, who were Charles Torrey's grandchildren. Seelye Bryant, the eldest son, graduated from Amherst College and Princeton Theological Seminary, then held pastorates in several Massachusetts towns. He had one child by his first wife and two by his second. In 1925 he attended the 175th anniversary celebration of the Congregational Church in West Medway and discussed the life of his grandfather. He died in 1954. Emmons Bryant, the second son, graduated from Amherst College, taught at private schools in New York and Newark, then worked for various businesses in New York State. He married, had two children, and died in 1942. The daughter, Ethel Charlotte Bryant, was born in 1875, but no information was found on her. The youngest son, Arthur Alexis Bryant, graduated from Harvard and later received a PhD in classics. He taught Latin in private schools in New York, Boston, and Baltimore and was an active member of the Socialist Party. He married twice but apparently had no children. No information was found on his date of death.[1]

If Charles Torrey returned today, he would find Scituate still surrounded by "wide marshes, covered with short salt grass" and its southern boundary defined by "the winding banks of a little river, famed for its excellent fisheries." The house in which he was born stands but is now adjacent to the train station, from which town residents commute to Boston. However, his grandparents' "dear old mansion" in Norwell, where Torrey went to live after his parents' deaths, has long since been replaced by a modern house, and many of the childhood fields in which Torrey played have reverted to woodlands.[2]

If Torrey traveled to Annapolis, Baltimore, or Washington, he would recognize very little. The Annapolis and Baltimore jails and Maryland penitentiary have been replaced, as have the boarding houses in which he lived and the slave pens he knew so well. In Baltimore, Greenmount Cemetery, behind which Torrey collected slaves for trips north, is larger but otherwise unchanged. In Washington, Torrey would of course recognize the Capitol, where he worked as a congressional reporter. Four blocks behind the Capitol, at the corner of Fourth and D Streets SE, he would find the Ebenezer United Methodist Church, the contemporary version of the black church he regularly attended and where he issued many tickets for passage on the Underground Railroad. The original building was replaced in 1870 and again in 1897, but the church's mission has not changed, and the church has been designated a historical landmark.

Traveling north from Baltimore on the route he used most commonly, Torrey would initially be perplexed by the McDonalds and

Mattress Discounters on the Bel Air Road, which is now U.S. Route 1, but he would immediately recognize the terrain when he got to the Gunpowder River. Farther north, he would have to turn off the present road at Kalima to find the old road down the steep and wooded gorge to Deer Creek. Except for a modern bridge, the crossing appears unchanged from the June morning in 1844 when Robert Rigdon stood on the old bridge watching Torrey watering his horses and the Heckrotte slaves eating crackers and sausage they had brought from their master's tavern.

Continuing on to Peachbottom, Torrey would encounter two visual shocks. The Susquehanna River would appear to be more than twice as wide as when he knew it, a consequence of the downstream Conowingo Dam, built in 1928. The home of the free black who used to row slaves across the river is, in fact, now underwater. Even more perplexing to Torrey would be the Peachbottom Nuclear Power Plant at the site, built in 1958 and employing eight hundred workers. The heavily armed guards at the plant would discourage Torrey from lingering. Most of the safe houses in Pennsylvania used by Torrey are no longer standing except for the Samuel Mifflin house in Wrightsville. That has been designated as an Underground Railroad site by the York County Historical Society and is advertised by the society as the house "in 1843 that Reverend Charles T. Torrey made his last trip south."[3]

If Torrey returned to Boston, he would find many things familiar. Marlboro Chapel, the scene of his defeat by William Lloyd Garrison, is no longer standing, but the Park Street Church, where his funeral was denied, and the Tremont Temple, where it was held, are unchanged in appearance except for being surrounded by taller buildings. The Tremont Temple advertises itself as the "first integrated church in America," which would have pleased Torrey. Faneuil Hall, where Torrey attended the memorial service for Elijah Lovejoy and where his own memorial service was held, is still there but would appear modestly changed, since it was rebuilt in 1898.

Mount Auburn Cemetery, where Torrey was laid to rest in 1846, is now enveloped by Boston's suburbs. Torrey's monument is designated by a "P" on a cemetery map made for visitors as one of the

"Memorials or Lots of Interest" and is referred to by cemetery personnel as "the slave monument." It is prominently situated on a small plot in the middle of the intersection of Spruce and Fir Avenues. The path to the site passes directly by the grave of Dorothea Dix, who visited the Maryland Penitentiary while Torrey was being held there. Among Torrey's other neighbors are Amos Phelps; Mary Baker Eddy; Oliver Wendell Holmes; Winslow Homer; Samuel Gridley Howe, who was one of the secret six that bankrolled John Brown's raid; Henry Wadsworth Longfellow; and James Russell Lowell, who wrote the poem read at Torrey's funeral.

Torrey's grave is prominent and well maintained. Text engraved on the three-sided monument acknowledges that it was erected by "the friends of the American Slave . . . to his memory, as a Martyr for Liberty." On one side are details of Torrey's arrest and death: "Charles Turner Torrey was arrested for aiding slaves to regain their liberty. For this humane act he was indicted as a criminal, convicted by the Baltimore City Court, and sentenced to the Penitentiary for six years. While on his death bed he was refused a pardon by the Governor of Maryland and died of consumption after two years confinement, a victim of his sufferings."

On the second side is a poem:

> Where now beneath his burthen,
> The toiling slave is driven
> Where now a tyrant's mockery
> Is offered up to heaven.
> THERE shall his praise be spoken
> Redeemed from falsehood's ban.
> When the fetters shall be broken,
> And the SLAVE shall be a MAN.

Beneath the poem is an image of a seated female slave looking toward the ground.

On the front of the monument is a bronze bust of Torrey. Below is a list of the dates of Torrey's birth, college graduation, ordination, arrest, and death. Above the bust, crowned by a laurel wreath, are Torrey's words from an 1846 letter:

It is better to die
    in prison
with the peace of God
    in our breasts,
than to live in freedom
    with
a polluted conscience

A NOTE ON SOURCES

The single best source of information on the abolitionist career of Charles Torrey is the work of historian Stanley Harrold, especially "On the Borders of Slavery and Race: Charles T. Torrey and the Underground Railroad" (2000), and *Subversives: Antislavery Community in Washington, D.C., 1828–1865* (2003). Also useful is Joseph Lovejoy's *Memoir of Rev. Charles T. Torrey,* compiled shortly after Torrey's death. The major limitation of Lovejoy's book is that it was compiled under the supervision of Torrey's wife, who was understandably anxious to protect her husband's reputation; thus, Torrey's bitter fight with William Lloyd Garrison and other important matters are not mentioned. Less useful is Torrey's autobiography, titled *Home! Or the Pilgrim's Faith Revived* (1845), written as a fund-raiser for his family while he was in prison. Although it includes some useful details of his childhood, it otherwise attempts to present Torrey in a pious and idealized light. It is also known that Mary Torrey destroyed many of her husband's letters (September 15, 1846, letter from Mary Torrey to Amos Phelps). The lack of a large collection of surviving letters, in contrast to the legacies of Garrison and many other abolitionists, has also made it more difficult for historians to assess Charles Torrey's contribution. Other important sources on Torrey are Catherine S. Brown's *Memoir of Reverend Abel Brown* (published by the author in 1849) and Thomas Smallwood's *A Narrative of Thomas Smallwood, (Colored Man),* published in Toronto in 1851.

Especially important are Torrey's letters to Phelps, his closest friend, in the Phelps Collection at the Boston Public Library. A few letters in the Torrey Collection at the Congregational Library in Boston are also helpful, as are occasional letters in the Gerrit Smith Collection at the Syracuse University Library. Beyond these, one must rely on scattered letters in other collections and published pieces by and about Torrey in the abolitionist newspapers of that era, especially the *Albany Patriot, Emancipator,* and *Evangelist.* To take these literary scraps and pieces and mold them into coherent flesh and blood has been both a challenge and a pleasure.

NOTES

Preface

1. Stanley Harrold, "On the Borders of Slavery and Race: Charles T. Torrey and the Underground Railroad," *Journal of the Early Republic* 20 (2000): 273–92.

2. Henry Stanton, Funeral Address, *Emancipator*, May 27, 1846.

3. William L. Miller, *Arguing about Slavery: The Great Battle of the United States Congress* (New York: Alfred A. Knopf, 1996), 38–39.

Chapter One

1. Maria Weston Chapman, *Right and Wrong in Massachusetts* (Boston: Dow and Jackson's Anti-Slavery Press, 1839), 95–96; David M. Kennedy, "Editor's Introduction," in Daniel Walker Howe, *What Hath God Wrought: The Transformation of America, 1815–1848* (New York: Oxford University Press, 2007), xiii–xv.

2. Richard H. Sewell, *Ballots for Freedom: Antislavery Politics in the United States, 1837–1860* (New York: Oxford University Press, 1976), 30; Dorothy Sterling, *Ahead of Her Time: Abby Kelley and the Politics of Antislavery* (New York: W. W. Norton, 1991), 67.

3. Henry Mayer, *All on Fire: William Lloyd Garrison and the Abolition of Slavery* (New York: St. Martin's Press, 1998), 260; Sterling, *Ahead of Her Time,* 97, quoting a letter from Maria Chapman.

4. Mayer, *All on Fire,* 33; James Brewer Stewart, *William Lloyd Garrison and the Challenge of Emancipation* (Arlington Heights, Ill.: Harlan Davidson, 1992), 16, 24; Dwight L. Dumond, *Antislavery: The Crusade for Freedom in America* (Ann Arbor: University of Michigan Press, 1961), 283; Stewart, *William Lloyd Garrison,* 22.

5. F. G. De Fontaine, *American Abolitionism from 1787 to 1861* (*New York Herald,* Feb. 1861; New York: D. Appleton, 1861), 20; Stewart, *William Lloyd Garrison,* 44–47; James L. Huston, "The Experiential Basis of the Northern Antislavery Impulse," *Journal of Southern History* 56 (Nov. 1990): 609–40. The value of the dollar in the nineteenth century compared to its current (2010) value was calculated by using the Consumer Price Index, 1830 to 2010, www.westegg.com/inflation/.

6. Stewart, *William Lloyd Garrison,* 50–51.

7. Richard S. Newman, *The Transformation of American Abolitionism: Fighting Slavery in the Early Republic* (Chapel Hill: University of North Carolina Press, 2002), 107, 104; Stewart, *William Lloyd Garrison,* 44.

8. Newman, *Transformation*, 120, 115; Lawrence J. Friedman, *Gregarious Saints: Self and Community in American Abolitionism, 1830–1870* (New York: Cambridge University Press, 1982), 162, 175.

9. William Goodell, *Slavery and Anti-Slavery: A History of the Great Struggle in Both Hemispheres with a View of the Slavery Question in the United States* (New York, 1853; New York: Augustus M. Kelley, 1970), 556; James Brewer Stewart, *Wendell Phillips: Liberty's Hero* (Baton Rouge: Louisiana State University Press, 1986), 63–64; also see Irving H. Bartlett, *Wendell Phillips: Brahmin Radical* (Boston: Beacon Press, 1961). Sterling, *Ahead of Her Time*, 39.

10. Friedman, *Gregarious Saints*, 49; Stewart, *Wendell Phillips*, 65–66; Chapman, *Right and Wrong*, 87, quoting a Phillips letter; Bertram Wyatt-Brown, *Lewis Tappan and the Evangelical War against Slavery* (Cleveland: Press of Case Western University, 1969), 200.

11. Louis Ruchames, ed., *The Letters of William Lloyd Garrison, Volume II: A House Divided Against Itself* (Cambridge: Harvard University Press, 1971), hereafter cited as Ruchames, ed., *Letters*, 407 (letter to Mary Benson, Dec. 23, 1838), 422 (letter to George Benson, Jan. 14, 1839); Wendell P. Garrison and Francis J. Garrison, *William Lloyd Garrison 1805–1879* (1885–1889; New York: Arno Press, 1969), hereafter cited as Garrison and Garrison, *WLG* 2: 283; Ruchames, ed., *Letters*, 415 (letter to Samuel May, Jan. 4, 1839); William Lloyd Garrison, "Annual Meeting," *Liberator*, Jan. 18, 1839; Chapman, *Right and Wrong*, 55–56, 78.

12. Amos Phelps, *Lectures on Slavery and Its Remedy* (Boston: Massachusetts Anti-Slavery Society, 1834), v; Mayer, *All on Fire*, 269.

13. Mayer, *All on Fire*, 254; Bruce Laurie, *Beyond Garrison: Antislavery and Social Reform* (New York: Cambridge University Press, 2005), 39, quoting a Birney letter of Sept. 14, 1837; Sewell, *Ballots*, 27–28, quoting a Wright letter of Oct. 17, 1837.

14. Sewell, *Ballots*, 27; Laurie, *Beyond Garrison*, 3.

15. Mayer, *All on Fire*, 204–5; Goodell, *Slavery and Anti-Slavery*, 405; De Fontaine, *American Abolitionism*, 32; Mayer, *All on Fire*, 215, 222.

16. Sterling, *Ahead of Her Time*, 72; Garrison and Garrison, *WLG* 2: 437.

17. Mayer, *All on Fire*, 261; Sewell, *Ballots*, 31, quoting a Wright letter of Feb. 18, 1839.

18. Merton Lynn Dillon, *The Abolitionists: The Growth of a Dissenting Minority* (New York: W. W. Norton, 1979), 117; Mayer, *All on Fire*, 223; John L. Thomas, *The Liberator: William Lloyd Garrison, A Biography* (Boston: Little, Brown, 1963), 226; Stewart, *William Lloyd Garrison*, 91–92.

19. Richard O. Curry and Lawrence B. Goodheart, "The Complexities of Factionalism: Letters of Elizur Wright, Jr., on the Abolitionist Schism, 1837–1840," *Civil War History* 29 (Sept. 1983): 245–59.

20. Howe, *What Hath God Wrought*, 845; Newman, *Transformation*, 148; Mayer, *All on Fire*, 237; Friedman, *Gregarious Saints*, 142.

21. Sterling, *Ahead of Her Time*, 53; Kathryn Kish Sklar, "'The Throne of My Heart': Religion, Oratory, and Transatlantic Community in Angelina Grimké's

Launching of Women's Rights, 1828–1838," in Kathryn Kish Sklar and James Brewer Stewart, eds., *Women's Rights and Transatlantic Antislavery in the Era of Emancipation* (New Haven, Conn.: Yale University Press, 2007), 211–41; Sterling, *Ahead of Her Time*, 55; Curry and Goodheart, "The Complexities of Factionalism," quoting a Wright letter to Amos Phelps, July 11, 1838; Friedman, *Gregarious Saints*, 87.

22. Sterling, *Ahead of Her Time*, 145, 3; Friedman, *Gregarious Saints*, 137; Sterling, *Ahead of Her Time*, 58, 4.

23. Leslie M. Harris, "From Abolitionist Amalgamators to 'Rulers of the Five Points': The Discourse of Interracial Sex and Reform in Antebellum New York City," in Patrick Rael, ed., *African-American Activism before the Civil War: The Freedom Struggle in the Antebellum North* (New York: Routledge, 2008), 250–71; J. Thomas Scharf and Thompson Westcott, *History of Philadelphia, 1609–1884* (Philadelphia: L. H. Everts, 1884), vol. 1: 651; James Brewer Stewart, *Abolitionist Politics and the Coming of the Civil War* (Amherst: University of Massachusetts Press, 2008), 47–48.

24. Ronald G. Walters, "The Erotic South: Civilization and Sexuality in American Abolitionism," *American Quarterly* 25 (May 1973): 177–201; Stewart, *Wendell Phillips*, 72.

25. Sterling, *Ahead of Her Time*, 78–79.

26. Stewart, *William Lloyd Garrison*, 39; Lawrence Lader, *The Bold Brahmins: New England's War Against Slavery, 1831–1863* (New York: E. P. Dutton and Co., 1961), 118; Torrey letter in the *Liberator*, Jan. 25, 1839; letter from A. Farnsworth to A. W. Weston, June 11, 1840, Garrison Collection, Boston Public Library, courtesy of the Trustees of the Boston Public Library/Rare Books; Kathryn Grover, *The Fugitive's Gibraltar: Escaping Slaves and Abolitionism in New Bedford, Massachusetts* (Amherst: University of Massachusetts Press, 2001), 184; Stanley Harrold, *Subversives: Antislavery Community in Washington, D.C., 1828–1865* (Baton Rouge: Louisiana State University Press, 2003), 98; Garrison, "Annual Meeting"; letter from Theodore Weld to Gerrit Smith, Oct. 23, 1839, in Gilbert H. Barnes and Dwight L. Dumond, eds., *Letters of Theodore Dwight Weld, Angelina Grimké Weld and Sarah Grimké, 1822–1844* (New York: DaCapo Press, 1970), hereafter cited as Barnes and Dumond, eds., *Letters of Weld, Weld, and Grimké*, 810; Mayer, *All on Fire*, 279; Dillon, *The Abolitionists*, 120; letter from Mary Torrey to Amos Phelps, Sept. 15, 1846, Phelps Collection, Boston Public Library, hereafter cited as Phelps Collection, courtesy of the Trustees of the Boston Public Library/Rare Books. Among letters in the Garrison Collection in the Boston Public Library and the Torrey Collection in the Congregational Library in Boston, there is only one between Torrey and Garrison. This was a formal request from Torrey to Garrison asking for the return of some letters. The letter is dated September 25, 1841, and begins "Dear Sir," although Torrey had known Garrison for at least six years.

27. Parker Pillsbury, *Acts of the Anti-Slavery Apostles* (Concord, N.H.: Clague, Wegman, Schlicht and Co., 1883); Joseph C. Lovejoy, *Memoir of Rev. Charles T.*

Torrey (Boston: John P. Jewett, 1847; New York: Negro Universities Press, 1969), 142; Charles T. Torrey, *Home! Or the Pilgrim's Faith Revived* (Salem, Mass.: J. P. Jewett, 1845), 107, 135.

28. Michael D. Pierson, *Free Hearts and Free Homes: Gender and American Antislavery Politics* (Chapel Hill: University of North Carolina Press, 2003), 18; Howe, *What Hath God Wrought*, 341–42.

29. Friedman, *Gregarious Saints*, 147; Mayer, *All on Fire*, 254; Friedman, *Gregarious Saints*, 149; Pillsbury, *Acts of the Anti-Slavery Apostles*, 243–44.

30. Mayer, *All on Fire*, 236, 229; James Brewer Stewart, "The Emergence of Racial Modernity and the Rise of the White North, 1790–1840," in Rael, ed., *African-American Activism before the Civil War*, 220–49.

31. Garrison and Garrison, *WLG* 2: 262–63. Letter from Garrison to George Benson, Jan. 5, 1839; letter from Garrison to Mary Benson, Dec. 23, 1838, in Ruchames, ed., *Letters*, 418, 407.

32. Walter M. Merrill, *Against Wind and Tide: A Biography of William Lloyd Garrison* (Cambridge: Harvard University Press, 1963), 148, quoting the *Liberator* of Jan. 11, 1839; Mayer, *All on Fire*, 218.

33. Chapman, *Right and Wrong*, 76–77.

34. Chapman, *Right and Wrong*, 80–81; letter from Torrey to Amos Phelps, March 30, 1839, Phelps Collection; Aileen S. Kraditor, *Means and Ends in American Abolitionism: Garrison and His Critics on Strategy and Tactics, 1834–1850* (New York: Pantheon Books, 1968), 97, quoting a letter from Torrey to Phelps, March 21, 1839.

35. Thomas, *The Liberator*, 266.

36. Sewell, *Ballots*, 31; Chapman, *Right and Wrong*, 98–99, 107–9.

37. Sewell, *Ballots*, 31; Chapman, *Right and Wrong*, 100.

38. Mayer, *All on Fire*, 257–58; Garrison and Garrison, *WLG* 2: 273; Chapman, *Right and Wrong*, 100.

39. Thomas, *The Liberator*, 267–68; Mayer, *All on Fire*, 257.

40. Thomas, *The Liberator*, 269; Sewell, *Ballots*, 32.

41. Thomas, *The Liberator*, 264; Sewell, *Ballots*, 33–34.

Chapter Two

1. Charles T. Torrey, "The Dead Heart: A Tale of a Prisoner," *Emancipator*, Apr. 8, 1846; Torrey, *Home*, 15.

2. Lovejoy, *Memoir*, 1; Torrey, *Home*, 131–32, 193.

3. Lovejoy, *Memoir*, 2, 5; Torrey, *Home*, 14.

4. *Biographical Directory of the United States Congress, 1774–2005* (Washington, D.C.: Government Printing Office, 2005), 2067; Lovejoy, *Memoir*, 3, 4, 142. The information on Charles Torrey's name change was found at www.dunhamwilcox .net/ma/ma_names2.htm. The change was dated February 18, 1819, at which time Torrey would have been five years old.

5. Torrey, *Home,* 14. The list of early settlers in Scituate was found at scituate-historicalsociety.org/families_home.html.

6. Frederic C. Torrey, *The Torrey Families and Their Children in America* (Lakehurst, N.J.: n.p., 1924), 18.

7. Lovejoy, *Memoir,* 4.

8. Lovejoy, *Memoir,* 8, 9, 12; these diary entries were dated July 1831. Torrey, *Home,* 76, 79–80.

9. Lovejoy, *Memoir,* 19–21; Torrey, *Home,* 131.

10. Frank G. Beardsley, *A Mighty Winner of Souls: Charles G. Finney, A Study in Evangelism* (New York: American Tract Society, 1937), 25, 97; Howe, *What Hath God Wrought,* 188.

11. Lovejoy, *Memoir,* 6–7.

12. Torrey, *Home,* 95; Lovejoy, *Memoir,* 2.

13. Lovejoy, *Memoir,* 14, 17.

14. Lovejoy, *Memoir,* 20–21, 23.

15. Torrey, *Home,* 216–23.

16. Torrey, *Home,* 88, 149–54.

17. Miller, *Arguing about Slavery,* 13.

18. Miller, *Arguing about Slavery,* 16–19; Eliza Wigham, *The Anti-Slavery Cause in America and Its Martyrs* (London: A. W. Bennett, 1863), 67–68.

19. Howe, *What Hath God Wrought,* 131, 128; Harrold, *Subversives,* 1.

20. Stewart, "The Emergence of Racial Modernity"; Peter P. Hinks, *To Awaken My Afflicted Brethren: David Walker and the Problem of Antebellum Slave Resistance* (University Park: Pennsylvania State University Press, 1997), 246, 245; Robert H. Abzug, "The Influence of Garrisonian Abolitionists' Fear of Slave Violence on the Antislavery Argument, 1829–1840," *Journal of Negro History* 55 (Jan. 1970): 15–28.

21. De Fontaine, *American Abolitionism,* 22–24.

22. De Fontaine, *American Abolitionism,* 24; John Ashworth, *Slavery, Capitalism, and Politics in the Antebellum Republic, Volume 1: Commerce and Compromise, 1830–1850* (Cambridge: Cambridge University Press, 1995), hereafter cited as Ashworth, *Commerce and Compromise,* 139–40.

23. Wyatt-Brown, *Lewis Tappan,* 87; Stewart, *Abolitionist Politics,* 173.

24. Wyatt-Brown, *Lewis Tappan,* 89; Stewart, *Abolitionist Politics,* 173–74; Stewart, "The Emergence of Racial Modernity."

25. Lovejoy, *Memoir,* 6.

26. Lovejoy, *Memoir,* 27.

27. Lovejoy, *Memoir,* 27–30.

28. Homer Merriam, "My Father's History and Family," from *Annals of the Merriam Family as Gathered by Homer Merriam Commenced in 1862,* the Old Sturbridge Village website, www.osv.org/explore_learn/document_viewer.php?DocID=987; Lovejoy, *Memoir,* 29.

29. Lovejoy, *Memoir,* 28–29, 31.

30. Lovejoy, *Memoir*, 29.

31. Ashworth, *Commerce and Compromise*, 132; Gilbert H. Barnes, *The Anti-Slavery Impulse 1830–1844* (1933; New York: Harcourt, Brace and World, 1964), 48.

32. Laurie, *Beyond Garrison*, 21; Goodell, *Slavery and Anti-Slavery*, 396; Wigham, *The Anti-Slavery Cause*, frontsheet.

33. Newman, *Transformation*, 117, quoting the *Pennsylvanian*, Dec. 12, 1833.

34. Barnes, *The Anti-Slavery Impulse*, 64–73.

35. Barnes, *The Anti-Slavery Impulse*, 69–71, 34.

36. Newman, *Transformation*, 111, 113.

37. Phelps, *Lectures*, v–xi.

38. Phelps, *Lectures*, 209–11; letter from Amos Phelps to Charlotte Phelps, Aug. 31, 1835, Phelps Collection.

39. Phelps, *Lectures*, 16.

40. Phelps, *Lectures*, 52, 56, 57, 52.

41. Walters, "The Erotic South"; Howe, *What Hath God Wrought*, 57; John D'Emilio and Estelle B. Freedman, *Intimate Matters: A History of Sexuality in America* (New York: Harper and Row, 1988), 100; Julie Roy Jeffrey, *The Great Silent Army of Abolitionism: Ordinary Women in the Antislavery Movement* (Chapel Hill: University of North Carolina Press, 1998), 29.

42. Walters, "The Erotic South"; letter from Torrey to Amos Phelps, Sept. 13, 1839, Phelps Collection; Harrold, *Subversives*, 47; Stanley Harrold, *The Abolitionists and the South, 1831–1861* (Lexington: University Press of Kentucky, 1995), 73; Benjamin Lundy and Julius Rubens Ames, *The Legion of Liberty and Force of Truth*, 2nd ed. (1843; New York: Arno Press, 1969), n.p.

43. See, for example, the letter from Torrey to Phelps, July 2, 1835, Phelps Collection, MS.A.21.5.45; Howe, *What Hath God Wrought*, 426; Leonard L. Richards, *"Gentlemen of Property and Standing": Anti-Abolition Mobs in Jacksonian America* (New York: Oxford University Press, 1970), 52; David Grimsted, *American Mobbing: 1828–1861: Toward Civil War* (New York: Oxford University Press, 1998), 17; Ormond Seavey, ed., *The Moon Hoax* (Boston: Grigg, 1975), n.p.

44. Grimstead, *American Mobbing*, 114; Richard B. Morris and Jeffrey B. Morris, eds., *Encyclopedia of American History* (New York: Harper and Row, 1976), 209; De Fontaine, *American Abolitionism*, 30; Grimstead, *American Mobbing*, 29; Richards, *Gentlemen of Property*, 17; Howe, *What Hath God Wrought*, 429; Lawrence B. Goodheart, *Abolitionist, Actuary, Atheist: Elizur Wright and the Reform Impulse* (Kent, Ohio: Kent State University Press, 1990), 75.

45. Harrold, *Subversives*, 1; Stanley Harrold, *The Rise of Aggressive Abolitionism: Addresses to the Slaves* (Lexington: University Press of Kentucky, 2004), 14.

46. Barnes, *The Anti-Slavery Impulse*, 81, 86.

47. Grimsted, *American Mobbing*, 4; Richards, *Gentlemen of Property*, 91.

48. John Bunyan, *The Life and Death of Mr. Badman*, 1680, qtd. in Rene Dubos and Jean Dubos, *The White Plague: Tuberculosis, Man, and Society* (New Brunswick, N.J.: Rutgers University Press, 1987), 8; Lovejoy, *Memoir*, 33, 150.

49. Lovejoy, *Memoir*, 32.

50. Lovejoy, *Memoir*, 159 (Torrey's letter to his wife of February 2, 1846, refers to the year of illness as 1826, but this almost certainly was meant to read 1836); letter from Charles Torrey to Amos Phelps, Aug. 14, 1838, Phelps Collection.

51. Lovejoy, *Memoir*, 33.

52. Newman, *Transformation*, 121; Mayer, *All on Fire*, 221.

53. Miller, *Arguing about Slavery*, 138, 144.

54. The information on Jacob Ide is from Jameson, E. O., Norfolk County MA Archives, Biographies, 1886, files.usgwarchives.org/ma/norfolk/bios/ide-30gbs.txt; American Abolitionism: Officers of the American Anti-Slavery Society, 1833–1840, americanabolitionist.liberalarts.iupui.edu/officers%20of%20the%20american%20anti%20slavery%20society%201833%2040.htm; and American Abolitionism: Officers of the Massachusetts Anti-Slavery Society, 1835–40, americanabolitionist.liberalarts.iupui.edu/officers%20of%20the%20mass%20anti%2035%2040.htm. It can be assumed that Amos Phelps knew Ide, since Ide had been one of the signers of the "Declaration of Sentiment," signed by 124 clergymen and included in Phelps, *Lectures*.

55. Lovejoy, *Memoir*, 316; Alonzo H. Quint, Christopher Cushing, Isaac P. Langworthy et al., eds., "Congregational Necrology," *Congregational Quarterly* (Boston: Congregational Rooms), vol. 12, new series vol. 2 (1870): 59–60; Lovejoy, *Memoir*, 34.

56. Benjamin Quarles, *Black Abolitionists* (New York: Oxford University Press, 1969), 163; T. Stephen Whitman, *Challenging Slavery in the Chesapeake: Black and White Resistance to Human Bondage, 1775–1865* (Baltimore: Maryland Historical Society, 2007), 126–27.

57. Barnes, *The Anti-Slavery Impulse*, 104–5; Mayer, *All on Fire*, 230–31.

58. Letter from John E. Brown to Amos Phelps, Sept. 12, 1837; letter from Charles Torrey to Amos Phelps, July 22, 1839, Phelps Collection.

59. Letter from Anne Warren Weston to Deborah Weston, 1839; letter from Anne Warren Weston to M. Weston, 1839, Garrison Collection. Torrey, *Home*, 103, 54, 27, 66, 56.

60. Richards, *Gentlemen of Property*, 34; Lovejoy, *Memoir*, 39.

61. Lovejoy, *Memoir*, 44, 80, 68.

62. Letter from Amos Phelps to [no first name] Smythe, Oct. 24, 1837, Phelps Collection.

63. Richards, *Gentlemen of Property*, 101; Lader, *The Bold Brahmins*, 76–84; Richard O. Boyer, *The Legend of John Brown* (New York: Alfred A. Knopf, 1973), 308–11.

64. Boyer, *The Legend of John Brown*, 309–10; Goodell, *Slavery and Anti-Slavery*, 406.

65. Ashworth, *Commerce and Compromise*, 143; Louis Filler, *Crusade Against Slavery: Friends, Foes, and Reforms, 1820–1860* (Algonac, Mich.: Reference Publications, 1986), 80; Justus N. Brown, "Lovejoy's Influence on John Brown," *Maga-*

zine of History 23 (1911): 97–102; Herbert Aptheker, *Abolitionism: A Revolutionary Movement* (Boston: G. K. Hall and Co., 1989), 103.

66. I can find no documentation verifying Torrey's attendance at the Faneuil Hall meeting, but he almost certainly was there. He was between his two ministerial jobs and in Boston at that time. Lader, *The Bold Brahmins*, 82; Filler, *Crusade*, 80; John Stauffer, *The Black Hearts of Men: Radical Abolitionists and the Transformation of Race* (Cambridge, Mass.: Harvard University Press, 2002), 118; Stewart, *Wendell Phillips*, 58.

67. Thomas, *The Liberator*, 256; Mayer, *All on Fire*, 237; letter from Torrey to Amos Phelps, Apr. 20, 1842, Phelps Collection.

68. Lader, *The Bold Brahmins*, 89.

69. The Phelps circular, dated Dec. 1837, is in the Torrey Collection, courtesy of the Congregational Library, Boston, hereafter cited as Torrey Collection. Dillon, *The Abolitionists*, 121, quoting William Jay, an abolitionist active with the New York group.

Chapter Three

1. Stauffer, *Black Hearts*, 33.

2. Laurie, *Beyond Garrison*, 287, 122; Howard Temperley, *British Antislavery, 1833–1870* (London: Longman, 1972), 208; Reinhard O. Johnson, "The Liberty Party in Massachusetts, 1840–1848: Antislavery Third Party Politics in the Bay State," *Civil War History* 28 (Sept. 1982): 237–65; see also Reinhard O. Johnson, *The Liberty Party: 1840–1848: Antislavery Third-Party Politics in the United States* (Baton Rouge: Louisiana State University Press, 2009).

3. See, for example, the letter from Garrison to Elizabeth Pease, June 1, 1841, in Garrison and Garrison, *WLG* 3: 10; Mayer, *All on Fire*, 267; Sewell, *Ballots*, 35.

4. Sterling, *Ahead of Her Time*, 96; letter from Child to Ellis Gray Loring, May 7, 1840, in Milton Meltzer and Patricia G. Holland, eds., *Lydia Maria Child: Selected Letters, 1817–1880* (Amherst: University of Massachusetts Press, 1982), 130; letter from Garrison to George Benson, June 19, 1839, in Ruchames, ed., *Letters*, 493; Johnson, "The Liberty Party"; Johnson, *The Liberty Party*, 101.

5. Sewell, *Ballots*, 35.

6. Sewell, *Ballots*, 36.

7. Sewell, *Ballots*, 37–41; *Sixth Annual Report of the Executive Committee of the American Anti-Slavery Society* (New York: William S. Dorr, 1839), 47; Chapman, *Right and Wrong*, 145–46.

8. Johnson, "The Liberty Party"; Harrold, *Subversives*, 70; Sewell, *Ballots*, 42, 51.

9. Sewell, *Ballots*, 49–51.

10. Sewell, *Ballots*, 48–49.

11. Sewell, *Ballots*, 52–54.

12. Thomas, *The Liberator*, 277; Mayer, *All on Fire*, 275; Goodell, *Slavery and Anti-Slavery*, 469; Sewell, *Ballots*, 44.

13. "Biography of Charles Turner," *Biographical Directory of the United States Congress*, 2067; Torrey's dismissal from his position in Salem is verified by his letter to Amos Phelps of July 22, 1839, in the Phelps Collection; Lovejoy, *Memoir*, 42.

14. Letters from Torrey to Phelps dated July 22, 1839, and Aug. 3, 1839, Phelps Collection; letter from Torrey to Amos Phelps, Dec. 13, 1839, Phelps Collection.

15. Sewell, *Ballots*, 54, 58; Johnson, *The Liberty Party*, 14.

16. Sewell, *Ballots*, 59, 60.

17. Sewell, *Ballots*, 63.

18. Thomas, *The Liberator*, 279; Mayer, *All on Fire*, 277, 259.

19. Sewell, *Ballots*, 64.

20. Sewell, *Ballots*, 66. Regarding Torrey's role in the formation of the Liberty Party, see the letters from Edwin W. Clarke to Torrey, February 21, 1840, and Amos Phelps to Torrey, Jan. 24, 1840, Torrey Collection; letter from James Birney to Amos Phelps in Dwight Dumond, ed., *Letters of James Gillespie Birney 1831–1857* (New York: D. Appleton-Century Co., 1938), hereafter cited as Dumond, ed., *Letters of Birney*, 527. See also Hugh Davis, *Joshua Leavitt: Evangelical Abolitionist* (Baton Rouge: Louisiana State University Press, 1990), 155.

21. Johnson, *The Liberty Party*, 101, 224; Sewell, *Ballots*, 67.

22. "The Albany Convention," *Friend of Man*, Apr. 8, 1840.

23. Sewell, *Ballots*, 71.

24. Sewell, *Ballots*, 71; Alan M. Kraut, "The Forgotten Reformers: A Profile of Third Party Abolitionists in Antebellum New York," in Lewis Perry and Michael Fellman, eds., *Antislavery Reconsidered: New Perspectives on the Abolitionists* (Baton Rouge: Louisiana State University Press, 1979), 20; Dumond, *Antislavery*, 297; Garrison and Garrison, *WLG* 2: 342.

25. Johnson, *The Liberty Party*, 222–23, 61; Howe, *What Hath God Wrought*, 652; Laurie, *Beyond Garrison*, 82.

26. Johnson, "The Liberty Party," quoting a letter of May 24, 1840; Sewell, *Ballots*, 77.

27. Johnson, "The Liberty Party"; Sewell, *Ballots*, 75.

28. Sewell, *Ballots*, 75; Johnson, "The Liberty Party"; Sewell, *Ballots*, 69; *Ninth Annual Report of the Board of Managers of the Mass. Anti-Slavery Society* (Boston: Dow and Jackson, 1841), 4.

29. Sewell, *Ballots*, citing a letter from Torrey to Phelps, Nov. 8, 1839; Goodell, *Slavery and Anti-Slavery*, footnote, 465–65; Wyatt-Brown, *Lewis Tappan*, 198.

30. Wyatt-Brown, *Lewis Tappan*, 197; Mayer, *All on Fire*, 278–83; Johnson, *The Liberty Party*, 9.

31. Mayer, *All on Fire*, 280, 283.

32. Lovejoy, *Memoir*, 318–20.

33. Temperley, *British Antislavery*, 86–87, 208.

34. Sewell, *Ballots*, 63.

35. Johnson, *The Liberty Party*, 93; Goodell, *Slavery and Anti-Slavery*, 393–94, 488–89.

36. Howe, *What Hath God Wrought*, 576; Johnson, *The Liberty Party*, 93.

37. Howe, *What Hath God Wrought*, 590.

38. Lovejoy, *Memoir*, 86–87; letter from Amos Phelps to Gerrit Smith, June 27, 1840, Gerrit Smith Collection, Syracuse University; Ralph V. Harlow, *Gerrit Smith: Philanthropist and Reformer* (New York: Henry Holt, 1939), 150. The reference to Torrey's land in Maine is in a letter from Torrey to Amos Phelps, July 28, 1844, Phelps Collection.

39. Garrison and Garrison, *WLG* 3: 10, 37; Goodell, *Slavery and Anti-Slavery*, 511; Stewart, *Abolitionist Politics*, 22; letter from Pompey Cesar to Torrey, June 24, 1841, Torrey Collection.

40. Johnson, *The Liberty Party*, 229, 376.

41. Lovejoy, *Memoir*, 86–87.

42. "Extraordinary Case of Kidnapping," *Liberator*, June 11, 1841, rpt. from the *Boston Daily Mail*.

43. Charles Torrey, "The Kidnapper Released!" *Boston Free American*, June 10, 1841.

44. Letter from Maria Child to Ellis Gray Loring, June 17, 1841, in Meltzer and Holland, eds., *Lydia Maria Child*, 144; Charles T. Torrey, "The Boston Vigilance Committee," *Liberator*, July 2, 1841; letter from Joshua Leavitt to Torrey (no date), Torrey Collection (Garrison's comment is under an item labeled "Boston Vigilance Committee," *Liberator*, June 18, 1841).

45. Torrey, "The Kidnapper."

46. Letter from Torrey to Lewis Tappan, Dec. 13, 1840, Amistad Collection, American Missionary Association Archives, Tulane University.

47. Goodell, *Slavery and Anti-Slavery*, 440-41; "Death of Alanson Work," *Hartford Courant*, July 8, 1879; Harrold, *The Rise of Aggressive Abolitionism*, 114.

48. Laurie, *Beyond Garrison*, 75; Johnson, "The Liberty Party."

Chapter Four

1. Torrey's request for a desk in Congress is in the Torrey Collection. See also Lovejoy, *Memoir*, 356.

2. P. P. [Torrey], "Correspondence from Washington," *New York Evangelist*, hereafter cited as Torrey, "Correspondence," Dec. 11, 1841; Fergus M. Bordewich, *Bound for Canaan: The Underground Railroad and the War for the Soul of America* (New York: HarperCollins, 2005), 299; Charles Dickens, *American Notes for General Circulation* (London: Chapman and Hall, 1842), www.fullbooks.com/American-Notes-for-General-Circulation3.html; Torrey, "Correspondence," Dec. 18, 1841.

3. Walter C. Clephane, "The Local Aspect of Slavery in the District of Columbia," in *Records of the Columbia Historical Society* (Washington, D.C.: Columbia Historical Society, 1900), vol. 3: 235–40, books.google.com/books?id=V2TENHr9D10C;

Harrold, *Subversives*, 54; Charles L. Blockson, *The Underground Railroad* (New York: Prentice Hall, 1987), 152; Ernest B. Furgurson, *Freedom Rising: Washington in the Civil War* (New York: Knopf, 2004), 103; Harrold, *Subversives*, 107, quoting the *Pittsburgh Gazette*.

4. Letitia W. Brown, *Free Negroes in the District of Columbia, 1790–1846* (New York: Oxford University Press, 1972), vi; Howe, *What Hath God Wrought*, 480.

5. Robert H. Abzug, *Cosmos Crumbling: American Reform and the Religious Imagination* (New York: Oxford University Press, 1994), 135; Harrold, *Subversives*, 31; *Sixth Annual Report of the Executive Committee of the American Anti-Slavery Society*, 47; Howe, *What Hath God Wrought*, 652; Harrold, *Subversives*, 5–6.

6. Letter from Torrey to his wife, Dec. 13, 1841, in Lovejoy, *Memoir*, 89–90; C.T. [Charles Torrey], "Free People of Color in Washington, D.C.," *Emancipator and Free American*, Sept. 8, 1842.

7. Davis, *Joshua Leavitt*, 148, 69–70, 88.

8. Davis, *Joshua Leavitt*, 41, 45, 108.

9. James B. Stewart, *Joshua R. Giddings and the Tactics of Radical Politics* (Cleveland: Press of Case Western Reserve University, 1970), 3–36.

10. James B. Stewart, "Joshua Giddings, Antislavery Violence, and Congressional Politics of Honor," in John R. McKivigan and Stanley Harrold, eds., *Antislavery Violence: Sectional, Racial, and Cultural Conflict in Antebellum America* (Knoxville: University of Tennessee Press, 1999), 173–74.

11. Stewart, "Joshua Giddings," 173, 176; Stewart, *Abolitionist Politics*, 130; George Julian, *The Life of Joshua R. Giddings* (Chicago: A. C. McClurg and Co., 1892), 172; Stewart, *Joshua R. Giddings*, 43.

12. Stewart, *Joshua R. Giddings*, 40–41; Stewart, "Joshua Giddings," 183; William H. Siebert, *The Underground Railroad from Slavery to Freedom* (1898; New York: Arno Press, 1968), 105.

13. Harrold, *Subversives*, 44; Stewart, "Joshua Giddings," 185; letter from Torrey to his wife, Dec. 13, 1841, in Lovejoy, *Memoir*, 88. An example of the Torrey-Giddings correspondence is a letter from Giddings to Torrey, Apr. 27, 1842, in the Torrey Collection. Also in this collection is a letter from Myron Finch to Torrey addressed "Care of Hon. J. R. Giddings."

14. Barnes and Dumond, eds., *Letters of Weld, Weld, and Grimké*, 882–85; Lovejoy, *Memoir*, 89.

15. Torrey, "Correspondence," Dec. 18, 1841.

16. Torrey, "Correspondence," Dec. 18, 1841; Jan. 13, 1842; Dec. 18, 1841.

17. Grimstead, *American Mobbing*, 166; Howe, *What Hath God Wrought*, 485; Miller, *Arguing about Slavery*, 134, 178; D'Emilio and Freedman, *Intimate Matters*, 96; Harrold, *Subversives*, 76, quoting the *Albany Patriot*, March 6, 1844; Kevin McQueen, *Offbeat Kentuckians: Legends to Lunatics* (Kuttawa, Ky.: McClanahan Publishing, 2004), 19.

18. Harrold, *Subversives*, 71.

19. Torrey, "Correspondence," Dec. 11, 1841; Christopher Phillips, *Freedom's Port: The African-American Community in Baltimore, 1790–1860* (Urbana: University of Illinois Press, 1997), 184.

20. Charles Torrey, "Case of Rev. Mr. Torrey," *New York Evangelist,* Feb. 3, 1842.

21. Torrey, Letter to the Editor, *Emancipator and Weekly Chronicle,* Aug. 29, 1844, in Lovejoy, *Memoir,* 143; letter from Torrey to his wife, Dec. 26, 1842, in Lovejoy, *Memoir,* 104. Details of the slaveholders' convention and Torrey's arrest are in the *New York Evangelist,* Feb. 2, 1842; *Baltimore Sun,* Jan. 15, 1842; and *Emancipator and Free American,* Feb. 4, 1842.

22. Torrey, "Case of Rev. Mr. Torrey"; Torrey letter in the *Emancipator and Free American,* Feb. 4, 1842, cited in Harrold, *Subversives,* 76; *A Guide to the History of Slavery in Maryland* (Annapolis: Maryland State Archives and University of Maryland, 2007), 11.

23. See, for example, the *Lynn Register,* Jan. 28, 1842. "The Slaveholders' Convention," *Emancipator and Free American,* Jan. 20, 1842; Mr. Torrey, *Emancipator and Free American,* Jan. 27, 1842.

24. Letter from Torrey to his wife, Jan. 19, 1842, in Lovejoy, *Memoir,* 100–101.

25. Letter from Torrey to his wife, Feb. 2, 1842, in Lovejoy, *Memoir,* 101–3; letter from Theodore Weld to his wife, Jan. 25, 1842, in Barnes and Dumond, eds., *Letters of Weld, Weld, and Grimké,* 903; Torrey, "Correspondence," Feb. 10, 1842.

26. Lader, *The Bold Brahmins,* 87; Leonard L. Richards, *The Life and Times of Congressman John Quincy Adams* (New York: Oxford University Press, 1988), 3.

27. Richards, *The Life and Times of Congressman John Quincy Adams,* 9; Lader, *The Bold Brahmins,* 88, 92.

28. Richards, *The Life and Times of Congressman John Quincy Adams,* 3, 9; Stewart, *Joshua R. Giddings,* 431; Richards, *The Life and Times of Congressman John Quincy Adams,* 3.

29. Davis, *Joshua Leavitt,* 191; Richards, *The Life and Times of Congressman John Quincy Adams,* 141.

30. Miller, *Arguing about Slavery,* 495; Barnes and Dumond, eds., *Letters of Weld, Weld, and Grimké,* 288, note 6, quoting a letter from Weld to his wife.

31. Davis, *Joshua Leavitt,* 189; Miller, *Arguing about Slavery,* 405; Gerda Lerner, *The Grimké Sisters from South Carolina: Pioneers for Women's Rights and Abolition* (New York: Oxford University Press, 1967, 1998), 215; letter from Weld to his wife, Jan. 18, 1842, in Barnes and Dumond, eds., *Letters of Weld, Weld, and Grimké,* 896.

32. Grimstead, *American Mobbing,* 72; Torrey, "Correspondence," Feb. 10 and 17, 1842; Miller, *Arguing about Slavery,* 429–44.

33. Barnes, *The Anti-Slavery Impulse,* 186; Richards, *The Life and Times of Congressman John Quincy Adams,* 142–43.

34. Julian, *The Life of Joshua R. Giddings,* 108.

35. Letter from Weld to his wife, Feb. 6, 1842, in Barnes and Dumond, eds., *Letters of Weld, Weld, and Grimké,* 913; Giddings letter in Richards, *The Life and*

Times of Congressman John Quincy Adams, 144; Torrey, "Correspondence," Feb. 17, 1842; letter from William Lloyd Garrison to Richard Webb, Feb. 27, 1842, Garrison Collection.

36. Miller, *Arguing about Slavery*, 446.

37. Miller, *Arguing about Slavery*, 449; Barnes, *The Anti-Slavery Impulse*, 188.

38. Barnes, *The Anti-Slavery Impulse*, 188; letter from Torrey to Amos Phelps, May 5, 1842, Phelps Collection; Julian, *The Life of Joshua R. Giddings*, 128; Torrey, "Correspondence," June 9, 1842.

39. Barnes, *The Anti-Slavery Impulse*, 189; James M. McPherson, "The Fight against the Gag Rule: Joshua Leavitt and Antislavery Insurgency in the Whig Party, 1839–1842," *Journal of Negro History* 48 (July 1963): 177–95.

40. Torrey, "Correspondence," March 17 and 24, and June 2 and 6, 1842.

41. Lovejoy, *Memoir*, 356–57.

Chapter Five

1. Harrold, *The Rise of Aggressive Abolitionism*, 75.

2. Harrold, *The Rise of Aggressive Abolitionism*, 37, 155.

3. Harrold, *The Rise of Aggressive Abolitionism*, 157–60.

4. Howe, *What Hath God Wrought*, 480; Harrold, *The Rise of Aggressive Abolitionism*, 76–77.

5. Thomas Smallwood, *A Narrative of Thomas Smallwood, (Coloured Man) Giving an Account of His Birth—The Period He Was Held in Slavery—His Release—and Removal to Canada, etc.: Together With an Account of the Underground Railroad. Written by Himself* (1851; Ithaca: Cornell University Library Digital Collections), 18.

6. Siebert, *The Underground Railroad*, 33; Larry Gara, *The Liberty Line: The Legend of the Underground Railroad* (Lexington: University of Kentucky Press, 1996), 101.

7. Karin Coddon, *Runaway Slaves* (Farmington Hills, Mich.: Greenhaven Press, 2004), 135; Henry Wilson, *History of the Rise and Fall of Slave Power in America*, 4th ed. (Boston: James R. Osgood, 1875), vol. 2: 80; Delaware History Online, Hall of Fame, Thomas Garrett, www.hsd.org/DHE/DHE_who_garrett.htm; Ann Hagedorn, *Beyond the River: The Untold Story of the Heroes of the Underground Railroad* (New York: Simon and Schuster, 2002), frontsheet, 47.

8. Gara, *The Liberty Line*, 82–83; Siebert, *The Underground Railroad*, 150; Gara, *The Liberty Line*, 73; Harrold, *Subversives*, 63.

9. Harrold, *The Rise of Aggressive Abolitionism*, 38, 108; Quarles, *Black Abolitionists*, 146.

10. Barnes, *The Anti-Slavery Impulse*, 109; Torrey, in *Tocsin of Liberty*, Oct. 27, 1842, qtd. in Harrold, *Subversives*, 5; Harrold, *Subversives*, 89; Torrey, in *Tocsin of Liberty*, Oct. 27, 1842, qtd. in Harrold, *Subversives*, 10.

11. Letter from Torrey to Amos Phelps, May 5, 1842, Phelps Collection.

12. Harrold, "On the Borders," 273–92. Letter from Joshua Giddings to Joseph A. Giddings, Aug. 14, 1842; letter from Seth Gates to Joshua Giddings, Dec. 5, 1848, MIC 7, Joshua R. Giddings Papers, Ohio Historical Society. Harrold, *Subversives,* 82–83.

13. Smallwood, *A Narrative,* 18–20. Catherine S. Brown, *Memoir of Reverend Abel Brown* (Worcester, Mass.: published by the author, 1849), 114. Circular to the Eastern New York Anti-Slavery Society, May 31, 1842; letter from Abel Brown to Torrey, June 24, 1842, Boston, Mass., Torrey Collection. Harrold, *Subversives,* 83, quoting a letter from Samivel Weller [Smallwood] to the editor, *Tocsin of Liberty,* Dec. 8, 1842.

14. Smallwood, *A Narrative,* 21–24; Harrold, *Subversives,* 81; Harrold, "On the Borders," 284.

15. John Hope Franklin and Loren Schweninger, *Runaway Slaves: Rebels on the Plantation* (New York: Oxford University Press, 1999), 285; Harrold, *Subversives,* 83; Harrold, *The Abolitionists and the South,* 77.

16. Harrold, *Subversives,* 55; "Notes of Southern Travel by a Negro Stealer," *Albany Patriot,* Feb. 7, 1844; Elwood L. Bridner, "The Fugitive Slaves of Maryland," *Maryland Historical Magazine* 66 (Spring 1971): 33–50; Carol Wilson, *Freedom at Risk: The Kidnapping of Free Blacks in America, 1780–1865* (Lexington: University of Kentucky Press, 1994), 20–33; Margaret Hope Bacon, *Rebellion at Christiana* (New York: Crown Publishers, 1975), 5–8.

17. Smallwood, *A Narrative,* 20; Harrold, *Subversives,* 80; Wilson, *History of the Rise and Fall of Slave Power* 2: 445.

18. William J. Switala, *Underground Railroad in Delaware, Maryland, and West Virginia* (Mechanicsburg, Pa., Stackpole Books, 2004), 99; Smallwood, *A Narrative,* 20; Switala, *Underground Railroad,* 137; Constance R. Beims and Christine P. Tolbert, *A Journey through Berkley Maryland: A Tapestry of Black and White Lives Woven Together over 200 Years at a Rural Crossroads* (Baltimore: Gateway Press, 2003); R. C. Smedley, *History of the Underground Railroad in Chester and the Neighboring Counties of Pennsylvania* (Mechanicsburg, Pa., Stackpole Books, 2005), 48–52.

19. Wilson, *History of the Rise and Fall of Slave Power* 2: 50–51.

20. Marianna G. Brubaker, "The Underground Railroad," *Lancaster County Historical Society Journal* 15 (1911): 95–119; Smedley, *History of the Underground Railroad,* 80 (see also 67–84 and 227–36).

21. "Diary of Caleb Swayne Cope, 1842–1846," Ms. 3085, Chester County Historical Society, West Chester, Pa., courtesy of Diane P. Rofini, librarian; published with permission.

22. Nat Brandt and Yanna Brandt, *In the Shadow of the Civil War: Passmore Williamson and the Rescue of Jane Johnson* (Columbia: University of South Carolina Press, 2007), 45–46; Emma Jones Lapansky, "'Since They Got Those Separate Churches': Afro-Americans and Racism in Jacksonian Philadelphia," in Rael, ed., *African-American Activism before the Civil War,* 100–118.

23. Brandt and Brandt, *In the Shadow of the Civil War,* 43–44; Lapansky, "Since They Got Those Separate Churches."

24. Daniel Alexander Payne, *Recollections of Seventy Years* (1888; New York: Arno Press, 1969), 73; Julie Winch, *Philadelphia's Black Elite: Activism, Accommodation, and the Struggle for Autonomy* (Philadelphia: Temple University Press, 1988), 117, 122; Laurie, *Beyond Garrison,* 148.

25. Martin Robison Delany and Robert Steven Levine, *Martin R. Delany: A Documentary Reader* (Chapel Hill: University of North Carolina Press, 2003), 118; Payne, *Recollections,* 73; Roberta Gupta, "Protest in History from the Black Perspective," *The Crisis* 87 (Nov. 1980): 373–79.

26. William Still, *The Underground Railroad* (1871; Chicago: Johnson Publishing Co., 1970), 760; obituary of Charles D. Cleveland, *Philadelphia Telegraph,* Aug. 10, 1869, rpt. in the *New York Times,* Aug. 20, 1869.

27. Still, *The Underground Railroad,* 755–56; Joseph Sturge, *A Visit to the United States in 1841* (London: Hamilton, Adams, and Co., 1842), 39.

28. Still, *The Underground Railroad,* 753; obituary of Charles D. Cleveland; Still, *The Underground Railroad,* 754.

29. *Boston Daily Mail* (no date), in Lovejoy, *Memoir,* 357; "Underground Railroad," *New York Times,* June 4, 1899; Gara, *The Liberty Line,* 144, footnote.

30. M. Marks, "Funeral of Mr. Torrey," *Emancipator,* June 17, 1846; Wigham, *The Anti-Slavery Cause,* 61–62; Siebert, *The Underground Railroad,* 125.

31. Letter from Torrey to Amos Phelps, Apr. 20, 1842, Phelps Collection.

32. Harrold, *Subversives,* 88; Smallwood, *A Narrative,* 22.

Chapter Six

1. Brown, *Memoir of Reverend Abel Brown,* 129–30.

2. Brown, *Memoir of Reverend Abel Brown,* 86, 99, 104, 87, 94; Tom Calarco, *The Underground Railroad in the Adirondack Region* (Jefferson, N.C.: McFarland and Co., 2004), 68.

3. Calarco, *The Underground Railroad,* 68; Brown, *Memoir of Reverend Abel Brown,* 118, 199.

4. Smallwood, *A Narrative,* 25, 29.

5. Tom Calarco, *The Underground Railroad Conductor: A Guide for Eastern New York* (Schenectady, N.Y.: Travels Thru History, 2003), hereafter cited as Calarco, *The Conductor,* 37; Brown, *Memoir of Reverend Abel Brown,* 150, 114.

6. Siebert, *The Underground Railroad,* 35; Calarco, *The Conductor,* 44.

7. Calarco, *The Conductor,* 50, 72, 78; Calarco, *The Underground Railroad,* 123, 222; "The Reverend Abel Brown," *People and Places: Lake Champlain: Gateway to Freedom* (Ausable Chasm, N.Y.: North Country Underground Railroad Association), northcountryundergroundrailroad.com/lake-champlain.php?page=5.

8. Smallwood, *A Narrative,* 60, 63; "Notes of Southern Travel," May 1, 1844.

9. Brown, *Memoir of Reverend Abel Brown,* 119–24; "Forwarding Business,"

Albany Patriot, Oct. 10, 1843; letter in the *Albany Patriot,* June 15, 1843, qtd. in Harrold, *Subversives,* 90; Smallwood, *A Narrative,* 60–61.

10. Harrold, *The Rise of Aggressive Abolitionism,* 73; Brown, *Memoir of Reverend Abel Brown,* 150.

11. Harrold, *The Rise of Aggressive Abolitionism,* 39, quoting a March 21, 1842, Torrey letter.

12. "The Reverend Abel Brown"; Brown, *Memoir of Reverend Abel Brown,* 147–48.

13. Brown, *Memoir of Reverend Abel Brown,* 151; "The Reverend Abel Brown."

14. Smallwood, *A Narrative,* 31–32.

15. Smallwood, *A Narrative,* 33–36.

16. Lovejoy, *Memoir,* 242; Gerrit Smith makes reference to Torrey's visit in his letter of Feb. 7, 1845.

17. Stauffer, *Black Hearts,* 75.

18. Elizabeth Cady Stanton, *Eighty Years and More: Reminiscences 1815–1897* (1898; New York: Schocken Books, 1971), 59, 51, 52–53.

19. Stauffer, *Black Hearts,* 76.

20. Harrold, *The Rise of Aggressive Abolitionism,* 49, 11, 183–88.

21. Jane H. Pease and William H. Pease, "Black Power—The Debate in 1840," in Rael, ed., *African-American Activism before the Civil War,* 50–57; Harrold, *The Rise of Aggressive Abolitionism,* 49; Thomas, *The Liberator,* 324–25.

22. Brown, *Memoir of Reverend Abel Brown,* 173–74; Owen Lovejoy, *His Brother's Blood: Speeches and Writings, 1838–64,* ed. William F. Moore and Jane Ann Moore (Urbana: University of Illinois Press, 2004), 62; Friedman, *Gregarious Saints,* 225.

23. Morris and Morris, *Encyclopedia of American History,* 226–27; Ronald G. Walters, *The Antislavery Appeal: American Abolitionism after 1830* (Baltimore: Johns Hopkins University Press, 1976), 26.

24. "The National Liberty Convention," *Emancipator and Free American,* Sept. 14, 1843; Harrold, *The Rise of Aggressive Abolitionism,* 123; Stewart, *William Lloyd Garrison,* 153–54; letter from Garrison to Helen Garrison, Nov. 21, 1842, Garrison Collection.

25. Brown, *Memoir of Reverend Abel Brown,* 174.

26. Smallwood, *A Narrative,* 37.

27. Lovejoy, *Memoir,* 105, 86–87, letter from Charles Torrey to his wife, Aug. 21, 1841.

28. Smallwood, *A Narrative,* 37–38.

29. Smallwood, *A Narrative,* 38–39.

30. Smallwood, *A Narrative,* 39–40.

31. Letter from Torrey to Gerrit Smith, Jan. 23, 1844, Gerrit Smith Papers, Special Collections Research Center, Syracuse University; Smedley, *History of the Underground Railroad,* 81.

32. Letter from Torrey to Gerrit Smith, Jan. 23, 1844, Gerrit Smith Papers; "Rev. C. T. Torrey," *Boston Daily Mail*, May 14, 1846, rpt. in the *Emancipator*, May 20, 1846; Payne, *Recollections*, 98.

33. Harrold, *Subversives*, 85–86; Lovejoy, *Memoir*, 106–26; "Notes of Southern Travel," March 6, 1844; Harrold, *Subversives*, 80.

34. Letter from Torrey to Gerrit Smith, Jan. 23, 1844, Gerrit Smith Papers.

35. "Notes of Southern Travel," Feb. 7 and March 6, 1844.

36. Joseph A. Baromé, "The Vigilant Committee of Philadelphia," *Pennsylvania Magazine of History and Biography* 92 (Apr. 1968): 320–51; letter from Torrey to Amos Phelps, July 28, 1844, Phelps Collection.

37. Stewart, *Abolitionist Politics*, 133; Stewart, *Joshua R. Giddings*, 89–90.

38. "Notes of Southern Travel," May 1, 1844; Brown, *Memoir of Reverend Abel Brown*, 133; letter from John C. Calhoun, *Liberator*, Jan. 3, 1845.

39. Lovejoy, *Memoir*, 176–81; "Torrey's Case," *Emancipator and Weekly Chronicle*, July 12, 1844; Harrold, *Subversives*, 46; "Big Ben," *Pennsylvania Freeman*, June 6, 1844.

Chapter Seven

1. Letter from Torrey to the Essex County Abolitionists, July 29, 1844, in Lovejoy, *Memoir*, 131.

2. Harrold, *Subversives*, 91; Lovejoy, *Memoir*, 167.

3. Letter from Torrey to Gerrit Smith, Jan. 23, 1844, Gerrit Smith Papers.

4. Harrold, *Subversives*, 87; Charles T. Torrey, *Pennsylvania Freeman*, July 18, 1844; "The case of Mr. Torrey," *Emancipator and Weekly Chronicle*, Aug. 7, 1844; Harrold, *Subversives*, 87; Filler, *Crusade*, 164; letter from Torrey to the Essex County Abolitionists, 134; Davis, *Joshua Leavitt*, 214–15.

5. "The Case of Mr. Torrey," *Emancipator and Weekly Chronicle*, Aug. 7, 1844.

6. Charles Torrey, "To the Public," *Baltimore Sun*, Aug. 30, 1844.

7. "Imprisonment of Charles T. Torrey," *Liberator*, Aug. 23, 1844; "Imprisonment of Mr. Torrey," *Emancipator and Weekly Chronicle*, July 3, 1844; S. P. Andrews, "Rev. Chas. T. Torrey," *Emancipator and Weekly Chronicle*, Oct. 2, 1844, originally published in the *Baltimore Sun*; Torrey, "To the Public."

8. Andrews, "Rev. Chas. T. Torrey"; "C. T. Torrey—a Card," *Pennsylvania Freeman*, Sept. 19, 1844.

9. Davis, *Joshua Leavitt*, 215, quoting a letter from Lewis Tappan to John W. Alden, July 8, 1844; Norfolk, "Mr. Torrey's Case," *Emancipator and Weekly Chronicle*, July 17, 1844.

10. "Imprisonment of Charles T. Torrey," *Liberator*, July 26, 1844; C. T. Torrey *Liberator*, Aug. 9, 1844.

11. Norfolk, "Mr. Torrey's Case."

12. "Shocking Depravity in a Philadelphia Editor," *Pennsylvania Freeman*, Oct.

16, 1844; Charles Torrey, "My Justification of My Attempt to Break Jail," *Emancipator and Weekly Chronicle*, Oct. 9, 1844, rpt. in Lovejoy, *Memoir*, 152–59.

13. Torrey, "My Justification," 156.

14. Letter from Torrey to Gerrit Smith, Aug. 3, 1844, Gerrit Smith Papers; letter from Torrey to Amos Phelps, July 28, 1844, Phelps Collection.

15. Torrey, "My Justification," 156.

16. Letter from Torrey to Amos Phelps, July 28, 1844, Phelps Collection.

17. Lovejoy, *Memoir*, 186.

18. C.W.D., "Notes of a Traveler," *Emancipator and Weekly Chronicle*, Nov. 13, 1844; letters from Charles Torrey to Mary Torrey, Sept. 14, 1844, and J. W. Alden, Oct. 10, 1844, in Lovejoy, *Memoir*, 148–50, 160–62.

19. Letter from Charles Torrey to Samuel E. Sewall, Sept. 28, 1844, in Lovejoy, *Memoir*, 151–52.

20. Lovejoy, *Memoir*, 158–59; *Albany Patriot*, June 15, 1843.

21. "Daring and Audacious Attempt of the Rev. Charles T. Torrey to Escape from Jail," *Baltimore Sun*, Sept. 14, 1844; Lovejoy, *Memoir*, 153.

22. Letter from Charles Torrey to Samuel E. Sewall, Sept. 28, 1844, in Lovejoy, *Memoir*, 151–52; letter from Charles Torrey to Mary Torrey, Sept. 22, 1844, in Lovejoy, *Memoir*, 150–51.

23. Lovejoy, *Memoir*, 152–59; letter from Torrey to Amos Phelps, Nov. 4, 1844, Phelps Collection; letter from Torrey to Gerrit Smith, Nov. 16, 1844, Gerrit Smith Papers.

24. Bordewich, *Bound for Canaan*, 209; letter from Torrey to Gerrit Smith, Nov. 16, 1844, Gerrit Smith Papers.

25. Brown, *Memoir of Reverend Abel Brown*, 219.

26. Letter from Torrey to Gerrit Smith, Nov. 16, 1844, Gerrit Smith Papers.

27. The letters between Lewis Tappan and Charles Torrey concerning the debt are in the Lewis Tappan Collection, Library of Congress; see especially October 10, 1839, and March 20, 1840. Tappan addressed Torrey as "Dear Sir," in contrast to how he addressed Amos Phelps, as "Brother Phelps" (letters from Lewis Tappan to Amos Phelps, Oct. 28, 1844, Dec. 31, 1844, and Jan. 24, 1845, Phelps Collection).

28. Lovejoy, *Memoir*, 156, 159, 151, 152; A. B. King, "Some Unusual Cases of Cerebral Tuberculosis," *Bulletin of the Johns Hopkins Hospital* 104 (Feb. 1959): 75–88; P. Lesprit, A.-M. Zagdanski, A. de La Blanchardiere et al., "Cerebral Tuberculosis in Patients with the Acquired Immunodeficiency Syndrome (AIDS): Report of 6 Cases and Review," *Medicine* (Baltimore), vol. 76 (Nov. 1997): 423–31; J. E. Vidal, A. C. Penalva de Oliveira, F. Bonasser Filho et al., "Tuberculous Brain Abscess in AIDS Patients: Report of Three Cases and Literature Review," *International Journal of Infectious Diseases* 9 (July 2005): 201–7.

29. Letter from Torrey to Amos Phelps, July 28, 1844, Phelps Collection; Lovejoy, *Memoir*, 169; letter from Torrey to Amos Phelps, Nov. [no day], 1844, Phelps Collection.

30. "Torrey's Trial Postponed," *Liberator*, Sept. 13, 1844, quoting the *Baltimore*

Visiter, no date; letter from Torrey to Gerrit Smith, Nov. 16, 1844, Gerrit Smith Papers; letter from Torrey to Amos Phelps, Nov. [no day], 1844, Phelps Collection.

31. Wilson, *History of the Rise and Fall of Slave Power* 2: 78; Bernard C. Steiner, *Life of Reverdy Johnson* (Baltimore: Norman, Remington Co., 1914), 19–20; Lovejoy, *Memoir,* 172.

32. The account of Torrey's trial is from the *Baltimore Sun,* Nov. 30, Dec. 2, and Dec. 3, 1844, rpt. in Lovejoy, *Memoir,* 173–202.

Chapter Eight

1. Letter from Torrey to the *Boston Morning Chronicle,* Dec. 3, 1844, rpt. in Lovejoy, *Memoir,* 202–14 (note that, at least in my copy of this book, the letter is erroneously dated November 21, 1844); "Death of Mr. Torrey," *Emancipator,* June 10, 1846; Goodell, *Slavery and Anti-Slavery,* 442; L. A. Chamerovzow, ed., *Slave Life in Georgia: A Narrative of the Life, Sufferings, and Escape of John Brown, a Fugitive Slave, Now in England* (London: W. M. Watts, 1855), 219.

2. Torrey, *Home,* iv, 254–55; letter from Torrey to the *Boston Morning Chronicle,* Dec. 3, 1844.

3. Letter from Torrey to the *Boston Morning Chronicle,* Dec. 3, 1844; letter from Torrey to Elias Smith, Aug. 19, 1844, in Garrison and Garrison, *WLG* 2: 132. For an example of a historian who believed that Torrey had a change of heart toward Garrison, see Ruchames, ed., *Letters,* 410, note 2.

4. Nath'l Colver, "Our Brethren in Prison," *Emancipator and Weekly Chronicle,* Jan. 29, 1845.

5. Letter [no author] dated Dec. 16, 1844, *Emancipator and Weekly Chronicle,* Jan. 1, 1845.

6. Miller, *Arguing about Slavery,* 477.

7. Johnson, *The Liberty Party,* 95; Laurie, *Beyond Garrison,* 61.

8. Lovejoy, *Memoir,* 215; E. C. Wines, *The State of Prisons and of Child-Saving Institutions in the Civilized World* (Cambridge, Mass.: John Wilson and Son, 1880); Wallace Shugg, *A Monument to Good Intentions: The Story of the Maryland Penitentiary 1804–1995* (Baltimore: Maryland Historical Society, 2000); J. Thomas Scharf, *History of Baltimore City and County* (Philadelphia: Louis H. Everts, 1881), 202–5.

9. Lovejoy, *Memoir,* 216–20, 231; "Mr. Torrey in prison," *Emancipator and Weekly Chronicle,* May 21, 1845, rpt. from the *Baltimore Saturday Visiter.*

10. Letters in Lovejoy, *Memoir*: from Joshua Leavitt to Torrey, Jan. 1, 1845, 238–39; from Gerrit Smith to Torrey, Feb. 7, 1845, 240–42; from Charles Torrey to Mary Torrey, Sept. 28, 1845, 269.

11. C. T. Torrey, *Emancipator and Weekly Chronicle,* Dec. 25, 1844; Mary Torrey's letters to Charles Torrey, Jan. 15, 1845, and Feb. [no day], 1845, in Lovejoy, *Memoir,* 243–47.

12. Harrold, *The Abolitionists,* 76, 80.

13. Stewart, *Joshua R. Giddings*, 108; Stewart, "Joshua Giddings," 167–92; Julian, *The Life of Joshua R. Giddings*, 172, 174.

14. Bridner, "The Fugitive Slaves," 41.

15. Mayer, *All on Fire*, 304.

16. Letter from Charles Torrey to Mary Torrey, Sept. 28, 1845, in Lovejoy, *Memoir*, 266–71, 225; R. G. Lincoln, "Visit to Rev. Mr. Torrey," *Emancipator*, Oct. 29, 1845 (his visit had been on Sept. 8, 1845).

17. Charles Torrey, letter to the *Baltimore Morning Chronicle*, Dec. 3, 1844, in Lovejoy, *Memoir*, 207.

18. Hazel C. Wolf, *On Freedom's Altar: The Martyr Complex in the Abolition Movement* (Madison: University of Wisconsin Press, 1952), 90; letters from Charles Torrey to Samuel E. Sewall, Sept. 28, 1844, in Lovejoy, *Memoir*, 151–52, and to J. W. Alden, Oct. 10, 1844, in Lovejoy, *Memoir*, 160–62. Letter from Charles Torrey to Mary Torrey, July 9, 1844, in Lovejoy, *Memoir*, 127–28; John Adair, *Founding Fathers: The Puritans in England and America* (London: J. M. Dent and Sons, 1982), 57.

19. Letters from Charles Torrey to Mary Torrey, March 2, 1845, and Apr. 29, 1845, in Lovejoy, *Memoir*, 222, 229–30; letter from Mary Torrey to Charles Torrey, Apr. 1, 1845, in Lovejoy, *Memoir*, 247.

20. Letter from Mary Torrey to T. Salisbury, Jan. 7, 1845, *Emancipator and Weekly Chronicle*, Apr. 2, 1845; letter from Mary Torrey to Amos Phelps, Sept. 5, 1845, Phelps Collection.

21. The information on Thomas Pratt is from Caleb C. Magruder, *Thomas George Pratt, Governor of Maryland, 1845–1848; United States Senator, 1850–1857* (Baltimore: Waverly Press, 1913).

22. Siebert, *The Underground Railroad*, 341; letter from Charles Torrey to Mary Torrey, March 2, 1845, in Lovejoy, *Memoir*, 224.

23. Letter from Mary Torrey to Amos Phelps, Sept. 5, 1845, Phelps Collection; "Petition for the Release of Rev. Mr. Torrey," Mrs. Torrey's letter, *Liberator*, Feb. 27, 1846, rpt. from the *Boston Daily Star*.

24. The negotiations for Torrey's release are described in multiple letters in Lovejoy, *Memoir*, 214ff; letter from Amos Phelps to James Birney in Dumond, *Letters*, 997; Harrold, *The Abolitionists*, 140; Wolf, *On Freedom's Altar*, 91–93; A. A. Phelps and C. D. Cleveland, "The Case of Rev. Charles Torrey," *Liberator*, Apr. 3, 1846, rpt. from the *Baltimore Saturday Visiter*; letter from Charles Torrey to Mary Torrey, Dec. 30, 1845, in Lovejoy, *Memoir*, 274–75.

25. Visit of Dr. Ide to the governor of Maryland, in Lovejoy, *Memoir*, 286–87; "Congregational Necrology," *Congregational Quarterly*, Jan. 1870, 60.

26. "Torrey's Case," *Emancipator*, Apr. 29, 1846; R. G. Lincoln, "Visit to Rev. Mr. Torrey," *Emancipator*, Sept. 29, 1845; "Rev. C. T. Torrey," *Emancipator*, May 20, 1846; "Charles T. Torrey about to Die," *Emancipator*, May 20, 1846.

27. Letter from Mary Ide to Charles Torrey, in Lovejoy, *Memoir*, 280–81; letter from Jacob Ide to John Codman, Torrey Collection.

28. Death of Mr. Torrey, *Emancipator*, June 10, 1846 (the account is signed "H.,"

but there is also a letter in Lovejoy's *Memoir* describing a May 8 visit by Porter H. Snow, so they are almost certainly the same); Lovejoy, *Memoir*, 293–94, 292.

29. "Death of Rev. Charles T. Torrey," *Emancipator*, May 27, 1846; Lovejoy, *Memoir*, 293.

30. Letter from Garrison to Samuel E. Sewall, May 15, 1846, in Walter M. Merrill, ed., *The Letters of William Lloyd Garrison, Vol. 3: No Union with Slaveholders, 1841–1849* (Cambridge: Harvard University Press, 1973), 338; letter from Charles Torrey to Mary Torrey, Jan. 9, 1837, in Lovejoy, *Memoir*, 35–36, 294; "Death of Charles T. Torrey," *Liberator*, May 15, 1846; Records of the Park Street Church, Congregational Library, Boston, 1846.

31. Records of the Park Street Church, Congregational Library, Boston, 1846; Lovejoy, in his *Memoir of Rev. Charles T. Torrey* (294), mistakenly said that the funeral took place on Monday, May 19, and that mistake has been repeated by many historians. The correct date was Monday, May 18; Wolf, *On Freedom's Altar*, 95; "Park Street Church," *Albany Patriot*, May 27, 1846; Goodell, *Slavery and Anti-Slavery*, 443.

32. "The Funeral of the Rev. Chas. T. Torrey," *Emancipator*, May 27, 1846; "The Funeral of Torrey," *Emancipator*, July 1, 1846, rpt. from the *Essex Transcript*; Lader, *The Bold Brahmins*, 101.

33. "The Funeral of the Rev. Chas. T. Torrey," *Emancipator*, May 27, 1846; Lovejoy, *Memoir*, 296; "The Funeral of Charles T. Torrey," *Emancipator*, June 17, 1846, rpt. from the *Gospel Fountain*.

34. Lovejoy, *Memoir*, 300–308; John Berendt, "How We R.I.P.: The Cemetery as a Mirror of Society," Book World, *Washington Post*, June 15, 2008.

35. Lovejoy, *Memoir*, 308–13.

36. Wilson, *History of the Rise and Fall of Slave Power* 2: 79–80; James R. Lowell, "On the Death of Charles Turner Torrey," *The Complete Poetical Works of James Russell Lowell*, Project Gutenberg EBook #13310, www.gutenberg.org/files/13310/13310.txt.

37. "Torrey Commemoration Meetings," *Emancipator*, May 27, 1846; Wolf, *On Freedom's Altar*, 96; John Niven, ed., *The Salmon P. Chase Papers, vol. 2: Correspondence, 1823–1857* (Kent, Ohio: Kent State University Press, 1994), 124–25; Lovejoy, *Memoir*, 360–61.

38. "A Standard Bearer Fallen," *Emancipator*, July 8, 1846, rpt. from the *Ohio Standard*; William Goodell, "Martyrs and Their Persecutors," *Christian Investigator* 4 (1846): 345–50; Lovejoy, *Memoir*, 335, 329–30; "The Great Murder," *Emancipator*, June 3, 1846, rpt. from the *Liberty Standard*.

39. Lovejoy, *Memoir*, 318–20; John W. Blassingame et al., eds., *The Frederick Douglass Papers* (New Haven, Conn.: Yale University Press, 1979), vol. 1: 308

40. Harrold, *Subversives*, 65–66; Wolf, *On Freedom's Altar*, 97; "Meeting in Aid of the Torrey Monument," *Liberator*, July 10, 1846.

41. Sterling, *Ahead of Her Time*, 4; "Refuge of Oppression," *Liberator*, Aug. 7, 1846, taken from the *Emancipator* (no date).

42. "The Monument to Charles T. Torrey," *Emancipator*, Sept. 9, 1846; "Rever-

end Charles T. Torrey Monument," Art Inventories Catalog, Smithsonian American Art Museum, Smithsonian Institution Research Information System (SIRIS), siris-artinventories.si.edu/ipac20/ipac.jsp?uri=full=3100001~!19958~0.

Chapter Nine

1. Lader, *The Bold Brahmins,* 111; Bordewich, *Bound for Canaan,* 159; letter from Henry Stanton to James Birney, June 25, 1837, in Dumond, ed., *Letters of Birney,* 388.

2. Harrold, *Subversives,* 60, 97.

3. Lovejoy, *Memoir,* 283; letter from Lewis Tappan to Amos Phelps, Dec. 31, 1844, Phelps Collection; letter from Torrey to the *Boston Morning Chronicle,* Dec. 3, 1844, in Lovejoy, *Memoir,* 211–12; letter from Chaplin to J. C. Jackson, Jan. 3, 1845, *Albany Patriot,* qtd. in Harrold, *Subversives,* 99; letter from Chaplin to the *Albany Patriot,* Dec. 26, 1846, qtd. in Harrold, *The Abolitionists,* 72.

4. Harrold, *The Abolitionists,* 105; Harrold, *The Rise of Aggressive Abolitionism,* 107; *The Case of William L. Chaplin* (Boston: Chaplin Committee, 1851), Samuel May Collection, Cornell University; Harlow, *Gerrit Smith,* 290.

5. Siebert, *The Underground Railroad,* 172; Bordewich, *Bound for Canaan,* 296.

6. Harrold, *Subversives,* 118–21.

7. Bordewich, *Bound for Canaan,* 302–4; Aptheker, *Abolitionism,* 111.

8. Stewart, *Joshua R. Giddings,* 153; Harrold, *Subversives,* 142; Stewart, *Joshua R. Giddings,* 152; Harrold, *Subversives,* 152–53; Stewart, *Joshua R. Giddings,* 152.

9. Letter from Chaplin to Gerrit Smith, May 17, 1848, qtd. in Harrold, *Subversives,* 144–45; letter from Giddings to his wife, Apr. 20, 1848, qtd. in Harrold, *Subversives,* 145; Harrold, *The Rise of Aggressive Abolitionism,* 120–21.

10. Harrold, *Subversives,* 154; Charles L. Blockson, *The Underground Railroad in Pennsylvania* (Jacksonville, N.C.: Flame International, 1981), 145; "Who's Who in Pennsylvania Underground Railroad," afrolumens.org/ugrr/whoswho/cnames.html.

11. Harrold, *Subversives,* 156.

12. Bordewich, *Bound for Canaan,* 317; *The Case of William L. Chaplin,* 25; "William L. Chaplin arrested!" Historical Marker Database, www.hmdb.org/Marker .asp?Marker=3969; Harrold, *Subversives,* 147.

13. Harlow, *Gerrit Smith,* 291–95; "Glen Haven Water Cure," Cayuga County Historian's Office, www.co.cayuga.ny.us/history/ugrr/report/PDF/5q.pdf. Harlow's book described Theodosia Gilbert as "a lady of questionable morals" (293), based on some letters, and this assessment has been repeated by other historians. For example, in *American Mobbing,* David Grimstead referred to Gilbert as "a brothel madam" (73). That impression may have come from the fact that Ms. Gilbert was very active in the women's rights movement and published an article recommending that women dress more comfortably.

14. Wigham, *The Anti-Slavery Cause,* 79.

15. Harrold, *The Rise of Aggressive Abolitionism,* 126, 131.

16. Harrold, *The Abolitionists,* 78; Harrold, *The Rise of Aggressive Abolitionism,* 189–96; Stauffer, *Black Hearts,* 163.

17. Gara, *The Liberty Line,* 154; Harrold, *The Abolitionists,* 154.

18. Gara, *The Liberty Line,* 133; David S. Reynolds, *Mightier than the Sword: Uncle Tom's Cabin and the Battle for America* (New York: W. W. Norton, 2011), 65; Pierson, *Free Hearts,* 174–75; Newman, *Transformation,* 181.

19. Brandt and Brandt, *In the Shadow of the Civil War,* 89; Bordewich, *Bound for Canaan,* 333–40; Bacon, *Rebellion,* 132; John Demos, "The Anti-Slavery Movement and the Problem of Violent Means," *New England Quarterly* 37 (Dec. 1964): 501–26.

20. Bacon, *Rebellion,* 132.

21. Demos, "The Anti-Slavery Movement."

22. David S. Reynolds, *John Brown, Abolitionist: The Man Who Killed Slavery, Sparked the Civil War, and Seeded Civil Rights* (New York: Alfred A. Knopf, 2005), 60, 37, 61, 249.

23. Reynolds, *John Brown,* 34; Brown, "Lovejoy's Influence."

24. Siebert, *The Underground Railroad,* 166; Frederick Douglass, *Autobiographies* (New York: Library of America, 1994), 715–19; Reynolds, *John Brown,* 249.

25. Stauffer, *Black Hearts,* 169.

26. Boyer, *The Legend of John Brown,* 435–38.

27. Reynolds, *John Brown,* 288, 290; Stauffer, *Black Hearts,* 240; Reynolds, *John Brown,* 362, 290, 208.

28. Stewart, *Abolitionist Politics,* 29, 164; Garrison and Garrison, *WLG* 3: 486; Stewart, *Abolitionist Politics,* 163–64; Wigham, *The Anti-Slavery Cause,* 136.

29. Reynolds, *John Brown,* 51; Stewart, *Wendell Phillips,* 203; Stewart, *Abolitionist Politics,* 30.

30. Reynolds, *John Brown,* 354; Friedman, *Gregarious Saints,* 208.

31. Gara, *The Liberty Line,* 154.

32. The information on Charles Torrey Jr. was obtained from the Medway (Massachusetts) Historical Society, courtesy of Ms. Margaret Maxwell; Friedman, *Gregarious Saints,* 213.

33. Thomas, *The Liberator,* 419, 422.

34. Stewart, *William Lloyd Garrison,* 192.

Chapter Ten

1. Stauffer, *Black Hearts,* 27; Laurie, *Beyond Garrison,* 5.

2. Johnson, "The Liberty Party."

3. Harrold, *Subversives,* 88; Wolf, *On Freedom's Altar,* 98.

4. Reynolds, *John Brown,* 99; Reynolds, *Mightier than the Sword,* 119.

5. Bordewich, *Bound for Canaan,* 351, 5–6.

6. Bordewich, *Bound for Canaan,* 437–38.

7. Letter from Torrey to Amos Phelps, July 28, 1844, Phelps Collection.

8. Examples of twentieth-century histories of the abolitionist movement that

do not mention Charles Torrey include Jesse Macy's *The Anti-Slavery Crusade* (1919); Gilbert Barnes's *The Anti-Slavery Impulse 1830–1844* (1933); Henrietta Buckmaster's *Flight to Freedom: The Story of the Underground Railroad* (1958); Martin Duberman's *The Antislavery Vanguard* (1965); Gerald Sorin's *Abolitionism: A New Perspective* (1972); Dillon's *The Abolitionists* (1974); Walters's *The Antislavery Appeal* (1978); and Paul Goodman's *Of One Blood: Abolitionism and the Origins of Racial Equality* (1998). Wolf, *On Freedom's Altar*, 80–98; James B. Stewart, *Holy Warrior: The Abolitionists and American Slavery* (New York: Hill and Wang, 1976), 137.

9. Lader, *The Bold Brahmins*, 101; Gara, *The Liberty Line*, 161; Filler, *Crusade*, 163–164; Harrold, "On the Borders"; Harrold, *Subversives*, 64–93.

10. Lovejoy, *His Brother's Blood*, 75.

11. Brown, *Memoir of Reverend Abel Brown*; Smallwood, *A Narrative*; Chamerovzow, *Slave Life*, 214–17; Wigham, *The Anti-Slavery Cause*, 61–64; Siebert, *The Underground Railroad*, 168–69.

12. Goodell, *Slavery and Anti-Slavery*, 444; Wilson, *History of the Rise and Fall of Slave Power* 2: 77.

13. Stewart, *Joshua R. Giddings*, 270; Reynolds, *John Brown*, 429, 362; Stauffer, *Black Hearts*, 240; Harlow, *Gerrit Smith*, 415–18.

14. Davis, *Joshua Leavitt*, 285; Henry B. Stanton, *Random Recollections* (New York: Harper and Bros., 1887).

15. Brandt and Brandt, *In the Shadow of the Civil War*, 161; Julie Roy Jeffrey, *Abolitionists Remember: Antislavery Autobiographies and the Unfinished Work of Emancipation* (Chapel Hill: University of North Carolina Press, 2008), 67; Gara, *The Liberty Line*, 177.

16. Still, *The Underground Railroad*, 691–97; Gara, *The Liberty Line*, 175.

17. Jeffrey, *Abolitionists Remember*, 5; Friedman, *Gregarious Saints*, 213; Garrison and Garrison, *WLG* 3: 10, 33, 131.

18. Portraits of American Abolitionists, 1850–1890, Massachusetts Historical Society, www.masshist.org/findingaids/doc.cfm?fa=fap014.

19. Thomas, *The Liberator*, 268; Stewart, *William Lloyd Garrison*, 115; Mayer, *All on Fire*, 268.

20. Samuel J. May, *Some Recollections of Our Antislavery Conflict* (Boston: Fields, Osgood and Co., 1869), 33.

21. Pillsbury, *Acts of the Anti-Slavery Apostles*, 172, 303; Jeffrey, *Abolitionists Remember*, 195, 194.

22. Kraditor, *Means and Ends in American Abolitionism*, 115.

23. Davis, *Joshua Leavitt*, 214; Harold D. Tallant, "Torrey, Charles Turner," in John A. Garraty and Mark C. Carnes, eds., *American National Biography* (New York: Oxford University Press, 1999), 757–58; letter from Theodore Weld to Angelina Grimké, Jan. 18, 1842, in Barnes and Dumond, eds., *Letters of Weld, Weld, and Grimké*, 896; Harlow, *Gerrit Smith*, 275; G.H.B., "Torrey, Charles Turner," in Dumas Malone, ed., *Dictionary of American Biography* (New York: Charles Scribner's Sons, 1936), vol. 18: 595–96.

24. Dumond, *Antislavery,* 299.

25. Jeffrey, *Abolitionists Remember,* 54, 25, 229, 242.

Postscript

1. Information on Charles Torrey's children and grandchildren was taken from the records of the Medway (Massachusetts) Historical Society (courtesy of Ms. Margaret Maxwell); *Who's Who in New England*; and the alumni bulletins for Amherst College and Harvard University. The complete information on the grandchildren is as follows:

Seelye Bryant, born in Turkey on December 11, 1866. Graduated from Amherst College in 1887 and from Princeton Theological Seminary in 1890. Married Margaret MacLean in 1891 and Kate Wheeler Skeele in 1897 in Scituate, Massachusetts. Held pastorates in several Massachusetts towns. Had one child (Agnes Lee, born December 29, 1892) by his first wife and one (Dorothy Emmons Bryant, born September 2, 1898) by his second. He died in Pawtucket, Rhode Island, on January 18, 1954, age eighty-seven.

Emmons Bryant, born July 10, 1871. Graduated from Amherst College in 1895. Was a teacher at Staten Island Academy in New York and at Newark Academy, Newark, New Jersey, then worked for companies in Syracuse, Niagara Falls, and New York City. Married Dorothy Lyon on June 21, 1899. Had two children (Katherine and Emmons). He died on March 7, 1942, age seventy.

Ethel Charlotte Bryant, born in November 29, 1874. Died June 22, 1876.

Arthur Alexis Bryant, born Nov. 10, 1877. Graduated from Harvard University in 1897 and later received a PhD in the classics. Taught Latin at a series of private schools in New York, New Jersey, Baltimore, and Boston. Joined the Socialist Party and was an active member. Married Louise Stevens December 26, 1908, but divorced, and then married Helen Lund in 1913; apparently no children. No information found on date of death.

2. Torrey, "The Dead Heart," 14, 16.

3. Mifflin House, www.millersville.edu/~ugrr/yorkugrr/mifflin.htm, accessed Oct. 15, 2009.

INDEX

Note: Throughout the index, CTT refers to Charles Turner Torrey; page numbers followed by "n" indicate endnotes.